PRAISE FOR

THE LAST HOUSE BEFORE THE SEA

"The mission of preservation is, like the land itself, murky and muddied, a product of progress and growth both triumphant and misguided; urgency swells and subsides like waters amid daily livelihoods. Martínez's account, in content, structure, and style, mirrors this nuance and complexity, resisting myopic quick fixes and even easy catastrophizing. A steady, tempering, enigmatic chronicle of a polarizing, and ultimately personal, ending."

— *KIRKUS REVIEWS*

"*The Last House Before the Sea* is a revelation . . . a prophetic meditation on the aching precarity of our impossibly beautiful world. Martínez transforms the island of Buda into a microcosm of our world and our future if we do not find in ourselves the love to act. A profound book by one of our finest writers."

— JUNOT DÍAZ, AUTHOR OF *THIS IS HOW YOU LOSE HER*

"One of the most extraordinary cases of the new travel literature. . . . A cross between Laurence Sterne and Paul Theroux."

— ANDRÉS BARBA, *EL MUNDO*

"Deltas are conversations between forces so much larger than the self: between land and sea, between saltwater and fresh, and, in today's climate changed world, between the past and the future. Gabi Martínez pays watchful attention to all who occupy one such landscape in northeastern Spain, asking, how do we hold on to what has defined us even as it disappears beneath our very feet? The result is a thoughtful mix of elegy, prayer, and poetry, and in this day and age, we need all three."

— ELIZABETH RUSH, AUTHOR OF *THE QUICKENING: ANTARCTICA, MOTHERHOOD, AND CULTIVATING HOPE IN A WARMING WORLD*

"Gabi Martínez has invented a new literary genre: one that speaks of nature from within."

— KIRMEN URIBE, AUTHOR OF *BILBAO–NEW YORK–BILBAO*

"From the Nile to the Ganges to the Mississippi, deltas not only form a vertebral column throughout human history, but are also essential sources of biodiversity in the planet's balance. *The Last House Before the Sea* addresses this fascinating and often overlooked topic with exceptional originality, certain of the urgency of its testimony. Like Claudio Magris with the Danube, Gabi Martínez offers his life experience, erudition, and sensitivity on a journey to the heart of the Iberian Mediterranean, which unveils before our eyes the overwhelming evidence of the climate crisis as a collapse of the natural spaces that sustain life on Earth."

— MICHEL NIEVA, AUTHOR OF *DENGUE BOY*

"*The Last House Before the Sea* is a book to reconnect with nature, with naturalist literature, with the vibrant story of a present that yearns for a different, better future. Time passes, the year 2023 slips away, but another will come. In *The Last House Before the Sea*, however, as if it were an ecological thriller, time is the killer, and everything points to it getting away with murder."

— GINÉS J. VERA, *LA GONZO MAGAZINE*

"Gabi Martínez has written his best nonfiction work to date, no doubt about it, but it's as action-packed as a novel. Monologues and voices as vivid as those in theater, and all the beauty of lyric poetry that moves anyone who delves into the pages of his book."

— CHUS GARCÍA, *REVISTA MERCURIO*

"A monumental book, outstanding, unusual, magnetic, rich, thoughtful, intense, and fascinating."

— JORDI CERVERA, *DIARI DE TARRAGONA*

THE LAST HOUSE BEFORE THE SEA

GABI MARTÍNEZ

THE LAST HOUSE BEFORE THE SEA

One Year on the Ebro Delta

Translated from the Spanish by
Ezra E. Fitz

RESTLESS BOOKS
NEW YORK • AMHERST

This book is based on real events, though it incorporates elements of narrative fiction. Certain facts and details have been modified and the names of people who appear in this book have been changed in order to preserve their identities and their right to privacy.

Published in agreement with Casanovas & Lynch Literary Agency

First Restless Books paperback edition November 2025

Paperback ISBN: 9781632064035
Library of Congress Control Number: 2025940558

This work has been published with a subsidy from the Ministry of Culture and Sport of Spain.

MINISTERIO DE CULTURA Y DEPORTE
DIRECCIÓN GENERAL DEL LIBRO Y FOMENTO DE LA LECTURA

Cover design by Richard Ljoenes
Cover photograph by Dylan Rabbit / Shutterstock
Text and interior design by Tetragon, London

Printed in the United States

1 3 5 7 9 10 8 6 4 2

RESTLESS BOOKS
NEW YORK • AMHERST

www.restlessbooks.org

To my father.

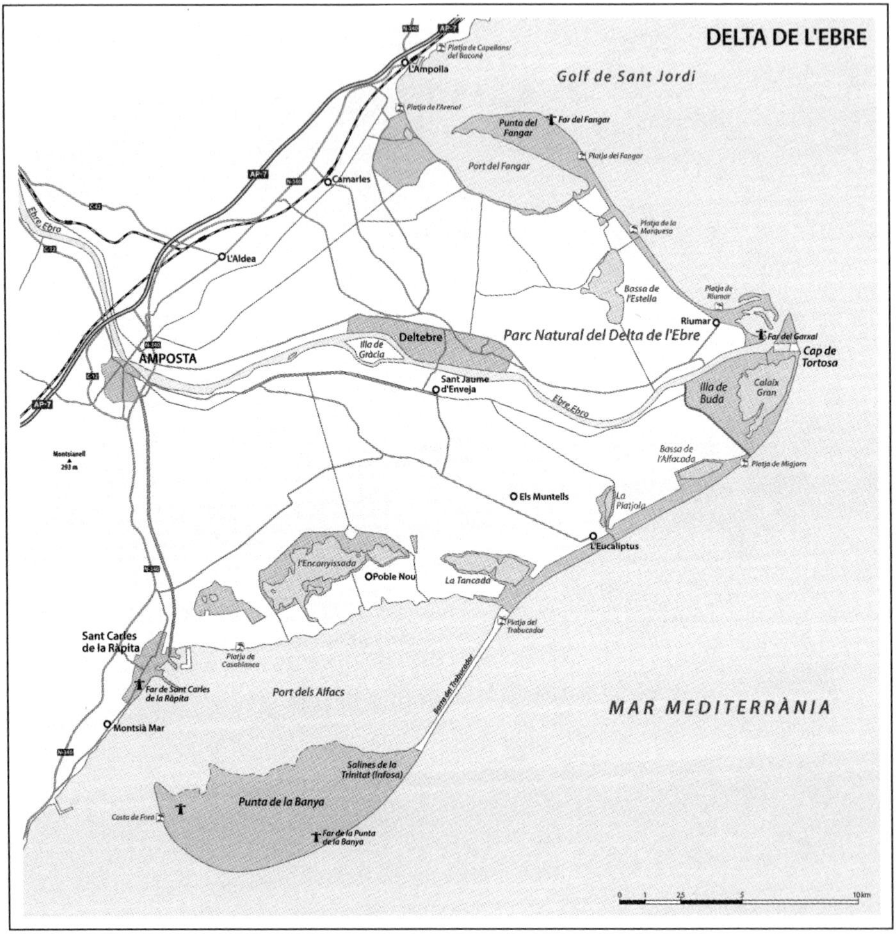
DELTA DE L'EBRE
Golf de Sant Jordi
L'Ampolla
Platja de Capellans/
del Bocone
Platja de l'Arenal
Punta del
Fangar
Far del Fangar
Platja del Fangar
Port del Fangar
AP-7
N-340
Camarles
C-42
Ebre, Ebro
C-12
L'Aldea
Platja de la
Marquesa
Bassa de
l'Estella
Platja de
Riumar
Riumar
Far del Garxal
Cap de
Tortosa
Parc Natural del Delta de l'Ebre
Deltebre
Illa de
Gràcia
AMPOSTA
Sant Jaume
d'Enveja
Illa de
Buda
Calaix
Gran
Montsianell
293 m
Bassa de
l'Alfacada
Platja de Migjorn
Els Muntells
La
Platjola
L'Eucaliptus
l'Encanyissada
Poble Nou
La Tancada
Platja del
Trabucador
Sant Carles
de la Ràpita
Platja de
Casablanca
Far de Sant Carles
de la Ràpita
Port dels Alfacs
Barra del Trabucador
MAR MEDITERRÀNIA
Montsià Mar
Salines de la
Trinitat (Infosa)
Punta de la Banya
Costa de Fora
Far de la Punta
de la Banya
0 1 2,5 5 10 km

CONTENTS

LIGHT

VOICE

Come on, I say to the creek, surprise me; and it does, with each new drop. Beauty is real. I would never deny it; the appalling thing is that I forget it.

— ANNIE DILLARD, *PILGRIM AT TINKER CREEK* (1974)

Perhaps the Delta is, in reality, a battlefield between man and nature.

— JOAN TODÓ, *GUIA SENTIMENTAL DEL DELTA DE L'EBRE* (2018)

Translated from the Spanish by Ezra E. Fitz

water still risin, land shrinks, heat sokin in to us. walkin west.

— PAUL KINGSNORTH, *ALEXANDRIA* (2020)

Why, being able to go singing toward death, go in silence?

— GONZALO ESCARPA, *QUIERO DECIR* (2024)

Translated from the Spanish by Ezra E. Fitz

THE LAST HOUSE BEFORE THE SEA

INTRODUCTION

"How much time are you thinking of spending here?" the island's owner asked me. We were standing in front of the last house before the sea, the first that would flood when the waters advanced a few meters more. The house where I hoped to settle, completing a journey begun fourteen years earlier when, while visiting the Barcelona aquarium with my two-year-old son, we saw a coral from the Great Barrier Reef alongside a plaque warning that if the planet's temperature were to rise just two degrees, almost all these reefs would die. The rapid increase in global temperatures suggests that the earth will soon reach that threshold, and since coral turns white when it dies, I wondered if my son would ever see the Great Barrier Reef in color.

The aquarium episode occurred while I was traveling around the world, writing about what drives people, regardless of where they're from. What I hadn't done much was write about places closer to my city. It was fascinating to me how that antipodean coral half an hour from my sofa had precipitated reflections on the future, leading me to think differently about what I held closest to me and about the environmental changes already shaking the ground beneath us all.

I began to focus a different sense of attention on what was happening at home, in more familiar territory. After writing about the tensions of living in a city as densely populated as Barcelona, I spent a lot of time with shepherds in the pastures of central Spain where my mother was born; the book *Un cambio de verdad* was written during this period. Having grown up near the Mediterranean coast, my father's part of the country, I'd eventually need to manifest that universe to close the circle I had opened with my son and the corals.

My father was a great aficionado of the Ebro Delta, of its space and its light. It's a place under the ever-increasing threat of rising sea levels, which are eroding the coastline at such a frenzied pace that experts have identified it as the imminent ground zero for Europe's first climate refugees. *Delta* is a word that inherently carries with it the idea of an ending, that of a river, and a beginning, that of the sea. But it's also synonymous with frontier, with change, with blending. The forces at play in those vast expanses so influenced by the wind, the sand, the flamingos, and by the weathered and exceptionally tough people, imply a story that could only be expressed by the voices of not only a human chorus but also a biodiverse one, a chorus touched by expectation, pain, joy, and challenges. One in which all members share a single aspiration: to survive.

The delta became an obsession when a friend told me about the first house the waters would engulf. A place where one could still experience that boundary from the outermost edge. That house was on an island and belonged to a family clan. The owner kindly asked me how long I wanted to stay. "Three months?" I asked. I wanted to be discreet, not presumptuous of his potential generosity. Nobody lived in that old fisher's house, but occasionally a member of the owner's family would spend a few days there. The man shook his head disapprovingly and replied, "If you want to truly understand this, I think you should stay for a full year." I couldn't help but grin. I thanked him, realizing that, in accepting this invitation, I'd be celebrating my fiftieth birthday on the delta. Fifty. An age that would undoubtedly invite a different engagement with concepts like *life* and *finality*.

DELTA

TONIGHT I'LL SLEEP ALONE ON BUDA, the largest island in Catalonia at the southeastern tip of Spain, where the Ebro Delta meets the sea. The water gently laps at the sand along the sharp leading edge of the delta, some two hundred meters from La Casa de la Pantena, where I'm settling down. The tender sound of the sea spreads across the lagoons and hectares of rice fields inhabited by frogs, catfish the size of dolphins, mosquitoes, and cattle egrets in a spectacle that won't last, because this pleasant murmuring only precludes the bellowing roar soon to be cast by the sea before it floods a new stretch of coastline. The peaceful murmur is experienced as a truce, perhaps the last for La Pantena. The storms, destroying sandbars and urgently built jetties, engulf a hundred and fifty meters of land at a clip. According to its owner, La Pantena is three squalls away from becoming an underwater relic. It's a tense waiting game, one which has an inexorably natural epilogue: the flood.

Flooding can be considered "natural" because the planet is going through a warming cycle that, combined with an unprecedented increase in human activity, has brought about changes to the global climate, increasing temperatures and in turn the tides, causing sea levels to rise from the Mediterranean to Polynesia, and chipping away at coastlines at a speed never previously recorded. All this is happening here at the mouth of the Ebro Delta.

It's also a natural response to the proliferation of artificial dams and the diversion of water for irrigation, which prevent the river from delivering the sediment that keeps the delta sufficiently compact to resist the battering waves of the sea. The water flowing downstream is so clear it's almost pristine, so sorely lacking in dissolved solids that the few deposits that accumulate at the river's mouth are unable to counteract the force of an advancing Mediterranean. And without the deposited sediment, there is no resistance.

Deltas, symbolically, are welcoming spaces. Little has been written about them, though. To understand most people's notions of deltas, we must go back to the letter where everything begins. The fourth letter of the Greek alphabet, delta, is what Herodotus pictured while contemplating the arcuate triangle forming the mouth of the Nile. He didn't merely think about it, he wrote it, and thus unwittingly bequeathed both the image of the D and the name to all posterity.

Delta.

The D is also the initial letter of Zeus's name in modern Greek. In that numeration it has a value of four. This number poses something of a paradox, because the geometric representation of a delta is the triangle, a shape associated with the pyramids or the All-Seeing Eye, and in many belief systems this equates to another number: three.

Whatever the case, the delta is a confluence, where interchanges and paradoxes abound. It's a place where the three and the four intermingle, the surf shops and farmhouses, the bulls and the eels, a place where environmentalists, fishers, and hunters enjoy the environment in different ways. Furthermore, it's a place where the end (of the river) and the beginning (of the open sea) are amalgamated into a mire rife with life, often amphibious, that adapts to both salt and fresh water. Die, be reborn. Walk. Swim. Fly. Bike, too.

Awash in fragmentary novelties and hyperpublicized modern concepts, we have begun to overlook death. This is precisely why the delta has now taken on a riptide-like value: it brings together the beginning and the end.

The primordial Greek concept of a delta as a door, as a "luminous delta," falters here. In theory, the delta is a generator of life and light . . . until sediment stops flowing downstream because the water is dammed or diverted to nearby towns, cities, and farms. With this, the delta is stripped of its nature and condemned to a quick death.

Dams and irrigation are depriving many of the world's deltas of vital sediment. Today, they are all under threat of flooding. When it comes to the Ebro, the sea captures ten meters of beach every year: a frenetic advance. On a geological timescale, the tides are galloping toward us—not with the visual drama of a tsunami but through an unstoppable onslaught, accelerating at an unprecedented rate. The Mediterranean is one of the seas where coastal regression has become overwhelming. Apart from the Ebro, there is Valencia's Albufera, where the residents of El Saler, El Cabanyal, and Malvarrosa are begging for the construction of breakwaters and artificial reefs to hold back the advancing sea, as well as the Rhône and the Po deltas, where crops, beaches, and even cities are sinking—Venice being the most well-known and most dramatic example.

Farther away, Cyclone Aila brought a tremendous amount of stress to the mouth of the Ganges, which is spilling out like never before. In New Orleans, plans continue to be drawn up for evacuating the city when the Mississippi eventually begins its definitive flooding, while land managers watching over the Rhine calculate the continued costs of the infrastructure that allows them to keep the river six meters below sea level. The rebellions these deltas are waging have sediment as a common origin, though humankind is the main culprit.

While it might make an impression to list the names of a few famous rivers in distress, only 9 percent of the roughly eleven thousand deltas on the planet are suffering from regression, according to the scientific journal *Nature*. In fact, the number of rivers expanding is greater, standing at 12 percent, though this is due to continued and historical deforestation in countries like China and Brazil, where the Huang He, the Mekong, and the Amazon have been turned into emblems of senseless logging. Tons of discarded vegetation, branches, and tree trunks are dumped into rivers, where they wash downstream into deltas that are then forced to widen and grow.

But here we will talk about the others.

The ones that are retreating.

In 2021, the Nile experienced the greatest decrease in sediment being brought to its delta. Second on the list of rivers was the Ebro. The thirty million cubic meters of sediment the Ebro originally carried has dropped to one hundred fifty-nine thousand. That's not a typo. Thirty million. Against one hundred fifty-nine thousand. You don't have to be an oceanographer to see that number as an end point.

And yet . . .

"I'm not just going to stand around and watch. I might not accomplish anything, but I'm going to fight for it," Mateo Gallart told me the day he gave me the keys to La Pantena.

Pantena is the style of fishing historically practiced in the canal near the house, and it's from this art that La Casa de la Pantena got its name. Mateo has offered the house to me as a place I can live for the next year. He inherited Buda, and he manages the island on his family's behalf. He liked my idea of portraying life on this frontier and agreed to lend me the outermost house. The day he first showed it to me, four donkeys were crossing the wide, rectilinear path that leads to the sea, silhouetted against the twin hues of blue in the background and a single, intermediate palm tree in a perfectly Nilotic image. Another African parallel.

Buda is part of the delta that sustains the most direct blows from the scourge of the storms. Its coastline is shrinking rapidly, and while the sea hasn't invaded the rice fields yet, it might when the next gale strikes. If this happens, it's almost certain that La Administración, the multiheaded entity encompassing nearly everything within the Generalitat de Catalunya, will allege that this land is now useless, declare the public spaces flooded, and the local Buderos will watch as their rice fields are expropriated and made part of the Parc Natural.

"The same thing is going to happen to plenty of other farmers. They're going to lose their land. It'll only happen to us sooner because Buda sits on the easternmost edge of the delta and is more exposed," Mateo said in the doorway of my new refuge before going on to explain how little attention he was paid when he first began calling for a coalition between farmers, fishers, and other residents of the delta that could stand up to coastal regression and demand the return of sediment in an alternative manner to what La Administración had proposed.

That radiant morning, nobody doubted that managing the sediment was the biggest issue. Nevertheless, Mateo found himself wondering how he hadn't realized long, long ago what was happening. From day one, he'd devoted himself wholeheartedly to Buda, attending to the tiniest details, but not—as he'd later come to understand—rising high above the island to get a more complete, bird's-eye view. He understood its footprint well, and he was conscious of its internal dynamics. Sometimes, when you are deeply enmeshed within something, you lose focus on other, more distant forces that also determine your existence. Mateo hadn't yet understood how so much time had passed without him identifying the underlying disorders, ignoring warning signs and examples of changes already underway, not only in the Mediterranean but also in deltas such as the Niger River, or the impending disappearance of islands forming the archipelagos of, for example, Vanuatu, Kiribati, or the Maldives. He never thought such remote disturbances could affect him.

Until 2017.

"I saw it. I'm not exactly sure why, but I saw it. I realized that something, everything, was changing. The sea was pushing inland. There was no doubt whatsoever. The sea was encroaching, it was going to continue to do so, and intervention was necessary. I didn't know how, but something had to be done." He embarked on a campaign, using Buda as an example to warn neighbors about what was heading their way.

The nightmare Mateo Gallart has been conveying to other Ebrencs is in his opinion La Administración's wet dream: a delta flooded by the sea, a breeding ground for mosquitoes, pirates (another feature of this seaboard is drug trafficking), and diseases, a place where the only visible humans will be biologists collecting data and banding birds. The inhabitants of Terres de l'Ebre will, according to him, see a return to the delta of two hundred years ago, where there were no humans, no fishing, and no rice cultivation, because such exploits will have become illegal.

For three years, the locals listened to him, oblivious and indifferent to the fiery speeches of someone they considered an armchair apocalyptic, because, as Mateo put it: "I'm a landowner, the guy who historically must be taken down. They saw me as Little Mateo and his island, and many of them still do. As if the problems I'm exposing won't affect them too. As if I'm asking them to help me and nobody else. But they're not supporting each other, either. There's this feeling here that if things aren't going well for you, then it's better for me, but people should be worried—if your neighbor's about to go under, the next to do so might be you."

His insistence led him to hold public meetings about protecting the delta, though the differing interests of the unions, mayors, and government officials prevented any agreements. Mateo felt overstressed and powerless, making him effectively a lit fuse. In one meeting he stood up and said: "We mustn't celebrate when our neighbors are struggling. If we do that, we're dead meat. Look, here's what I'm saying. I'm from Barcelona. That's where I grew up. I've been in Buda for nineteen years, okay? But if things really start going downhill, I can pack up and leave. You're all from here. And whatever happens to Buda will happen to you. If Buda falls, we lose the entire delta, because it's the linchpin of the ecosystem we all share. If you don't defend this island, you won't be able to defend the others. In Barcelona they're studying us like lab rats to be disposed of when we're no longer useful. La Administración has time on its side. They're infinite, and we're finite. They're just waiting us out. The exodus won't be a sudden, violent one, but each one of you will gradually be made to realize you should slink humbly away, as if it were logical, as if it were something inevitable. But that's not true! We can and we must continue to defend this space."

The people listened to him with their standard indifference. Later, when the representative supporting the 1988 Coastal Act revealed plans for the delta that completely ignored Gallart's proclamations, the majority of those in attendance applauded.

Exactly one week later, something happened that Mateo described as a stroke of luck despite the misfortune that came with it: Gloria arrived. Winter Storm Jacob, as it was named in the United States and Canada, apparently underwent a sex change in the middle of the Atlantic Ocean and killed five people, forced seawater three kilometers inland, flooded 15 percent of all rice fields, razed mussel beds, vaporized Trabucador beach, and engulfed the one in Bassa de l'Arena. A few hours later, it had left a satellite image of destruction by drowning. True, experts had already predicted this would happen, but their prognoses were directed between thirty and fifty years in the future.

Older residents affirmed that they'd never seen anything like it. One declared that the Ebrencs would now become Spain's first climate refugees. Mateo Gallart began receiving calls from farmers, fishers, stockbreeders, restaurateurs, scientists, and environmental activists to get together and talk. The first item on the agenda was the sediment.

In mathematics, a capital D signifies differentiation. Change. The mouth of the Ebro is immersed in it. This space which until recently was a symbol of fertility is now both a limit and a risk. At these latitudes, a storm is assumed to be devastating when it reaches a magnitude of twelve on the Beaufort wind force scale, which is where it maxes out. Thanks to Gloria, we know that even an ordinary storm is enough for the water to overwhelm poorly reinforced sandbars and rocky jetties, destroying miles of coastline as if it were nothing.

It's easier to ponder these risks through La Pantena's lens. Storms have killed many in those waters. More information changes the tone, adding a menacing vibrato to the quiet lapping of the waves.

All deltas exist in a state of flux, though the Ebro does to a greater extent because it receives air from three different regions as well as the sea, experiencing constant and varied changes depending on wind direction. In addition to the peat moss, calcareous soil, seaweed, and sand that have been flowing down the river for centuries, there are also fighting bulls and the jota, the Aragonese dance fishers still perform to this day, its various leaps and physical displays contrasting sharply with the minimalism of the traditional Catalan sardana. The bulls and jota are the sediment that has drifted down from the upper Ebro to stay, and they seem more fixed and permanent than the earth on which they tread. They've taken root with the same adaptability as seaweed and will undoubtedly endure, because sentimental sediment isn't swept away by one storm, or two, or ten. For years now, many Ebrencs have been claiming the jota as part of their region's character, and ever since Gloria hit, they seem to be trying to reinvent themselves in the wake of that blow using their own sediment, regardless of where it came from.

The sediment itself is a root of a different sort, which is why I find myself thinking of my father as I settle in. When I was writing *Un cambio de verdad* and living for a year in the open pastures of Spain where my mother grew up, trying to understand her history from a different point of view, I became even more aware of something: my father, my siblings, and I belong to the space where land and sea meet. Soon enough, I'll be half a century old, an age with connotations of crossings and thresholds that until fairly recently people associated with life's final stretch. My father is still impaired by a tumor he's been living with for the past decade, but despite occasional somber intimations, the two of us still seize every opportunity to visit the coast. Now his condition has made many things difficult for him, he's stopped wading in the surf, though he still wants to keep it close at hand because the sand, the salt in the air, the glinting light, and the incredible mass of water all invite him to dredge up memories and imagine the future there, under the sun.

In my family, this aquatic boundary has always been an effervescent strip of present and future. On a sunny beach, it can seem as if the past no longer exists. That's how my father lives it, at least, and his devotion to the coast meant he and my mother were among the first Barcelonians to regularly take to the water in the regenerated Llobregat Delta. This is why discovering the Ebro was a sentimental milestone. My father had been a house painter capable of creating the shades his clients envisioned, and the light from these even more expansive spaces captured his eye and expanded the diversity of his palette.

Just a few strides from a duck making a taut line across the channel perpendicular to La Pantena, a gray heron pecks apart the shell of a crayfish, flaying the tail meat with its beak. In front of the house, half sunk into the banks, lie a couple of traps for catching eels. They're empty, and they'll stay that way for a good while. La Administración has banned eel fishing in Buda. Mateo considers it revenge for pending complaints. "La Administración is strong with the weak and weak with the strong," he says. "So they're beginning with Buda and my family."

Many Ebrencs consider hunting and fishing to be traditional in the delta and synonymous with balance and biodiversity, which is why they're outraged by the indiscriminate, modern stigmatization of both these practices, especially when those wielding the branding irons aren't paying attention to the details of why they're hunting here or fishing there. Sweeping criminalization, uninformed denunciation, and displays of political correctness that go beyond the bounds of common sense are new norms irritating the direct descendants of pirates and Vikings who are faithful to the rough-hewn characters of their ancestors and always willing to reveal the formidable wealth of invectives in their arsenal. These include *pixapins* ("pine pisser," used for city folk who leave Barcelona on weekends to get out into nature), *pela este préssec* ("peel that peach," meaning "do it now"), *maria bruta* ("dirty Mary," meaning something disgusting), *mal te caigue* ("you're fucked"), *pareixes de mas* ("you look like a hick"), or *quedarse loco* ("go crazy with something") and are deeply rooted words and expressions, a fertile vocabulary which comes from both upstream and the sea: pure oral sediment.

As with any true frontier, this delta sits on a simmering bed of creative expressions and words which are used to settle territorial showdowns in which great powers can intervene with hidden intentions. But sometimes words aren't enough, and the instinct is to evoke that phrase once attributed to a Prussian general: "The banks of the Ebro would be a true paradise if only man did not live on them."

When Mateo leaves, I go over to where three horses are grazing under a sun that doesn't seem to belong to the winter. The susurrous sea lies some two hundred meters away. I need to get a bicycle. When a squall is in the offing, even if it's not a magnitude twelve, you should have a bike at the ready and pedal fast, leaving the Mediterranean behind you in hope that the rising river hasn't cut off the meager arm of sand which, during dry periods, connects the island and mainland.

FRESH WATER

SEDIMENT

LA PANTENA HAS A HIPPED ROOF: an architectural design where rainwater runs down all four sides toward the walls. Similarly, it's situated between four bodies of water: a river, a sea, a lagoon, and the channel connecting the two freshwater bodies. The salt is always there, seeping inland or blown upstream by Buda's sweeping winds. Everything else on this final strip of the island is rice fields which, in March, are still dry and flecked with scrubs that grow at will.

It's ten steps from the porch to the canal. Across the strip of water, four donkeys and three horses graze freely. Roughly a quarter mile beyond them is the sea.

They say the inexorable advance of the sea will soon flood a significant part of the delta, and that Buda and La Pantena in particular will be the first part of Spain to founder. This land is receding while also sinking at a rate of three millimeters a year, though the last two winters were due more to the catastrophic double spectacle of storms Gloria and Filomena. The havoc wreaked by the latter is still evident on the beach, which is littered with glass and plastic bottles, cans, fishing nets, shattered hulls of boats, twisted iron, torn sailcloth, and cables, in addition to the branches, tree trunks, and spent cartridges strewn about the rest of the island. Since January is the heart of cyclone season, I figure I have a year's worth of calm during which I can settle into island life before the next storm catches me forewarned.

Simona, the supervisor, said yesterday that when the waters rise they can reach half the height of a tractor, and that the storms don't go easy on the houses. She's a tall woman with a strong, sinewy build, dark skin, a short, boyish haircut, and a face almost garnet in tone from having absorbed so much ultraviolet light. She speaks commandingly, ordering me to ask for permission before visiting the lagoon or the sea, or if I want to leave Buda, because I don't have a vehicle. Unless you have a boat, it is impossible to get off the island at this time of year unless you follow the road that runs through a mile or more of the Parc Natural. This road is impassable by bike or on foot; you can only travel it by car, and only if authorized by the guard. This is the same road by which I arrived with Mateo and which will connect me to the mainland for a few more months until I have to resort to the ferry. A mile of land with no rice fields, a wetland flocked with the delta's iconic and relentlessly promoted flamingos, mallards, glossy ibises, herons, and cattle egrets that often alight on the backs of French Camargue horses: when La Administración banned fighting bulls, which they considered dangerous, it also imported a herd of fifty horses which now offer a mammalian counterpoint to the horizon. As Mateo drove me to the house that first time, a western swamphen trotted across the road toward an eddying bend in the river into which black-winged stilts submerged their lengthy beaks, capturing worms and frogs.

"This used to be an Eden," Mateo said. "But it's getting overwhelmed."

I suppose I lacked the perspective to judge how far that landscape was from being Edenic. After two fantastical kilometers, the birds continued spreading across the wild rice paddies until we reached La Pantena, where I dropped off my luggage a few minutes later. Lined up in the canal were a number of half-sunken black traps and a couple of mud boats.

"Look," said Mateo, jutting a finger at the water, where a dozen massive crustaceans were floating. "Blue crabs. They're a plague now. Try not to fall in there."

He flashed a mischievous smile, tapping the rim of his unobtrusive glasses, which befitted his shirt and jacket, which were as monotonously formal as his trousers. His shoes shone and his close shave revealed a smooth complexion with a healthy tan that suggested a balanced life with long helpings of sun . . . though skin can, at times, be deceiving.

"It keeps me up at night to think how all of this will one day be gone," he muttered, standing in front of his porch.

We walked toward the beach. When we passed the last patch of rice, he pointed to the embankment he built himself, having invested "seventy thousand euros along with a lot of time and energy" into it, and launched into an elaborate description of the disputes he'd had with environmentalists about how best to protect the delta, lamenting that there seems to be no way of reaching an agreement with them, that these people argue about everything, that all they know how to do is go on and on about how dikes, breakwaters, and jetties—any fast, fixed structures—are no longer able to protect anything. Always criticizing "anything rigid, anything rigid" . . . only to find out that many of them wouldn't even be able to define what a delta is, what *this* delta is, or how it was formed.

It's been said that the Ebro Delta as we know it took shape thanks to industrial logging motivated by the need for lumber with which to build the Invincible Armada back in the sixteenth century. However, experts in hydraulics and sediment believe most existing deltas began to form around six thousand years ago. The rest is down to legend.

In the early twentieth century, the Ebro Delta was advancing ten meters a year due to sediment being carried downstream through the force of a watershed that cut diagonally across Spain without impediment until 1946, when new water regulations coincided with the beginning of the massive hydroelectric energy industry, supported by the construction of dams in the Pyrenees. And the delta has been receding ever since. In Riumar and El Serrallo, the beaches have been cut back by over three hundred meters, some of the more serious examples of regression.

All this was foreseeable, Mateo said from his vantage point atop the embankment. It had been twenty-three years since he first voiced his concerns about the upstream dams and the need for sediment to continue flowing down to the mouth of the delta so it could remain more or less where it was.

"But they didn't listen to me. The environmentalists wanted water. Everyone was talking about water. They made ball caps, T-shirts, and flags featuring the famous logo with the knotted pipeline. That's great, I told them, but instead of blue the pipe should be brown, the color of the sediment. Because that's what the delta needs, sediment. That's what mattered at the time. But nobody listened to me. Now here they are, all begging for sediment, all asking me why I changed my mind. *Isn't that what you wanted?* they're asking. Of course I did. Twenty years ago. Now there's no time left. It's too late for that now. If we want to save Buda, if any of us want to save these lands, we need sand now. Tons of sand and concrete to build dikes, like the Dutch do."

Standing there on the embankment, Mateo pointed to the areas where he'd extend the dikes and where he'd pile up the sand while rattling off a dizzying list of figures on the delta, from the two thousand nests built by yellow-legged gulls and cataloged by the forestry each year in Buda, to the 1,200 dams stemming the flow of Spain's waterways, 135 of which are specifically along the Ebro.

The numbers dance in the head of this sentimental scientist who manages a fantastic property, as large as it is beautiful, one in which he perceives bits of data alongside every taxonomic group. *Tadorna tadorna*, 109. *Anas platyrhynchos*, 12,609. *Pandion haliaetus*, 4. *Anas crecca*, 17,582. *Danaus plexippus*, 4 in Buda. *Larus audouinii*, 1,531 in the delta. It's not what he wants, but, having managed the island for so long, he now understands that survival, including his own, depends largely on statistics. It's even more dependent on morality, of course, though statistics offer a version of reality which can be used to justify certain arguments and actions that might otherwise fly in the face of that vaguest of entities known as Public Opinion. Or can it? Because when Mateo learned about the huge drop in sediment received by the Ebro between 1877 and 2015, he wondered what more objective proof would be needed by the bigwigs at La Administración—the fucking Administración—for them to take action on the Ribarroja, Flix, or Mequinenza dams, which hold back the vast majority of sediment. The statistics sang the clearest of songs. What, then, was the response?

He wound down his own speech by concluding that there are other numbers which count even more: numbers which correspond to the shares owned in hydroelectric companies. There was little to be done against those, at least in the short term. It would involve intense negotiations with sharklike executives and mayors of distant towns, and to achieve what exactly? It took him fifteen years and a major storm to convince the neighboring mayors of Sant Jaume d'Enveja and Deltebre that they had to change the nature of their dynamics and face their receding shorelines as a united front; he wasn't about to put his nose right back to the grindstone to entice some strangers upriver. Nor was it his job to do so. That's the purpose of La Administración. Those two words were forever at the tip of his tongue: La. Administración. He was aware he should swallow them, but that tentacular organism occupied everything, even his dreams, softly purring *I'm going to sink you . . . I'm going to sink you.* Quite literally.

"They want to sink us," he said from atop the embankment, contemplating the fields which would soon be flooded.

We stood a little more than a meter above the rice fields at our feet, and in a vastness as flat as this, that sliver of height was a vantage point. A purple heron emerged from an irrigation canal with a heavy flapping of its wings, zigzagging slowly and unsteadily into the wind until, having steadied itself, it changed direction, allowing a tailwind to carry it into the lagoon.

"Yes, now the environmentalists want more sediment," Mateo muttered. "They've commissioned who knows what kinds of studies, and they're saying a million and a half tons would be enough to get the situation back under control. But I don't have time."

He turned to face the sea. The lighthouse looked tiny, emitting flashes of red out in the middle of the water.

"I'm tired. I've been in charge of Buda for almost twenty years, and it's been a struggle. Nice, right? A constant struggle. My family bought the island in 1927, and I'd like to stick it out here at least long enough to celebrate a hundred years. I hope the island holds out until then. I hope the land isn't expropriated. We'll see. I'm retiring anyway. Going to live in Terra Alta. I'm not staying here."

In Giuseppe Tomasi di Lampedusa's novel *The Leopard*, Don Fabrizio, prince of Salina, the famous Sicilian nobleman whose family insignia was the leopard, alludes to what a hundred years meant to him back in the nineteenth century: "We live in a changing reality to which we try to adapt ourselves like seaweed bending under the pressure of water. Holy Church has been granted an explicit promise of immortality; we, as a social class, have not. Any palliative which may give us another hundred years of life is like an eternity to us."

Over the decades, this once-stable reality has slowly been dissolving into a liquid. A fluid reality. This is how the twenty-first century has come to define this world made of parts both solid and virtual, where everything seems to be floating and it's easy to doubt the firmness of the ground you walk on. The world is a grand, vast, insecure delta whose roots are known by another name, sediment, an engrossing, absorbing form of soil which advances as it vanishes, spanning waters, times, farms, stories that may well be true in one way or another, starring Fabrizios and Mateos until they form something completely new and which, like everything else, will not last.

From the air, the delta resembles an asymmetrical anchor or a giant fishhook. Buda is the point of that hook, the sharpest end, pierced by the blue stain of the lagoon separated from the sea by a faint yellow line: the sand. The island forms something of a triangle that seems almost integrated with the mainland until you notice the slight line drawn by the Migjorn, the river disconnecting it.

When it was a military port, the most valuable jewel in the Aragón crown, Buda was known as Port Fangós. It was abandoned during the fifteenth century due to the accumulation of sediment, and was still considered untamed as recently as the early twentieth century. The dictator Primo de Rivera advised several businesspeople that these uninhabited areas would soon become an opportunity to invest, and a handful of wealthy families responded to this alluring call.

José Facundo Gallart bought the island in 1927. In the deed he only included two of his sons, Marcelo and José, Mateo's grandfather, because the remaining heir didn't like to hunt: what good would so much nature have been for him?

Mateo affirms that his grandfather José Gallart amassed a considerable fortune importing British steel. During the long stretches of time he spent in London, he became friends with members of British high society, who invited him on safaris in their former colonies, affording him the opportunity to hunt in countries like Mozambique, Tanzania, Kenya, and India, thus sparking his desire to have his own lands on which he could reciprocate his English friends' offers with a few days in the fields, gun in hand. The delta turned out to be the ideal opportunity.

During the first half of the twentieth century, the Gallarts enjoyed the uninhabited wetlands, organizing the occasional hunting party and inviting aristocrats, lords, and other members of the British bourgeoisie they'd met at various receptions. But eventually the family thought about getting a return on their investment. And rice was the solution.

The younger José Gallart, the heir to the land, joined the wave of rice crops spreading across the delta, planting dozens of hectares, though his interest in and sympathy for the incipient environmentalist movement led him to ignore the prevailing trend of transforming the wetlands into paddies and growing rice only on elevated ground, respecting the existing lagoons. Instead, to protect the fauna, he built an embankment that separated the rice fields from the lagoons. The combination of grain and fishing began generating revenue. Seven families, all farm laborers and fishers, settled on the island, but there were no hands left for the immense wetlands, so supervisor Manel Bosch started recruiting workers in nearby La Cava. He offered them a thatched-roof shack, which would be rent-free until the crop was harvested, and all agreements were verbal.

Soon enough, over seventy families were planting and fishing on an island where, with the large central farmhouse known as El Mas as the epicenter, several homes had been built, along with a church, a school, and a tavern. Locals from around the delta began referring to Buda as La Capital.

Some describe that period on the island as a party. Others say they worked like slaves. Most of the houses still standing are known by the names of the people—well, the men—who inhabited them. Uncle Llull's shack, where they kept the rice harvesting tools. Nil's, Pas's, Paquito's, Perico de Claus's . . . and Ramon's La Pantena, where I am, and which refers to the father of Ramoneta, the woman who lived her entire life in the house with her husband Pep.

The grandson of Manel Bosch the recruiter is known in Spanish as Manuel Bosch, to distinguish him from his grandfather, and he was the one who took over from his grandfather as supervisor, meaning he experienced the transformation caused by machinery arriving on the island. Tractors sped up the harvesting process. Farmhands, who were once in scant supply, were now overly abundant, and many laborers who were unable to find work returned to their hometowns. Laia, Mateo's aunt, who inherited half the island, sold part of it to the Generalitat. Since then, that section has been managed by the Departament de Medi Ambient.

The island began to empty. The new means of industrial production traded fresh air for profit-and-loss statements, and when the numbers stopped adding up, Mateo's father, who had been tasked with administering Buda near the end of the twentieth century, wrote in his will that the island was to be sold upon his death. The decision had been made . . . or nearly so, because he'd added a clause that would allow this stipulation to be revoked if despite all the warnings one of his children chose to complicate their lives by accepting the inheritance of that deteriorating space. In rescuing the island on his family's behalf, Mateo was made aware of the bankruptcy he was then facing while at the same time being forced to come to terms with the expropriation of the lagoons by a state wielding the full force of the Coastal Act. They denied him permission to hunt or fish on those lands, a permit the Act itself had specifically established as compensation for those whose lands had been expropriated. Was the law acting in violation of the law just to bully him? They're plundering us, he thought. Either someone is collecting debts or simply abusing their power. He quickly concluded that he'd have to let go of the last remaining tenant farmers if he wanted to offset his losses and improve production.

Manuel Bosch left the island in 2003. For a few "painful" years, Mateo kept things more or less as they'd been when his father bequeathed them, but the 2008 global financial crisis drove costs even higher. To maintain profitability, it was no longer enough to rent farm machinery; you had to have specific equipment, a fleet of tractors to pull it, as well as increasingly expensive phytosanitary products or highly efficient water pumps, along with the fuel needed to run them. In 2009, there were fourteen families left on Buda, and they all received a letter informing them that they'd have to leave the island. Well, not quite. Not Ramoneta and Pep. They were the only ones who lived off fishing alone. And that was enough to keep them from devoting themselves to rice.

The entrance to La Pantena seems to belong to a different house entirely. The foyer turns out to be a long workbench with deep sinks and a tap primarily for cleaning fish. Around the other side of the wall lies the home: a spacious living room with a kitchen, a fireplace, a table for six, and a television situated next to one of the three windows filtering light into the room. All three are covered with mesh to protect against the mosquitoes which will come.

Across from the workbench is a room unused since Héctor, the couple's son, passed away. At the other end of the house, across from the living room, is my bedroom. The afternoon sun enters through the large double-paned window, bathing the room in an earthy ocher and making it the warmest space in the house. It will be a great refuge come winter. The roof is lined with chipboard to prevent leaks. I start a fire with the wood I collected on the other side of the canal after crossing a small bridge.

If I need more firewood or water, I'll have to ask Simona, though Buda's other two workers are also available to help. That's what the supervisor said. My first goal is to get a bike I can use to go shopping in town without depending on others. Sant Jaume is fourteen kilometers away, and the road back can be long when you're on foot carrying two weeks' worth of food. I could do a run every three or four days, but I want to spend as much time on the island as possible, the way Ramoneta and Pep did.

Pep's mother gave birth standing up because she didn't have time to get to the hospital. It was too far away. Pep married Ramona at the age of twelve, and they were together until the end. They had a house on the side of the Deltebre–Riumar road, but they hardly ever set foot in it, preferring La Pantena.

Pep always dressed for work: his corduroy pants, plaid shirt, work boots, in fact his whole appearance contrasted with Ramoneta's perfectly manicured metallic-pink nails, green eye shadow, and impeccable mascara. She was smart, vivacious, and vainglorious; he, calm, crafty, "with a brain like a computer." There always seemed to be a pot of fish stew on the stove, and whenever someone asked them what to bring, they'd reply: "Anything, really. We're poor."

They appreciated bread, sweets, oranges, and peanuts, and while visitors always brought something, Pep often found himself wanting more without being willing to offer much himself in return. But what can you say to people who live off the water while unable to swim? On stormy days, when the island shut down and it was impossible to cross to the other shore even by boat, they could go for days without bread. His stinginess, though, never left them short of friends. Whenever they went into town to go shopping or visit the bank, it was like embarking on an endless journey; at every step, they were stopped by neighbors wanting to know how life was going in that place which, over the years, had acquired an increasingly enigmatic character.

The couple from La Pantena lived most of their lives with a single electric generator; to save money they only turned this on when absolutely necessary. Pep got up three or four times a night to check how many fish were in the nets. Sometimes he even caught a few prawns and black shrimp, or fished for eels with a worm and a line. They had their fill of mullet, eel, sea bass, and gilthead bream, which the fishers washed down with whiskey while casting the occasional glance at the painting of three ducks which still hangs over the fireplace. In my room, above the headboard of my new bed, hangs another realistic representation of waterfowl, but this time only two.

Héctor, their son, died before the couple. He was the skipper of the restaurant Cava en Got, made a name for himself as a paella cook, ran a brothel he inherited, and frequented a "dangerous" dive bar in La Cava. When both his health and his business dealings went south, the crown of his head cleared itself of hair and he settled back in with his parents in La Pantena, following in his father's footsteps of dressing daily for work.

But manual labor wasn't enough to rid him of his darker self. He often argued with his parents; or, rather, he was the recipient of their indignant reprimands after showing up for work drunk or high. Héctor tried to temper his rage, came to terms with his highs and lows, and started to dredge, fish, and clean the canal. To this day, he's remembered on the island as an honest person who, regardless of his shortcomings, performed his duties.

One morning, Héctor got out of bed feeling a bit off. He'd been awake since the wee hours. He told Dylan, one of his coworkers, that he wasn't quite himself, but before long he was sinking his hoe into the ground as he always did. He worked all day. Before dinner, Simona told Héctor she'd like to invite him to a meal celebrating her son's first Communion on Saturday. Héctor said goodbye to the supervisor and went to have dinner with his parents on the porch. All of a sudden, he stood up so abruptly he knocked his plate to the floor. "I'm dying! I'm dying! Call Simona!" he cried to Ramoneta. "Get an ambulance here!" Stumbling, he reached for the door, pulled back the screen, took two steps into his room, and collapsed, face first, on the bed with his legs still on the ground. And with that he was gone.

They buried his ashes next to the eucalyptus tree he had planted a year before, along the road that leads from La Pantena to the last remaining bird observatory. After his passing, his parents deteriorated quickly. They were buried with him, though some of Pep's ashes were also scattered into the canal.

People remember Pep and Ramoneta's marriage with such sincere affection that it seems to come from an entirely different time. There are no rifts, no suspicious affectations whenever someone mentions them, despite the drugs and solicitation on their boy's résumé. In a few days, in this room, I'll be having a conversation with a man who'll be brought to tears when he sees the old swallow's nest hanging on a wall. "They never stole anything from anyone," that man will say. As if they were an exception.

Pep, Ramoneta, Juanito de Cardona, Duardet . . . this place is teeming with diminutive forms of names, workers' informal titles signifying proximity to the family if not outright affection. Affection is bestowed through physical touch. While its close contact can breed affection, it can also cause friction, so these diminutives are more an indication of those individuals who've had a long history here in the delta. The same is true with *malnoms*, nicknames, which summarize a person in a flash by seizing on physical or spiritual quirks and marking them once and forever. Diminutives and *malnoms* aren't commonly used when it comes to the landowners, some of whom are still referred to as *amos* or, above all, *siñors*.

Social strata are more mixed than the sediment beneath our feet. The layers of different clay, branches, sands, plants, and carrion only intermingle and meld on occasion, though local inhabitants would like the water to become even dirtier. There is a real thirst for turbidity, a desire to see the brown water that darkened the ancient fertile deltas. Here, murkiness is gold, but the true masters upriver, the Lords of Electricity, maintain the crystalline flow that's weakening the ground to the point it's almost evanescent: liquidating a part of history, as marine biologist Rachel Carson would say. "The sediments are a sort of epic poem of the earth. When we are wise enough, perhaps we can read in them all of past history," wrote Carson, who revolutionized environmental thinking with her book *Silent Spring*. Today, humans displace three times more sediment than the oceans receive, causing paradoxical situations like the one occurring now near the Ribarroja dam. There, accumulation has created an inland delta; the Spanish government has labelled this artificial delta a Natural Protected Area, while allowing the true natural delta to dissolve from a lack of that same sediment. Meanwhile, people living near the dam are protesting because the stench welling up from the retained silt is suffocating the town, having become so toxic it echoes India's Ganges, which feeds the largest delta on earth and whose supposedly purifying holy waters are being poisoned by the corpses and garbage thrown into its riverbed.

The Mississippi River is plagued by chemical spills in addition to the vertiginous coastal regression being fought with dredges working tirelessly to move tons of sand to prevent flooding in and around New Orleans, one of the most threatened cities in the world. Destrehan, a few miles outside New Orleans, is a perfect example. When you search for Destrehan online, it's not defined as a city or a town but as a place. This may be due to its inexact location, sitting atop a mass of shifting sand so unsteady that nobody knows how it manages to reappear year after year when hurricane season has ended. Or perhaps it's because the internet is anticipating the place's imminently foreseeable desolation, now the majority of inhabitants are moving out, having learned that methane, oil, and salt extraction companies have eroded the already ultrafragile subsoil, turning it into a sort of contaminated Gruyère where the risk of dying from cancer is eight hundred times the US national average. But what best explains the decision to label Destrehan a "place," a word both unaffiliated and imprecise, are the tensions and interests that benefit some while harming others. This is why it's important to be aware that, when the industrialists decided to take over even more space to continue drilling, they bought up the large plantations owned by white families who had evacuated an area where thousands of Black people still live. Thus, in the aftermath of Operation Destrehan, what could have been considered a town or small city is now a festering landscape pockmarked with boreholes and populated almost exclusively by Black families breathing such toxic air that it seems illogical to describe it using the same word we use to discuss communities where human beings live. Destrehan's conditions more closely resemble those of some distant planet or some other unlivable and therefore uninhabited territory: spaces no one could ever justify calling a "locality."

Unbridled extractivism and institutionalized poverty are common in many large deltas around the world. Until recently, they were considered lush, fertile paradises. Spring is already silent in Destrehan. Its sound is dwindling in Bangladesh, where the

Ganges Delta is neck and neck with Mississippi in the race to be the fastest-retreating waterway on the planet. In Liberia, the Mesurado Delta is a dumping ground with an ironic name ("mesurado" means "measured" in Spanish). And the Yellow River and the Rhône also confirm the silence of Rachel Carson's title: there, hydraulic despotism is the order of the day.

China's Yellow River is an excellent example of how arrogance and greed can waste a good solution. Our story begins in the third millennium BC, when Emperor Yao commissioned an engineer by the name of Gun to solve the problem of a river that kept overrunning its banks, flooding villages and crops alike, to say nothing of the thousands of farmers and animals killed, resulting in it being dubbed China's Sorrow and the Scourge of the Sons of Han.

Gun ordered the construction of dikes built with stones, wood, and clay. These walls were able to stand up against a few floods before eventually giving way to the force of the water. The emperor ordered that the expert be put to death and handed over the responsibility of solving the problem to a younger engineer by the name of Yu, who happened to be the now dead man's son.

Yu spent a lot of time on foot, roaming the river and its tributaries. He studied the banks, the land and surrounding mountains, the ravines, the strength of the currents, and the lines traced by the meandering branches, before finally concluding that he'd have to drain several sections of the river and lay a network of canals for irrigating fields and pastures. Thousands of people worked for thirteen years. To fulfill his promise of not seeing his family until he had completed his work, it has been said that Yu didn't visit his wife or son during this time. Once finished, he waited for the rains to come. When the sky opened, releasing torrents of water upon the land, the river swelled, its speed increasing to a breakneck pace, but the massive overflow was now drawn into a magnificent web of canals and plowed land. Yu himself was elevated to the status of legend.

There is no evidence Yu actually existed. Even if he did, there isn't anything to indicate that his actions had such a decisive effect on the river. Presumably, a myth had been created to anchor the notion that a single determined, well-informed person can tame even the wildest of elements. Since then, the Chinese have continued to drain and divert the Yellow River and its tributaries, building massive dikes and multiplying the number of dams. The most colossal of all such projects is the Three Gorges Dam: the pinnacle of hydraulic despotism, of human beings' efforts to tame nature, and a monument to the arrogance of our species, which imagines itself capable of imposing its artifices upon the dynamics of the cosmos.

What the passage of time shows us, however, is that when you alter the water's flow, the problems solved in one place trigger issues in another. "Thinking that current technology can nullify the danger would be even more of a mistake," biologist Alex Richter-Boix writes regarding another river in China, "because archeology and geology reveal that past actions have aggravated flooding in the long term: the construction of each new levee caused new sediment to accumulate in the riverbed, raising its level and increasing the likelihood of overflowing its banks. Higher river walls were then built, resulting in the accumulation of more sediment, in a process repeated ad infinitum. As soon as they first altered the course of the Yellow River, the Chinese people set in motion a vicious cycle from which they still haven't been able to escape."

The same gyre in which the Ebro also turns.

The sun is descending at La Pantena when I see a man in front of the porch. He pokes at the branches of the Siamese pine with the handle of a landing net.

"Hi. I'm Gonzalo, your neighbor. We came to pick up pine cones for the fire."

From inside the house, which is now my own, two women emerge. "The door was open," one of them says.

They introduce themselves as Gonzalo's ex and Teresa, with whom he now lives.

"But we're not screwing," Gonzalo clarifies, quietly enough for neither woman to hear.

They're a bit tipsy. They've had dinner at a restaurant on the other shore, and with the accompanying wine, there you have it. They separate Gonzalo from his net and, laughing, take turns trying to knock down the pine cones. Gonzalo says that when they go to the restaurant they have to get picked up by boat: a little business run by his cousin.

Gonzalo is the third of the seven Gallart siblings. He settled into Buda life a few months ago, though an illness he chooses not to specify requires that he frequently head up to Barcelona. His house is less than a mile from mine. We're the only two who sleep on the island, because Mateo and the workers don't spend the night unless it's fishing season or there are ducks to scare away. The rest of the family drops in on certain weekends or for a few days of vacation, and during these visits they stay in the old tenant farmers' shacks. And then there are the yogis, hunters, and other sorts of tourists who'll occasionally rent El Mas for a few days.

He recommends I leave the porch light on at night, because this can be a desolate place and it's helpful to let folks know there's someone at home. I doubt, though, whether announcing my presence is any more appropriate than hiding it. Meanwhile, Gonzalo goes on to add that tractors will soon begin to open up the furrows into which the rice will be sown, and that I'll be seeing some workers hired specifically for that purpose. "These people are whip-smart. I'm sure you'll learn a lot from them. Just don't pay any attention to Simona." Gonzalo views the supervisor the same way Mateo views La Administración. "That woman thinks she owns Buda," he says before heading off with his net full of pine cones.

The three of them head straight down the road to El Mas when Simona's 4x4 pickup appears, kicking up a cloud of dust. The truck passes the group, nobody waving to anyone, turns toward La Pantena, and parks in front of the porch. The supervisor asks if everything is good, if there's anything I need. She goes inside, plugs in the TV, and flips through the channels. Apart from the local delta programming, there are no stations in Catalan, the language Simona speaks with me. Gonzalo, his ex, Teresa, and Mateo all addressed me in Spanish, though soon enough I'll be hearing the two brothers speaking perfect Catalan.

After returning to the porch, Simona repeats the advice about keeping the light on, adding that we're in a stash zone: a drug shipment was seized on the beach not too long ago. As if on cue, a Guardia Civil patrol unit appears, parking directly behind the pickup because there's only room for one car on the narrow lane leading to La Pantena. Two uniformed men exit the vehicle; one agent says he's here to introduce the other, who's only recently joined the local corps. The new one identifies himself by his two last names, asks who I am, what I'm doing there, and concludes that, if you don't have a vehicle, there shouldn't be any moving lights in Buda, correct? Other than the headlights of your neighbor Gonzalo's truck, correct? But it seems like that gentleman, Gonzalo, isn't always home, correct? So if I notice any unusual activity, they expect me to report it to them.

"How?" I ask.

"Just call me, and that's it," Simona says.

By the time everyone has left, night has fallen. I leave the porch light turned off. The night, starless and still, unfolds enigmatically. The flickering of the distant lighthouse is the lone tear in the darkened curtain. What's invisible becomes pronounced: the splash of a sea bass in the channel, something scurrying through the reeds, croaking frogs, squawking herons hastening the night, birdcalls I don't recognize. What I don't hear is the sea. Nor the river. It's just twenty meters away, and yet the buffering thicket of reeds isolates me from its roar. I close the door behind me without turning on the light.

I wake up naturally after eight hours of sleep; in the city I'd only been getting five or six. A large bird is walking across the roof. Along the edge of the rice field, three glossy ibises stand in a line, unable to detect me through the window. Between the foggy glass and the anti-mosquito mesh, I can serenely contemplate the flocks of sparrows flying overhead after leaving the reedbeds in which they nestle. They add their loud trills to the symphony, which includes gentle songs with the more strident shrieks and squawks, the light spluttering of birds that seem to move in an almost mechanical way, the chattering cadence, the semi-ancient chirping, the chittering. Biodiversity is in the air, and the river isn't far behind. There is an effervescent movement of waters resulting from sudden immersions, frolicking splashes, the aerial pirouette of leaping fish silhouetted like daggers against the sun.

A restorative breeze blows, loosing purple herons like arrows and bringing the rumble of a tractor breaking up the sod. Along the edges of the rice I look for plants growing next to the canal and the drainage ditches, though the larger marsh herbs take root in the lagoon: huge formations resembling spiked feather dusters, walls of reeds, and the clusters of cattails that lent their name to Buda and which are now so widely scattered they're all but nonexistent. Because these grassy wetland plants were once so abundant that people referred to the island by alluding to its star flora, the *bova*, which is what they call cattails here, and thanks to people putting a modern spin on local pronunciation, the island of the *bovas* became Buda. Today it's hard to find cattails anywhere on the island. The advancing salt water has all but eradicated the Typhaceae family of plants, which are now even harder to find in La Pirenaica, the stretch of rice fields situated between the La Pantena channel and the sea.

La Pirenaica includes Buda's easternmost parcels of land: the area that will be first to flood and into which the salt seeps at will, though the overall effect is still muted by the freshwater pumps operating around the clock. This most vulnerable soil reminds us that a delta is forever young, proffering the certainty of renewable energy with 100 percent returns. And as with any frontier, change often takes place violently and in plain sight. It is all connected with this tender vastness being renewed out in the open, without deceit. Life here is so superficial it seems to hold no secrets, or perhaps secrets can't be kept because dawn reveals them all: this morning, during my walk, I discover the lagoon's embankment strewn with the claws and carcasses of crabs devoured by birds the night before. There are also the remains of amphibian victims of the marsh harrier, footprints of ducks that either mated or gathered in search of protein or warmth. The gangway of dead crabs, which ends at the ever-shrinking beach, is a tribute to life, to the everyday labors of those survivors who made do with what there was while knowing that, as soon as all this is flooded, they'll up and fly. The ibis doesn't put down any roots. Fifteen years ago, there weren't any, and today forty thousand come together without worrying about where they'll be having breakfast tomorrow. One of the advantages of having wings.

A trickle of water from the rice field flows into the sea, dividing the beach into two. The southern part belongs to the Parc Natural and the northern part to the extended Gallart family. Since the birds have begun to nest, I've been advised to avoid walking along the beach, and that if I do, to keep to the left bank.

"Pay attention, because if you don't, there'll be fines to pay, and we're the ones who have to pay them," Simona said.

But I've also been assured that if I don't go near the lagoons I'm not disrupting anything, so I walk along the shore, pointing my binoculars at the flocks of birds floating in the fresh water. Since winter is still rife with wind and cold, I entrench myself in a cluster of dunes shored up by plant growth. Lying on the sand next to a massive tamarisk tree, I can neither feel nor hear the wind, and even if I were to get a little closer to the birds, I'd say they're fine, because coots, flamingos, mallards, shovelers, and even a few cormorants are right there in front of me yet still calm. The sun beats down. After a while I take off my polar fleece.

This atmosphere is very dear to me. I spent my childhood on sandy beaches, toasting my half-naked body, and now the decades have passed, I realize the seaside was where my father and I learned to cherish the vastness. I once wrote that my father's name is Gabriel, that he's the son of a Gabriel, and that the third member of this list is me. Although my father followed in the footsteps of his house painter father and brother, he would have liked to have delved more into mathematics. In any case, whenever he found himself with brush in hand, he'd blend his paints until he achieved colors only he could see, and today I know and understand the lights and shores that inspired him to bring the Mediterranean to other people's homes.

The roller and the broad brush create atmospheres on a grand scale, which is why I can see my father's hand in the sky, in the rivers, in the hillsides, in the seas. Give my father wide spaces where he can stretch out his arm. And if he doesn't have them, he'll go looking for them, like when school theater festivals were being organized and he and his brother were put in charge of painting twenty-five square meters of stage curtains and wings. To make up for the disappointment of working in a profession he didn't enjoy at first, he spent five years studying piano, his thick painter's fingers dancing across the keys, releasing his repressed artistry. I've never heard him play the piano—we never had one in our house because there was "no money for that"—but it's clear he carries it inside him. Now he's retired, his old music has a calming effect on him now he sees his days diminished by the tumor which accompanies him and which he's accepted as one of the occupational hazards that comes with living. Immersed in the decline of his veteran body, he remains faithful to a particular ritual: the one place he always wants to be is by the sea.

I've fallen asleep among the dunes. When I open my eyes, I see dozens of seagulls flying over me, pondering whether it's time for me to be devoured. I sit up, and the gulls flap away.

On the beach I contemplate the theater of this world: the sphere is perfect, the sky is clear, and Nature herself can be seen for dozens of kilometers in all directions. From the north, where land and sea meet, the mountain chain stretches out as far as Montsià, forming a semicircle that connects with this great body of water, completing the impeccable circle of which I am the nipple. There are no margins here, or if there are, they seem so far away they might as well not exist. Everything is central, everything is always here. The periphery is something invented by others. It's up to you to live according to these people's fantasies or to grow from around your own two feet.

What exotic, global thoughts these are.

The sea is wonderful because it makes you think in a downward direction. We're so unused to its inverted immensity that practically everything there at the bottom remains yet to be discovered. We know a lot about airplanes but almost nothing about the limits of diving or underwater Everests, even though three-quarters of the globe's surface is covered in seas, even though we're descended from fish, our fins transformed into arms and legs, gills into lungs, even though the sodium, potassium, and calcium in our bloodstreams are in similar proportions to those found in seawater.

Humidity and darkness have complicated our relationship with the environment. Half the oceanic world receives no sunlight: no known form of plant life can survive beyond a depth of 120 meters. If plants form a key part of the animalic diet, it's certainly understandable that our ancestors found it difficult to comprehend the existence of beings in that soulless aquatic atmosphere. That is until the early nineteenth century, when a few innovative devices made it possible to collect clumps of pelagic silt which turned out to be filled with worms, thus beginning our enlightenment when it came to the existence of life in the abyss. In 1860, when the exploratory sloop HMS *Bulldog* hauled up a 1,260-fathom sounding line with thirteen starfish attached to it, experts declared, "The depths have delivered us a long-awaited message." There was indeed life down there.

Oceanographic vessels were designed to be equipped with advanced hydrophones which could detect remote sounds in the deep, and the frilled shark was heard at a depth of two thousand meters. But even with this new avalanche of information, it wasn't until the summer of 1947 that we ceased to believe the bottom of the sea was flat; this was when the Swedish ship *Albatross*, which had been chartered to explore the deepest reaches of the ocean floor, found massive elevations and depressions during its crossing of the Atlantic toward the Panama Canal. We now know of five trenches in the Pacific Ocean that plunge more than ten kilometers below sea level. We also know that the Atlantic basin has sedimentary layers more than four thousand meters thick. Imagine two and a half vertical miles of organisms that have been deposited with the telluric slowness of what has come to be described as "marine snow."

How does it snow underwater? Gravel, boulders, and shells, but mostly millions and millions of tiny bits of limestone and silicates, of the skeletons and cartilage that once characterized the bodies of whales, squid, dolphins, cod, octopuses, eels, halibut, sardines, shrimps, prawns, mahi-mahi, and tuna, in addition to birds felled while flying over the sea, captains, cooks, sailors, passengers of the *Wilhelm Gustloff* and *Titanic* as well as those of thousands of smaller vessels, fishing boats, pirates, Vikings, crashed planes . . . imagine all of them as particles filtering through the depths, day after day throughout the millennia, like flakes on the water, being dragged down by their own weight into the darkening abyss.

Tons of these flakes are gradually drifting toward the mouth of the Ebro. Before, the flakes from the sea intermingled with those flowing from upstream, merging to form a layer of substrate which is the delta. Now, most of the marine snow circulates at the mercy of the current, encountering no buildup of river flakes settled and compacted enough to stop it.

Who can say whether, by some magic, the Ebro Delta might have received some of the snow about which Henry Beston wrote in *The Outermost House*, the book I've begun to reread on the dune. I read it for the first time a few months ago to get a sense of what life in La Pantena might be like, and now I've returned to it in the knowledge that, in this environment which is also his, I may come to a better understanding of it. The book narrates his experiences after he managed to construct a retreat for himself, a little house perched atop the last cliff standing along the forearm of Cape Cod and exposed to all the winds and salt. The house, which he named the Fo'castle, enveloped him, making him part of it. Beston understood immediately that it wouldn't be enough for him to enjoy a few days or weeks ensconced there, deciding instead to stay and spend "a year of life" to both write about and write with his "outermost house." That's the root of this book, one which Rachel Carson said was the only book that ever influenced her writing and which Mary Oliver described as "the most timeless book I know."

Beston was clear about the sun being the one great dramatic opus which governs our lives. Inspired by this star and the rarity and wonder of his solitude, for the next twelve months he defined his own style as a writer capable of presenting nature with enduring words. "A day of rain, another bright week, and all earth will be filled with the tremor and the thrust of the new year's new energies." Such was his announcement of spring.

The Fo'castle shared a number of things with La Pantena: it had two rooms, it was the last house before the sea, and it was seriously threatened by an eroding beach.

Shortly after finishing the book, Beston married and significantly cut back on his visits to the Cape, but since the Fo'castle had become something of an icon thanks to his narrative, the writer bequeathed the cottage to the Massachusetts Audubon Society in 1960. Four years later, it was declared a National Literary Landmark. But by that time, the structure had been moved from the site upon which Beston had originally built it so it wouldn't succumb to the advancing waves. Not long after that, it was relocated again for the same reason, becoming a nomadic monument.

Henry Beston passed away in April 1968. Less than ten years later, in February 1978, a violent winter storm uprooted the Fo'castle from its final foundations and it disappeared into the sea. The only items recovered were the latrine and the metal plate commemorating the house's landmark status. The rest of the house lies in pieces somewhere on the ocean floor, but it also continues to exist, in a much more complete form, in the imagination of those who ever visited it or have read Beston's book. Who can say whether a few snowy flakes from the Fo'castle could have floated as far as here, or if one day, in the not-too-distant future, their disintegrated microparticles will have been deposited atop what will already have become the detritus of a flooded La Pantena?

Local author Jordi Gilabert has imagined the Ebro Delta in 2095, when the advancing waters are about to swamp several cemeteries. The inhabitants of the affected towns are divided between those who want to transfer the remains to a safer place and those who'd rather cremate them. This situation is antipodean to the one described by Ștefan Bănulescu, who recounts a child's funeral in the Danube Delta. A ferry steers along in search of dunes, hillocks, any sort of terrain elevated and sturdy enough to bury the young body while winter is sending an icy storm which threatens to alter the coastline, demolishing any slope, any bank. Even if they're able to find a point high enough to bury this child, how long will it last before the sea engulfs it?

To bury or not to bury? To exhume or leave at rest? Bănulescu and Gilabert both demonstrate how the unsteadiness of the ground beneath our feet can influence bodies even after death. Both writers invite us to consider the challenges unique to death in the delta, where sacred spaces can be flooded and memory is suddenly no longer welcome.

At Paquito's shack, eight men unwrap sandwiches comprised mostly of cured, sliced meats. Dylan, who was clearing an irrigation canal of algae and scrub three minutes ago, sinks his teeth into some chorizo. Like the others, he's dressed in green work overalls with a gaiter around his stout neck. Being a seasoned veteran lends him a commanding presence, punctuated by the smooth, brown skin of an Indigenous Peruvian and his shock of jet-black hair that's been soaking up vitamins for the past twelve years in Buda, where he arrived as a day laborer a year after Simona's career flushing birds from the rice fields took off. During those twelve months, Simona earned Mateo's trust, and both agreed that they needed an efficient worker. That's when Dylan showed up. He came from South America, so he didn't bring with him the prejudices or resentments harbored by candidates from neighboring towns whose families might still be feeling the sting of Mateo's order dismissing the tenant farmers, which he issued shortly after taking over Buda. In addition, Dylan proved to be the utility player the recruiters were hoping to find. He knew how to plant, he could fix water pumps and patch up boats, he tamed horses, he was strong and selfless. The only thing he hadn't been able to master was driving a tractor. But Simona and the occasional machine operators hired during planting and harvesting seasons were more than able to cover that.

The rice fields furthest from the sea, between El Mas and the Migjorn river, are leased to companies unconnected to Mateo's family, so strange faces will pop up for the rest of the year. Rice season has just begun. Tillers are already churning up the fields, and five seasonal workers are having breakfast with Simona, Dylan, and Quim, the third member of Team Buda, recruited seven years ago when Mateo and Simona realized that even Dylan's strengths weren't enough to maintain nearly six hundred hectares. All told, there are nine of us at the table.

Like Dylan, Quim focuses solely on his sandwich. He occasionally contributes to the conversation, but not often. He's a massive young man, strong and stout under a burly layer of fat, with a face somewhere between serious and suspicious. When the rest of them find out where I'm living, they laugh and ask what I think of the humidity at night, if I need a shotgun in case some drug traffickers show up, if I'm not worried about another storm like Gloria.

"The water reached as far as El Mas," one of them says, nodding toward the small window through which the slender white walls of the building are visible. El Mas is a scant two miles from La Pantena.

"If something like that happens in September, three thousand hectares of rice will be lost to the delta."

But that storm was in January.

Simona sidles closer to the warmth of the firepit. She's the only one who remains standing. The only woman. At the table, the seltzer, wine, and La Casera soda are flowing freely.

"I heard the storm wasn't much to write home about unless you were in Buda," I say.

"Like Sant Jaume d'Enveja, in the same municipality as Buda. They were pretty indifferent there. Most of them didn't believe what we told them."

"The locals have no idea what could happen at any time. Gloria opened their eyes a little bit, but still, wow . . ."

"Things are getting serious. The water is eating us up."

They speak as if they were the earth itself.

"Fifty years ago, you'd leave your bike on the sand at the edge of the beach, and you still had to hike for an hour to get to the sea. Now just look. The water is right there."

"It's normal to feel helpless. We're talking about the sea, after all. What can anyone do against that?"

Those in favor of solutions all agree on the need to build retaining dikes and levees.

"And then there are the people betting on sediment," I say.

"Sediment? Those people watching the problem on TV from their couches are delusional. What we need is a good solid system of dunes that the sea can't get past. They should plant more beach grass."

"It's too late for that."

"But not the sediment? It would be forty years before any of that would take effect. What will be left of Buda by then?"

"Well, in Barcelona, they're always spreading it around as needed."

"Those damn environmentalists. The Parc Natural has managed things as if the people here didn't exist. Ecology this, ecology that. Their vision is so . . . so ecological that it's like all they see are the bugs."

"The Parc Natural hasn't ever complained about the delta receding."

"Because they're the environmental version of weekend warriors," says Simona. "They're the kind of people who want to go down to the delta, hop off their bikes, and go for a hike before heading back to the city to go shopping. Fuck it all to hell."

They open a couple bags of peanuts and scatter them across the table to shell and snack on. Dylan makes the coffee while his thick-fingered companions uncork the cognac.

"They try to regulate everything to the point where they don't give you the permits for the things that need to be done," Simona adds from her spot next to the firepit. "You apply for a permit to hunt wild boars—one came out just the other day while we were scaring off the ducks—and they deny it. The Parc Natural is anti delta. Or at least they're not interested in helping. Here, the flamingos matter more than the people. These sons of bitches have no idea how the farmers are struggling, but they've the audacity to tell them how to work. They think agriculture is some kind of social gathering."

"Over the next fifteen weeks we're going to be putting in fifteen-hour days, but for us that's a vacation," says one of the tractor operators. "At least you get to spend the day sitting down. The real pain begins after planting, because you lie awake at night worrying about whether you're gonna get hit by a storm or by locusts or ducks or those fucking flamingos . . . and then there goes your rice."

Bringing up flamingos releases a string of jokes. Someone fantasizes about throwing one on the grill.

"You're not an environmentalist, are you?" another member of the crew asks me.

As they get ready to depart, Dylan brushes away the peanut shells with his hand, saying he'll drop off a couple jugs of water at La Pantena because I shouldn't be drinking from the tap. If I want bread, he can also bring a loaf every day, *només has de dir-ho*. Just give him the say-so. Dylan's a natural when it comes to mixing his Spanish and Catalan. He may strike up a conversation in one language or the other, he might sprinkle some Catalan words into a Spanish discussion. It's clear he has a perfect command of the esoteric, deltaesque version of Catalan several of his coworkers speak, because he always laughs, chimes in, and adds to the conversation at the right moments. No one could have predicted this when he first arrived from the mountains of Tayabamba seventeen years ago without having heard any language other than Spanish while growing wheat and tending to cows. But if you can understand cows, why wouldn't you be able to understand another person, even between intermittent hammer blows? The first few Catalan words he learned were while he was standing on scaffolding during his days as an immigrant working in construction. "I've been learning through the *soroll*, the noise," he tells anyone interested in his self-taught polyglotism. "If I don't understand, I don't work. You just have to get your shit together. That's all there is to it. And, well, that's what culture is all about, right?" Henry Beston, who once said he could think with equal ease in both French and English, felt much the same.

It takes me half an hour to walk back to La Pantena. I continue until I reach the beach, and from there to the dunes, where I pick back up again with Henry's prose and his Fo'castle. The wind is cold, the roar of the sea incessant. The seagulls squawk. And yet I fall asleep. I sleep next to La Pantena, in the outdoors, recovering the slumber my body had been craving. I wake surrounded by salt cedars and shells. Without opening my eyes, I remember the names of all the men I had breakfast with, which is strange, because in the city, whenever I'm introduced to more than three people at once, I have trouble retaining their names: my head gets distracted by trite stimuli or is simply saturated with information, with too many individuals. I tend to forget too much about the people right in front of me. But now, on the beach, I remember the eight people from the stand, their names and faces clearly separated from one another, as if the solitude of many hours in the open landscape allows us to better distinguish who's who.

As I round the dune of the great salt cedar, a lame flamingo with faded feathers walks along the seashore. Although old and out of its habitat, it's moving away from the lagoon at a determined pace. It would be easy to be reminded of those whales or elephants returning to communal cemeteries. But this bird doesn't want to die, at least not now, not in this way, because as soon as it discovers me, it musters a few quick, limping strides, takes flight, and scuds falteringly for a few meters until it lands atop a particularly rough swell that rocks it in such a way that it seems unsteady, uncertain. Perhaps the delta will soon enough be receiving a new dose of flamingo snow.

FLAMINGO

ON THE PATH WINDING along the river toward the beach, I find the fresh afterbirth of a recent delivery. It's spread out in the middle of the road, bright as day. The gelatinous placenta shimmers, soaked in blood and membranes. On the opposite side of the rice field, next to the lagoon's embankment, a trio of white horses surround a tiny black spot lying on the ground.

The ebony foal reminds me that all animals are new, that all are very different from their parents, though genes can eventually lend them a similar appearance. The young Buda flamingos first don black and white feathers, before changing to pink when they're about four years old.

Five adult flamingos sink their necks into the tide pool at the edge of the beach in search of algae and crustaceans. As I pass, they raise their heads. They remain still until, as I continue walking, parallel to the group, three of them stretch their thinnest of stilts, splashing toward the opposite end of the pool. The fourth propels itself into the sky by flapping its enormous wings, undertaking a halting flight which soon enough straightens out, heading directly for the Gran Calaix lagoon.

On the path that winds along the river toward the beach, a flock of coots has spotted me. Together they take off into the river, raising tiny trails of froth, as they prefer to flutter quickly across the surface of the water than to expend energy flying. It's amusing to watch them leaving a trace of their relative fear; however, they only sprint like this for twenty meters or so, aware that, having put so much water between them and me, there's no way I'm catching up with them. The foamy commotion of the fugitive coots contrasts with the parsimonious flight of the flamingo. Don't accelerate until you've reached an appropriate altitude. As if it knew it was protected by a superior force. Which it is. Such is the strength of Spain's Departament de Medi Ambient.

Last year, some forty thousand flamingos came to the delta, attracting thousands of tourists and irritating a handful of rice farmers like the ones plowing the land today, who mostly share contradictory feelings in the same vein as those expressed by Simona: "People are so fanatical about this protection and tourism stuff . . . I don't care if they put a goddamn ski slope on the Pyrenees that breaks up the landscape or if the tourists are being too loud. Just look and see, where's the money? Come on, man. Let the tourists come. Let 'em all come, spend their euros, and leave as fast as they got here. Thirty years ago, we were broke as rats. And now they're telling us we can't earn a living the way we used to? I'll tell them what they can't be doing—banning us from everything. No! Don't touch that land! There's a flamingo on it! There's an imperial eagle! I mean, really. We need to strike a balance."

Simona's first job in Buda was flushing ducks from the rice fields; she also hosted tourists at El Mas, and she more than anyone has made it profitable to grow rice, to fish, and to hunt. She's become the right-hand woman to Mateo, running one of the most influential and charismatic farms in the region. By all means protect the area, yes, but everything has its limit: do the environmentalists not see how the flamingos get into the rice fields and trample everything with their broad, webbed feet? Forty thousand of them . . . just imagine the destruction forty thousand flamingos can bring. And after that, who compensates the farmer? Fortunately, last year, after pressure from the farmers, they were compensated through *Déu mana*—"as God intended"—when they were able to demonstrate losses caused by the flamingos. Before then, La Administración paid them based on a per seed planted amount. But seeds don't cost much. The value lies in the harvest, the fruit of half a year's worth of work, tending to the grains, bearing the brunt of a gale that uproots or knocks down the plants, or of apple snails devouring the stems, or caterpillars boring into them, or or or . . . but it's fine now, because La Administración now compensates farmers based on the entire expected harvest. Bear in mind, though, that this law was implemented just a few months ago, and imagine the havoc the birds have wreaked throughout the years.

The flamingos and the ducks anchored Mateo to this island, he knows he should be grateful for that, but now all he gets from them is a headache. Now, to protect him from the protected species, Garrobud Associats spends a fortune on gassing up the vehicles patrolling all night, on lights, on batteries that power the sound cannons that fire intermittent bursts of noise month after month . . . and even so, the effectiveness of the lights, the cannons, the whistling which startles the security as much as it does the birds will last four days, more or less, depending on who you talk to. As soon as they learn the tricks, there's no other way to scare them away.

Flushing has been going on forever. The stories of traditional *flamenca* nights shooting up the sky or launching rockets and fireworks are pure local heritage. Pol says that when he was a kid, he shot a bird in the middle of one of the fields that turned out to be a flamingo. Afraid of getting busted, he didn't tell anyone, but he's not ceased his firing now he's grown. You must shoot to graze them, Pol says. Not to kill, but to graze. That way it just stings them, but enough that they've learned their lesson.

These are the tricks one learns after a lifetime of flushing. Spending the night out in the rice fields is exhausting, but you're compensated with good money and good stories. The problem is that, when Simona first started in Buda, she was on the other end of the delta food chain: she was the rented flusher. Now, however, when she crunches the numbers, she can see how much she's paying Carmelo to sleep most of the night (she's convinced he does more dozing than flushing). That, and the fortune she's paying for gas. In other words, she knows the farm's finances in detail, and the same task that enabled her to prosper in her day has now become a headache forcing her to pay close attention to her employees.

Mateo is truly appreciative that Simona has taken management so personally that she's come to feel as though the farm belongs to her. He appreciates that his supervisor is suffering for Buda. And that she enjoys it, of course, but most of all that she's suffering for it, because in that state of pain you most acutely perceive danger and react by taking the precautions to anticipate the next blow and either dodge it or make it a glancing one. It doesn't even bother him when his employee refers to "my" farm, "my" land, "my" tractors, because using the possessive denotes personal commitment, guaranteeing that the well-built fortysomething Santjaumera is going to defend Buda as if it were hers . . . which it is, to a certain extent. It's okay, you've earned it, he seems to say. No one besides the two of them knows how much it cost to sort out the mess Mateo inherited two decades ago. His father told him to think carefully about accepting this poisoned property, that bailing it out would be an exhausting process, that it would end up haunting his dreams. He immediately discovered that his old man was in the red, and if Mateo wanted to keep the space within the family, he'd have to make it profitable. This was behind his decision to say goodbye to the tenant farmers, who felt like Buda was partly theirs as well. Such is the island's magnetism: it draws you in, you blend into the place to the point where you feel as though you're a part of the ecosystem itself, like the water, the sand, the ducks. Telling a tenant farmer that, hey, I know how many decades you've lived here, but you're still human, you're not a coot, an eel, or a flamingo, you're not protected by the Parc Natural, and so you don't belong here, you have to give it all up . . . that's hard.

Other than the postcard everyone has come to know and love, toughness is the island's trademark. Rice farming is a hell of a business. Catching and selling fish will wear you out. Hunting . . . well, Mateo doesn't go hunting himself, though he earns a good amount from those who pay for the opportunity to do so. Aside from the recent bad press hunters have received—and, by extension, those who have offered up their private lands—it's nevertheless a great source of satisfaction, because it allows you to meet many fascinating people. Plenty of them are obsessed with slaughter, but more often than not those days spent hunting have allowed him to get to know the personal attorneys of Spanish royals, businessmen in the salt-producing and -processing industry, eccentric and astonishingly creative individuals, all of whom enjoy the old style of hunting that involves things like blowback shotguns and tracking a partridge for twenty-five kilometers or more. Yes, he's okay with that. Or rather he has been, because these days not even dinners with hunters are worth it. He's invested so much effort in building the farm, and at sixty, it may be time for him to retire. He could step down and let one of his brothers or cousins take over the day-to-day operations, but are any of them ready for such a task? Whenever a family member comes to him complaining about why business isn't better or why he hired this person instead of that one, he always counters with the same reply: well then, I'll leave and let you figure it all out. And what happens then? Not a peep out of anyone. Nobody wants to take charge, because they're all comfortable in their homes in Barcelona or wherever they live, far from Buda in any case, saving themselves from taking care of an island: a job that entails one sleepless night after another and battling every day with the fucking Administración. Just ask him. He'll tell you.

Mateo has been here nineteen years, not including the fifteen he spent in L'Ametlla running the sea bream and sea bass farm there. Thirty-odd years meticulously accumulating knowledge about the rhythms of the tides, the tendencies of the terns, or the nature of politicians and fish market auctioneers, all of which contributed to keeping the ocean liner that's Buda afloat. Navigating the waters seems simple enough, but when you're at the helm, there are many who can't even find their way back to the coast.

Simona started working with him early on, which is when the big changes took place. In other words, from the beginning . . . of the new era. She embodies all of it; after all, how many women can do what she does? Even Mateo had doubts when Simona's father suggested he hire her to flush birds on Buda. Being out in the fields at night had always been a man's thing, but this girl had desire, a contagious sense of strength, and such unusual energy levels that many people felt intimidated by her. She even drove tractors! Since he urgently needed someone from a nearby town, Mateo simply said, okay then, let's try it. And what a success it was. *Aquesta tia és un home*, some of the neighbors were overheard saying. That girl is a man. And she thinks it's great she's seen in such a light: it means she's earned the respect of an economic sector unused to seeing a woman in charge. Simona knows the land, the people, she knows when to raise her voice, and once you see her driving up and down Buda all day in a four-wheel-drive truck you know everything is under control. Quim and Dylan have had the occasional qualm about the way their supervisor treats them, but who doesn't complain about the boss? Mateo himself is subject to harsh criticism every now and then, even getting torn to shreds by neighbors and members of his own family. After all, many primarily consider him a landowner, and we're aware how toxic that word sounds today. When it comes to his family, he's the one in charge, which is synonymous with jealousy and bitterness. The human condition. You have to deal with it, not let it intimidate you. And Simona gets this. In a coarse way, sure, but she does what Mateo asks of her, and, more importantly, she's kept her word. When the decisive point came, when Mateo confirmed his father's fateful omens and the island began to eat away at his sleep, he went to his supervisor and said: "You know as well as I do what the prospects are like. If you want to stay, that's great. But you're going to have to shoulder the cross and climb the steps at Calvary with me."

Mateo frequently draws upon metaphors like this, which come to him spontaneously, inspired perhaps by Our Lady of the Forsaken, his favorite saint after having spent four years studying veterinary medicine in Valencia, or by the God to whom he prays daily in the town church, because the chapel at El Mas hasn't held Mass in some time.

"I'll be right here with you," Simona replied.

And that's how it's been. Nineteen years later, Mateo continues to feel Simona's loyalty, to the point where he hands over routine tasks that have recently started to either bore or overwhelm him. He's delegated so much that he only sets foot on the island if there's no other option, trusting fully in the reports he receives from his supervisor, with whom he's in constant contact via telephone.

Now planting season is beginning, those phones will be on fire. Consider, for example, who will be Carmelo's backup when it comes to scaring off the birds at night (after all, at some point he does have to rest), because there are forty thousand flamingos and sixty thousand mallards roaming around, plus the gray and purple herons, the egrets, and the glossy ibises who might nibble a bit here and there but do most of their damage by trampling the rice. Either way, they must be flushed.

Even the word itself, flamingo, conjures that photo of an old lighthouse keeper and his family holding up a dead one like a trophy. Nobody would dare pose for a shot like that today. Mateo certainly hasn't; he even got rid of a decades-old collection of bird eggs for fear of someone finding them and accusing him of something untoward, because these days he feels the environmentalists will crucify someone the first chance they get, him most of all. There's Luzia Galioto and representatives of the fucking Parc Natural who banned him from fishing for four years, laughing in his face, he says. Like the bastard running the Ministry of the Environment, who ran into Mateo one day on the street and said to him with a sneer, "You've got no idea how much it cost me to get you banned from fishing in Buda." That's what passes for an environmentalist these days. What harm were they doing by fishing the way his parents and grandparents had always done? he asks. The extent to which the island has remained wild is entirely thanks to private management. His grandfather wanted the lagoon embankment built specifically to isolate the wildlife, to make sure the rice fields wouldn't disturb the ecological balance. And that very rice feeds the birds that so fascinate so many bird-watchers and so-called environmentalists who know less about birds and plants than your average kindergartner. What exactly does it mean to be an environmentalist? Mateo studied veterinary medicine. He knows when and how the Gregale, Levant, and Tramontane winds blow, he recognizes the properties of hundreds if not thousands of plants, what a prawn needs to survive in a fish farm, and how the droppings from a cormorant's roost can kill off the surrounding vegetation and impair the nesting of other bird species. Mateo has treated bulls, he owns one of the most important collections of lepidopterans in the country, he was the first to document the African monarch's flight from Buda to Catalonia, and when it comes to caring for the environment, he's sustaining the second-largest wetland area in all of Spain, one flush with migratory species from all over the globe, while fighting harder than anyone so this land won't be lost. Is there any denying that he's this island's original environmentalist? Then again, his wetlands accommodate not only flamingos but also humans, whereas environmentalists are now saying that, no, there is no room for people. That we must let Nature express herself, advancing and spreading and swallowing up whatever she needs. It's easy to talk about something you haven't fought for. Something you haven't been taking care of for the past century. Easier still if there's a check worth millions of euros just waiting for Buda to flood so it can be cashed, because that's exactly what many of these executives who wrap themselves in eco-friendly colors want. Money. Like everyone else.

To be fair, though, Mateo thinks, not all environmentalists have the same mindset. There are some decent ones, like Rubén Pons. When he was first hired by the Parc team to work security in Buda, the neighbors called him every name in the book, beginning with "environmentalist." He wasn't made to feel welcome in town because, in these parts, "the Greenies" are usually the ones causing problems. But Rubén is astute and has a clever way of handling problems. He understands people's needs here, and in doing his job he respects the needs of others. Security officers like him show that coexistence is possible. If Rubén had found Mateo's clandestine collection of eggs, or perhaps one of the field notebooks in which he jotted down certain findings that may now be politically incorrect, he'd surely have checked the dates on the entries and chalked them up as belonging to a time in which extracting an egg from a nest didn't constitute an attack against all of humanity. There was no willful transgression of the law, perhaps because there weren't at the time any laws to be transgressed. But since Rubén is just one man, and one who doesn't ask for much, Mateo destroyed the eggs and burned the notebooks. "It's for my own reputation, and that of the family," he says. "Nowadays, if they catch you with any of that kind of thing, you can explain all you want about how it's been in your family a very long time, practically since the flea plague of the 1500s, but they're still going to pillory you. Publicly, too."

Simona has cultivated that same sort of grudge against established environmentalism. If environmentalists felt the same way about Buda as she and Mateo do, if they wanted a true balance, they'd have already agreed to reduce the flamingo population.

It wasn't so long ago that flamingo expert Alan Johnson told Rubén Pons that an acceptable bio load for the delta would be around fifteen hundred mating pairs. At that time, however, there were over four thousand. One of the reasons behind this is the simple life they lead in the vast expanses of rice fields and lagoons, where they can go about their lives unbothered. Pons knows there are thousands of them, but he doesn't make decisions on behalf of the Parc, much less the delta, limiting himself to tracking numbers, supervising official properties, sending reports, and ensuring no one oversteps the bounds of the Espacio Natural. His voice carries a bit of weight, but major decisions like whether to dispense with a few thousand flamingos aren't his to make, although he's the wisest of all the sages; political geometry often excludes those who know the most.

I met Rubén Pons the other day because I wanted to ask about birds. It was in the little Casa del Sifó, along the road that, after passing El Mas, ends at the ferry that shuttles back and forth across the Migjorn river in winter when the floodgates yawn wide, the water cuts through the arm of sand, and the isle of Buda—which is technically a peninsula—becomes an actual island. El Sifó takes its name from the hydraulic pipe which allows water from the main irrigation canal to enter the island's irrigation system, but before La Administración bought the property, it was a hog farm.

Pons was smoking a cigarette as he spread out nets for capturing birds. The self-taught ornithologist who's been smoking Ducados Negros since he was fourteen is the silent type. If I hadn't gone looking for him, or entered some part of the Parc Natural without advance notice, I don't think he'd have bothered introducing himself to me. Stocky, with a nomadic expression, five days' worth of beard, and hands like welder's gloves, he started watching over wildlife thirty-two years ago. All around him, dozens of house sparrows trickled through the trees, chasing one another. We were talking about the striking protuberance which adorns the beak of the male shelduck when Pons raised an index finger, his eyes focused on the top of a eucalyptus tree. "A starling," he said, though the trill sounded to me like that of a Cetti's warbler. "It doesn't have a song of its own, so it copies everything. A bastard mockingbird. Good enough to fool me from time to time."

The starling can imitate almost anything, from the buzzing of an electric saw to the dripping of a faucet. Everyone and everything. This false warbler continues its whistling ambush in the trees making up the row shading El Sifó. Buda is full of eucalyptus trees that were imported from Australia roughly a century ago with the intention of letting their thirsty roots soak up large areas of wetlands that facilitated rice cultivation. During the twentieth century, thousands if not millions of these trees displaced countless pine, poplar, and birch forests throughout Spain without adding much through their own presence, and they've often been blamed for drying out the landscape and harming the surrounding flora. This is why, a few years ago, a number of areas saw eucalyptus trees being cut down and old, native forests being restored. Today, the eucalyptus is considered an invasive species with a bad reputation for spreading, though Buda's residents aren't too worried about them. These are people with firm convictions and a voice of their own who'll never imitate the mockingbird, regardless of how mocking it may be: they like their eucalyptus trees. They've grown up with them, they've seen them adapt to the environment, and they see no reason to be cutting them down. It's true these trees are imports that did little if anything to improve what was already here. However, many are of the belief that, after a certain amount of time, if a change has done no harm, why not accept the organisms that have been transformed through adaptation to a place that has adapted to them? Many of these eucalyptus trees are at the century mark and beyond. And now they should be removed?

Rubén Pons, who originally comes from an inland town, adapted to the island and the delta like another eucalyptus. Adaptation requires time and therefore a sense of calm, and so, during those early days with the Parc, when neighbors began presenting him with the bodies of dead flamingos and ducks, he was accommodating.

"People came to me saying, 'You're not supposed to shoot these birds, right?' What was I going to do? Well, at first I just let it go. If they're bringing you something, it's because they know there's a problem that needs fixing. They're conscious that they need to learn something. It's a sign of goodwill. Again, what was I supposed to do? Report the hunters? No, that'd make me a son of a bitch. So that's how I earned their respect. And if they respected me, they'd respect the flamingos."

"But they'll keep hunting, and then there are the poachers," I said.

"Well, hunting isn't the worst thing that can happen."

In the eighties, seven hundred and fifty thousand birds would gather here. Today, if there are only some sixteen thousand-odd coots here, it's not due to hunting. Shooting a few ducks here and there pales in comparison to the damage caused, for example, by the apple snail. A female snail can lay sixty thousand eggs in a single night. Imagine the rate of reproduction. Not even a word like "plague" can convey the full weight of this situation. This slimy yet devastating gastropod is a newcomer to the delta, having arrived long after the first eucalyptus tree. They were bred in fish farms for the purpose of cleaning aquariums, as their adherent movements left the glass tanks clean as a whistle. Local experts say it would have been easy to round up the escapees and eliminate them, as was the case with a recent bullfrog outbreak. The problem was that the great escape occurred during the summer months when the officials supposedly in charge of capturing them were on vacation, and the eventual response took so long that the largest freshwater snail on earth, capable of reaching fifteen centimeters in length and considered one of the most harmful species in existence owing to its omnivorous and voracious appetite, spread through the delta, presumably in a way no one can stop. It can scarf down rice faster than a mallard duck, and here in the delta its table has been set.

Controlling the snails requires a considerable effort on the part of the rice farmers, who, in addition to resorting to certain pesticides, now hire snail smashers or have even started planting what's known as upland rice in dry soil to mitigate the damage, though when it comes to Mateo, he's more concerned about the western swamphens. "I can't even look at them," he says with a wince, because these Gruiformes have a penchant for eating the tender rice plant itself. As do the American red swamp crayfish, which burrow through the rice fields, causing the rows to collapse and water to be blocked or diverted, thus preventing the grain from growing well. These species began to appear in the eighties; they make succulent snacks for birds like the black-headed gull and the glossy ibis (a great consumer of apple snails, another reason for it to set up shop in the delta, which was never a destination a decade ago), but farmers are overwhelmed by their proliferation.

As if that weren't enough, six years ago the blue crabs went wild. In 2012, a specimen discovered in La Tancada was considered mildly exotic. Shortly thereafter, Dylan found another in La Pantena. Mateo immediately went to see what it was: they put it in a tank and showed it to tourists. The next spring, the blues were running roughshod across Buda, gobbling up anything that came within reach of their spiked tongues and pincers . . . including their fellow crabs, because these crustaceans are cannibals.

In the canal running past La Pantena, I observe how these blue wonders meander, suspended in the water. They sway back and forth like large underwater specks, giving them the mistaken impression of being adrift, chitinous structures occasionally bumping together, bouncing around under the murky water like idle marbles. In six years, their formidable pincers have made them dominators of the delta. During this extremely short period, the populations of several aquatic beings have been decimated, beginning with the region's most emblematic animal, one whose charisma is comparable to that of the flamingo: the eel. The reason for eels' declining numbers isn't due to the blue crabs alone, but the crabs' role is a significant one. Another reason is that there are barely any legal protections in place for eels, and fishing for them is encouraged.

In this new, frenetic order, the blue crabs are reproducing helter-skelter. In a short period, the old world has been replaced with strange, powerful pincers that can tear the locals to shreds. These new animals have imposed themselves upon the realm at a breakneck pace, devastating millions of older ones. Just six years. And no one can stop them.

It's a small consolation to walk along the embankment next to the Gran Calaix lagoon, which is strewn with crab carcasses crushed into the ground. To see that at least a few birds are out there trying to stave off the invasion while at the same time dispensing a sort of natural justice. Naturally, this is a moral vision of nature, but it may no longer be possible to view it through any other lens. It wasn't long ago that morality was an option, a game that depended on how much you wanted to expand your fantasy by finding parallels between the human and animal worlds. Today, you can't see blue crabs in the delta and avoid considering the ethics of it all.

Forty thousand flamingos. A delivery of sixty thousand snails per night. Six years to conquer a delta. These are transformative figures. They cut to the soul. Numbers that can change people's feelings, can make the flamingo as hated as the wolf or the bull. And one must ask why. Why do we single them out? Why do we feel this way?

The pink adult flies over the black calf lying there among the reeds and rice in a frame of emeralds, blues, and siennas. Of waters, sky, and earth. A few steps later, two mallards take off from the canal, flapping their wings loudly, startling me. The ducks, coots, and redshanks flee as soon as they spy me, but the gulls and herons hold their positions until I come within fifteen or twenty meters. Then there are the plovers, running along the shore pecking at the wet sand, holding out until I'm only five or six meters away, and even then they don't fly off: they're content with simply quickening their pace. Each animal knows its own strengths and has a temperament that determines a safe distance from potential predators. What risks are we willing to take? With ducks and coots, it's none. The ducks don't depart silently either, instead taking off screaming, gripped with a sense of amused terror. Now, also next to the canal, a purple heron rises with an elegant fluttering that belies its rugged screech. It flaps its wings slowly, struggling to gain altitude, its lanky legs attempting an aerodynamic posture while its beak points any which way. It wavers like a scribble in the sky before stretching out in slender alignment, giving meaning to its name.

I often surprise the birds tucked into a bed of reeds, reacting late to my presence even though they often alert each other. The tern, which can shriek without dropping its prey, is a wonderful sentinel of the beaches and rice fields, though the flamingos barely even flinch when hearing its warning. Neighbor Joan Todó calls them the divas of the delta, as they know danger isn't coming for them. This is why they've started settling there permanently, emulating their cousins at the Tour du Valat research institute on the southern coast of France, which for years represented the only fixed colony in the Mediterranean. By sharing in our decadence, flamingos are becoming bourgeois.

Now there is so much forewarning about imminent ends, and with the sea just thirty steps away, I wonder how we get to the finish line. Not all endings are the same: some are practically happy, abrupt, agonizing, and some don't seem like an end at all as they arrive on our doorstep. The culmination promised by these shores has been announced wide and far because it heralds many more, and who among us can say whether it will serve as a prologue to an even greater one: the grand finale. A Hindu fable points out that a formidable flood devastates the earth every four thousand years.

I go back to sleep on the dune, and I don't feel as though I'm wasting a wink of my time. Such is the change I've undergone. I'm old enough now that I sleep as soundly as when I was a child.

There's no wind today. The sea is a uniform sheet of green advancing without spume until it melts softly into the beach. There's nothing whiter than the crests of the three sublimely fine waves in which the water repeatedly ends. It's the color of this conclusion, as it is with mourning in China, like the dead corals, the driftwood, shells, reeds, skulls, bones, and excrement spread along the shore, bleached by erosion and the sun.

I spend the day on the dune.

At 4:46 p.m. the wind picks up. The seagulls arrive with their bellies full of stolen olives from Amposta or Camarles, plump and shiny after a bath in the freshwater ponds so the salt doesn't scorch their feathers. On the path back to La Pantena, a series of energetic songs arise, joined soon enough by other birds to create a warbling orchestra that envelops the afternoon. Meanwhile, the reeds bow in diplomatic greeting and the air that slips between them whistles in tune. Privilege is my quotidian reality. Days of exercise, reading, sun, wind, and black or pink animals.

SALT WATER

MEDITERRANEAN

MY FATHER SAYS if you want to mix colors, you must know how to play: another way of saying that all anyone needs is personality. And the sea has it. Green, black, indigo, earth, lilac, sludge. He says he can paint the sea however and whenever he wants. Without even using a brush. He says the sea speaks in the same way as the river, the mountain, or my dune, and that's why it's completely normal that New Zealand granted a river personhood status, opening up the path for trees, rocks, lagoons, and other parts of the natural world. He also says that he plays with colors the way I do with words, though he's being overly modest because not only has he played the piano and painted giant backdrops, I've also seen him, after the stage is set, writing scripts late into the night for plays to be performed by students' parents: plays in which he himself would appear, often dressed as a woman. So my father knows a bit about mixing letters, enough even to have removed some of his own when he was searching for an identity: since my grandfather was Gabriel, he was known as Gabrielín, until one day he'd had enough and decided his dearest friends would refer to him as everyone now refers to me. Which is why he's of the belief that names can be changed to sound more familiar.

If we consider the Mediterranean a person, a person we feel close to, we could give it a friend's name.

Medi.

While my father can no longer bathe in Medi, Medi is the keeper of untold traces of paint that have flaked from his skin over the years, and it reminds my father of lifting his children onto his shoulders before catapulting them into the water. Medi remembers my old man's most sensitive side, and now, as I'm thinking about it—among the infinite number of grunts he let out in his life—I can't picture him ranting about the sea.

Medi affirms that he'll temper anyone with his warm waters, his lulling waves. He's a sea that appeals to swimming and thinking, but he wouldn't have been the cradle of civilization if he hadn't shown his sour face sometimes. Humans, like anything else, learn best from tempests and tribulations. Medi confirms this, having gobbled up two and a half kilometers' worth of Buda's land over the last sixty years. The lighthouse seemed very close to the shore back then, but Medi has been moving it farther and farther out to sea, and he intends to keep on doing so, if not outright demolishing it the way he did with the old lighthouse on Christmas Day 1961, when José El Nano was participating in a coot hunt. He heard a sound, looked at the sea, and said, "Where did it go?" Ramon del Cadell remarked that the lighthouse was well built and hadn't been hit recently by any storms, so if it had collapsed it must have been for "structural" reasons. His suggestion was that, wave by wave, the sea had been weakening the base, shifting the sand on which its foundation rested. Until it came tumbling down.

The lighthouse that replaced it lasted five years. This story is reminiscent of the breakwater in the Scottish town of Wick, which lies on the same coast where Thomas Stevenson, father of author Robert Louis Stevenson, became the first person to measure the strength of a wave, estimating its power at thirty thousand kilos per square meter. The waves that crashed against Wick's primitive concrete blocks were able to break and displace an object that weighed in at 1,350 tons. As the *Glasgow Herald* reported, "The concrete block of a thousand tons, which was dislodged on Tuesday, is at times seen lying irregularly on the top of the loose rubble." After that, the Scots installed a new breakwater weighing in at around 2,600 tons. Five years later, the waves brought that down as well, as they did with Buda's replacement lighthouse.

These are other shores, but the seas form a single ocean thanks to the deep currents which communicate with and relate to them all. Being confined and exposed to many days of intense sun, the salinity of the Mediterranean increases as water evaporates and the sea level drops in comparison with the Atlantic. The lighter oceanic waters are increasingly infiltrating the Strait of Gibraltar in the form of intense surface currents, offsetting the difference and allowing the waters to continue advancing, as other seas across the globe have been doing. But how far can this go?

Here's a simple way of looking at it: without rock to break it up, and lacking sand consistent enough to contain it, the advance is all-encompassing. He is the sea, and he alone is the center of everything that happens. Surprising, then, is our desire for control and our illusion of taming him, as his dynamics are so unstoppable that no technology can make noticeable changes. For a few years, it might seem as if we've gotten the upper hand, but soon enough we will yield to his will. According to Medi, there are problems that require urgent attention, and he recommends we solve them by being aggressive and realistic in much the same way that a catfish is realistic: "It is advisable to set aside the ultrahuman point of view for a while."

To understand Medi's logic, the logic of the universe, we must look to the Southern Ocean. With neither coasts nor reefs for thousands of kilometers, the waves grow and roil endlessly. They don't die. Imagine what life without a coastline in sight would be like. The word itself, coastline, is synonymous with refuge. With arrival. With destiny. What might it be like to move in such a way as to never arrive, to live without obstacles, without a destiny driven by inertia? Such is the daily existence of millions of waves, which humans understand to a slight degree thanks to knowledge acquired by the needs of war: to carry out an invasion, armies had to predict the state of the sea, calculate the height of the waves, and thus we came to the "almost desperate lack of basic information on the fundamentals of the nature of the sea." These are the words of Rachel Carson in *The Sea Around Us*.

Mediterranean breakers tend to be minimalist, with licking waves not even suitable for surfing. In the Ebro Delta, however, the sea comes crashing in with extra impetus drummed up by the wind and currents. Even so, the violence is a Mediterranean one in the most marine sense of the word, one historically incomparable to the tsunamis, hurricanes, typhoons, and other such meteorological ensembles that transmute the oceans and other great spaces of open water. This isn't the Andaman Sea or the Bay of Bengal, but within the past year, this basin has been swept by unprecedented cyclones, leading many residents to understand, as Ramon del Cadell did, that something is different now. The great storms that once struck every fifty or sixty years have, in this new century, tightened their trajectories, becoming almost annual, bringing their respective destruction and advancing seas. And with this progression, how far will the sea go?

The largest marine invasion on record occurred during the Cretaceous period, roughly a hundred million years ago. True to its logic, the waters rose, and today, in the Himalayas, there are outcrops of marine limestone six thousand meters above sea level.

Many things have been blamed for the advancing sea, but during the last million years, all these have been dwarfed by the prevailing action of glaciers. We find ourselves in the midst of an interglacial period, where sustained melting is raising global sea levels. "Today we live at the beginning of a new geological cycle," Charles Schuchert said at the beginning of the twentieth century, "when the oceans are larger, higher, and grander in appearance. These oceans, however, have already embarked on a new invasion." Schuchert's "today" continues to be applicable here, in the present, since it's well established that the passing of a century is only marked by the second hand of the geological clock, and that the Mediterranean moves to the ticking of a more profound time.

The rhythm of this deeper time guarantees that, in a sidereal future, the days will be so long that the moon will no longer influence the tides. Long ago, the earth took much less time to rotate on its axis. Four hours were all it invested in a day. Now, it takes twenty-four. There will be a time when days will last fifty times longer. As the moon drifts farther away, its attraction wanes and the tides lose their friction. It's a question of mathematics, although we needn't worry about the answer: by then the human species will surely have disappeared.

Oceanic phases are measured in thousands of years; tides are so vast and prolonged that it's impossible to measure them any other way. Well, until now. Although glaciers have melted throughout the millennia, fulfilling a natural cycle, human-caused climate change has accelerated the process over the last two centuries. Today, snowfields and glaciers are disintegrating in plain sight.

The shifting of the earth's crust and the weight of its sediment on a humanly inconceivable scale—can you imagine something so heavy it's capable of sinking the bottom of the sea?—are key to understanding why the Mediterranean will flood a good part of the delta in just a few years.

In ancient Polynesia, they believed the stars were a set of lights that reflected those of the earth and sea, like an inverted abyss. Their understanding of depth and vastness was metaphorically accurate, their intuition of the forces that animate the world precise, which is why they could read the swells and surf long before modern scientists proclaimed that they had unlocked the language of the waves. The formula employed by these experts was to superimpose exorbitant numbers of successive wave photos until they were able to determine their speed. Scientists can now work out the reasons for the height, length, and period of a wave, or to what extent they depend on the wind, but all they've done is ascribe numbers to what the Polynesians already knew.

Since Mr. Palomar (as imagined by author Italo Calvino) has a Polynesian spirit, he began his attempt to understand his own universe by observing a wave on the beach. Italo Calvino has written that his dear Palomar then realized how difficult it is to isolate a wave by separating it from the one that either follows or precedes it. Or that it's even more challenging to concentrate on a wave, that one, single wave, and accompany it with your eyes as it undulates and separates, shrinking and accelerating. Or that there is a certain resemblance between that wave and you.

If the Mediterranean could write, I'd ask it to tell a story called *The Life of a Wave*, a chronicle detailing the travels of a newly created wave, watching it grow and describing the way it adorns its crest until it becomes a breaker. This story would be about a long wave, although Medi is simply a sea and the longest of waves need oceans in which to live. But this one would be just long enough, and like all itinerant waves it would grow as it approached the shallows, forming a massive crest along its extensive leading edge, gathering up all its strength before starting to curl forward until its formidable mass collapsed in a roar.

This wave's story would sound like others already told, because waves have been discussed extensively, though the fun here would lie in capturing the nuances of this wave's particular journey. Ultimately, the secret of the waves is that they repeat, they repeat, they repeat. And yet none are the same. Soon enough, there may well be one of such unthinkable proportions that it breaks over Buda during a storm, putting an end to it all.

Dumont d'Urville saw a thirty-meter wave near the Cape of Good Hope. In February 1933, the ship *Ramapo*, en route from Manila to San Diego, recorded one at thirty-four. The Moken, those semi-nomadic people often called "sea gypsies" who fish primarily in the Andaman Sea, know the beach will periodically be hit by a Laboon: a flesh-eating wave invoked, they say, by their ancestral spirits, to clear out the evils of the world.

There are coasts where fury is normal, such as Tierra del Fuego in South America, the Shetland and Orkney Islands of Scotland, and the American Pacific coast running from northern California to the Strait of Juan de Fuca and Vancouver Island. Places where the boundaries of sea and air are erased by sea spray that clouds the world in an aerial sediment, diluting everything.

The sea is infinite dissolution. One ending after another and then back to the beginning. The repetition of the waves is proof they exist outside our logic, our forces, creating perpetual motion. "Apparently only repetition reaches the heart," writes philosopher Byung-Chul Han, knowing the heart is key: without it, all other rhythms will stop. Rote memorization is, as the French say, *apprendre par coeur*. Repetition is distinguished from routine through its ability to generate focus and intensity by delving into the nuances and revealing that no repetition is truly identical. The sea is never boring; as Kierkegaard said, "Genuine repetition is recollected forward." I now understand that the songs my son memorizes will offer him warmth in the future. I've been writing about the same thing for a while now, and yet what I write is different. Repetition.

Spending time on the shoreline offers us a notion of limits. Sun-bleached carapaces lie everywhere, deposited by the waves as they die and die again. In a world where it is becoming increasingly difficult to finish anything, where it's becoming increasingly difficult to talk about endings, the sea continues with its natural cadence. It invites us to calmly converse with the vital part that is death. But tranquility is a spark which, today, we must remember how to strike, because what's become normal is the monotony of urgency, something that spreads with an imperial speed, as if there were no other rhythm. Tranquility has so much to do with the profundity of time that it has even been said it can lengthen life. There is a species of jellyfish, *Turritopsis nutricula*, which has, since the 1990s, been presented as the only immortal animal on earth. When this jellyfish reaches sexual maturity, it can return to the polyp stage and restart its life cycle from there. Its cells are rejuvenated time and again, perhaps by the cosmic calmness in which it floats, or perhaps by salt itself, like brown sargassum, which has also been described as virtually immortal and apparently favors areas of high atmospheric temperatures which receive no fresh water from rivers or melting ice, allowing for exceptional evaporation levels and giving the Sargasso Sea the highest salinity in the entire Atlantic, which is also the saltiest of the earth's great oceans. The jellyfish and the millions of tons of seaweed that spread across the underwater meadows of the Sargasso enjoy a deep sense of time, one which reminds me of Mateo Gallart telling me on my first day that La Administración are simply studying Buda's residents and biding their time.

Mateo believes La Administración is as devastating as one of these waves, repeatedly wearing away at inhabitants of the delta, and he's convinced nobody is going to stand up and fight, that all the Ebrencs will slink silently away, having chalked up the loss as inevitable. In his head, the story ends with the delta being converted into a theme park dedicated to tourism and subsidies, which will be enormous. When the salt water advances far enough to prevent rice from being cultivated, La Administración will integrate the area into the existing Parc Natural and finally have access to so many square kilometers of protected land that it will be able to generate "two hundred euros or more" in revenue, according to the figures Mateo has formulated in his head.

When pondering such things, Mateo's heart rate shoots up. It's almost painful, he thinks. How will his heart feel, then, when he sees local youths heading off for Barcelona, London, or Berlin? When nobody remains to dig their feet into the mud and defend what's theirs? Buda will soon turn one hundred, but there are landowners with even deeper roots than the Gallarts and still no one says a word, even as their fields flood. Where are the heirs, the successors? He can't fathom such indifference or resignation or cowardice from those who should be defending what's theirs. But when he looks at his own family, the simple truth is this: the only person who's breaking his back for Buda, for the delta, for the entire delta, is him. That's how he feels.

Karen and Natalia tell him he's taking things too personally. Maybe he's a masochist. Does he enjoy suffering? Let's put it this way: what he enjoys is seeing justice being done, seeing how the head honchos react when someone has a sense of pride and enough of a conscience to stand up to them. What else can any of us do? Lately, though, it hasn't been much of an issue because he's been minding his manners a bit more, and Karen has played a central role in changing his attitude. Yes, she's tempered his edge. Age must be playing a part too: when you're in your sixties you're not as forceful as you once were. He also recognizes that his partner, Karen, has instilled in him a sense of serenity that occasionally takes even him by surprise, allowing him to downplay situations that once upon a time would have been major aggravations. He needed someone like that by his side after many years of living alone in Buda. She imbued him with that Latina sense of self-confidence, and with it many nonsensical ideas and fears simply faded away. It's true that the constant onslaught from La Administración continues to leave him stressed and sleepless, but whether he's more grizzled or more enamored, he's tolerated defeat better since being with Karen. There's no comparison between their biographies: she grew up in a Colombian cesspool, had to flee her own family (not to mention a number of ex-partners), came to Spain without her daughter, and met him when she was an employee at El Mas. Yet he shares with her the energy and the will to live. Everything else depends upon basic connections like these. She's taught him so much about the relaxing powers of meditation that even Natalia has noticed a change.

Natalia came to La Pantena this morning to see her horses, which calm her as much as Karen's walks along the river. Mateo's eldest daughter recognizes that, while Karen isn't the stepmother of her dreams, she was good for her father in the beginning. There are nuances, of course. She thinks Mateo is too attached to his partner and occasionally jumps through unnecessary hoops, but on the other hand, Natalia has seen him too demoralized, sad, and alone not to appreciate his new positivism, if that noun is an option for describing her father. Yes, Karen has calmed him down a bit. It's a victory in itself that she knows how to manage Mateo's intensity. And yet she also shows a prodigious level of verbal incontinence, a sight to see once she gets talking. For two such intense people to get along is no easy feat, but there they are. Perhaps things couldn't be any other way, since Karen arose, so to speak, from Buda itself: she used to work as a cook at El Mas. This can't be a coincidence. Everything that comprises Mateo either is Buda or has to do with Buda, with the delta, and while it's hard to believe he could have found a partner on the island, where few women live, well, Karen happened to appear. Since she also lived in Deltebre, Mateo was able to keep his relationship with Buda intact. Until the couple made their relationship public.

Since Karen and Mateo went public, Natalia knows her father has been spending less time on the island, though he continues to keep a keen ear to its day-to-day life with his legendary passion even as Karen wants him to distance himself even more, seeing as she does how the island can weigh on him to the point where it almost brings him down. Natalia knows she's asking the impossible, because her father won't give up his sentimental attachment to the landscape, and she too is under Buda's spell.

Natalia associates the island with calmness, adventure, childhood, and although she settled in Barcelona and now lives some fifty kilometers from Buda, she's always felt an attraction toward the island. As much as her disillusion has steeled her, and as often as she's surprised by how detached she can feel from people and places that once meant something in her life, the delta is always there. When she first got together with Artur, she unloaded tons of old shit from her past, as if someone else had experienced it. Including her parents' separation. She's amazed at how poorly she remembers this stage of her life; after all, she was thirteen at the time, and it's believed that at that age people tend to retain hard-hitting events with exquisite clarity. But Natalia has some sort of beneficial self-mesmerism that blots out certain types of pain, keeping that chaos in limbo. Psychologists might interpret this as some sort of latent trauma that should be exorcised, but scientific theories don't matter much to her as long as she's well. Distancing herself from what others (including experts) say is also part of her newfound sense of detachment. If burying her parents' separation allows her to live better, it will continue to remain buried.

The one inescapable part of that memory is that the breakup took place in Logroño, where the family had moved a year or so before. Mateo was working at the L'Ametlla fish farm along Buda's north coast, but with the girls starting to grow up, it was better for him to settle down in a larger city with good schools and a hint of verve to enliven and inspire the teens. Mateo didn't like the hustle and bustle of Barcelona, and Rosa María came from Logroño, an affordable city in northern Spain that still retains a certain quaint village feel, so the girls and their mother moved there, with the stipulation that Mateo would travel to see them on weekends. It was a time of many hours in the car, driving up and down from Buda to L'Ametlla, from L'Ametlla to Logroño, with the stereo playing Cat Stevens, David Bowie, Elton John, Queen, and occasionally the classical music his mother preferred. That was until the adult world did its thing, in collaboration with the intemperate nature of their elders, Mateo in particular: the marriage fell apart. Thankfully—"thankfully" being the appropriate word here—Rosa María's mind was made up, because Mateo was and still is fully capable of enduring even the most unsustainable situations to sustain a relationship that's reached its expiration date. He in fact spent the next year pretending everything was fine, as if his wife hadn't told him they'd reached that point.

For Natalia and her sister the situation didn't change all that much, as they stayed in Logroño with their mother while Mateo continued driving up to see them. But he reduced the frequency of the visits to two weekends a month, respecting the terms of their shared custody. When Mateo was there to see the girls, their mother would leave the house to the three of them, and Natalia resigned herself to associating her father's visits with a specific menu, because, without fail, he'd bring a little slice of Buda along with him: packages of rice for paella. It was Mateo's signature dish, one that reflects the two things invariably on his mind and which are an eternal part of his life: rice and La Administración. Natalia hated it. That much she remembers. The damn rice on Saturdays, further evidence that her father was a man of his customs, a quintessential product of Opus Dei, the school where many members of the family had been educated. Go to Mass, be inflexible, eat rice. Mateo forced himself to repeat a series of obligations and routines as if there were no alternative. No matter how overwhelmed or bored he felt, there were certain things he simply had to do, and if he failed to comply with any of them he blamed himself, or at the very least he worried about the consequences of having avoided such atavistic customs.

Despite everything to the contrary, Natalia believes her father managed to hold up well in the face of the exhausting influence of religion and the unhealthy relationship with his parents, because instead of distancing themselves from their children, her own grandparents led separate lives. Or so she's been told. Her grandmother didn't want children and yet gave birth to seven, so nannies ended up parading around the house, looking after a bunch of kids and sharing the kitchen and rooms on the ground floor while the parents lived in the duplex upstairs.

Natalia has heard that, when everyone got together to eat, one of two things would happen: either a deathly silence would descend over the table, or they'd start going at each other and everything would go up in flames. It was then that Mateo convinced himself God wanted things to be that way. No matter what happened, it was all part of a divine decision, even if Grandpa Gallart disregarded the tributes, gestures, or other displays of affection from Mateo, the son who always went out of his way to please his father.

In this environment, expressions of love were outlawed, and those kids didn't stand much chance of emerging without garnering some scars along the way. Who knows if her father's chronic anxiety and destructive mentality are the result of that misery? And this is precisely why Natalia is so appreciative that Mateo has managed to stay sane enough to know how to convey affection to his own family. It couldn't have been easy for him. Natalia sensed the magnitude of the various crises that had plagued her father for years when, on one of the four bookshelves in the family's apartment in L'Ametlla, she found several old volumes on various religions, with one in particular being devoted to Buddhism. Buddhism in Buda. Through his connection with the island, my father is even capable of changing his religion, Natalia thought ironically as she stood there in front of the shelves, understanding that this unexpected library represented a sincere interest. Her father was not a frivolous man. He liked to joke around, but he'd never have bought books he didn't intend to read. And it made sense that the sort of hermit Mateo had become would look for options that might help him overcome suffering through inner strength, through wisdom cultivated in solitude which might bring him closer to some semblance of peace.

"Those books come from a time when I was studying different religions to see which one was best suited to what I was searching for: verity," her father explained. He was captivated by Zen Buddhism, which in Mateo's code translated into a fierce dedication to the doctrine, from yoga classes in Valencia to the practice of meditation.

It's not easy for Natalia to imagine her father alone on the island in the lotus position, his eyes closed, smiling at the sun, but she herself has experienced the same unforeseen sense of handing oneself over to Buda. On top of that, there's her father's compulsive nature and susceptibility to enthusiasm about things that can carry him off to unexpected frontiers. In Mateo's eyes, everything is scintillating, smashing, loving, so the separation with his wife led to an emotional earthquake he'd have to deal with alone in Buda. And earthquake is the appropriate word here, because for a deeply rooted Catholic shaped in the bosom of an ultraconservative family, ending a marriage sent shudders through the foundations. The early stages of the separation were painful for Natalia. After her parents informed her of their plan to divorce, she began experiencing severe abdominal pains that lasted a year, which she attributes to the anxiety caused by a situation that overwhelmed her as much as it did Mateo, the only difference being that he expressed it through grumpiness, stringing along one fight after another, wavering between distracted and disconcerted at this sudden and unfamiliar lack of control. And, as always, at the worst possible moment, Buda came to the rescue. Like an adviser, the island gave him the necessary pause, making him realize he needed to right the course. The temporary solution had been Buddhism.

Natalia would mull over all this later, because while her father was in Buda trying to reform himself in accordance with Zen teachings, she was trying to survive her teenage years in Logroño. There, she even gave up horseback riding, appalled by a militaristic instructor who demanded she keep her back straight as a stick in the saddle while completely ignoring that Natalia had been riding since she was eight, and that her desire was not to become some picture-perfect horsewoman but rather to enjoy those magnificent beasts. Hell, how would she have told her parents? *It's not my thing, Mom and Dad. If I like Buda so much it's because I can wear the same clothes three days in a row and nobody's gonna give it a second thought. I can ride a horse however I want, I've even learned to play the guitar all by myself. They're always harping on me . . . sit like this, put your foot there, call all the dogs Fosca because Dad likes that name. I don't like it.*

When she turned eighteen, she chose to go live with her grandmother in Pedralbes, Barcelona, to study philosophy at the Universitat Ramon Llull, where she experienced a somewhat disconcerting sense of liberation: something she had been craving so long that oftentimes she'd felt as though it would never come. The matriarch of the Gallart family left her to her own devices—no surprise, considering that she had foisted her seven children upon the nannies. But Natalia aspired to become even more independent, and the following year she moved into an apartment with a former high school classmate also studying in Barcelona. There she continued letting her hair down, almost literally, whether by dyeing it a different color every week, growing dreads, or shaving it off completely. The transgressive airs of the big city, combined with the repressions that had built up during the Harsh Years that started with the Civil War and only ended with Franco's death in the mid-1970s, spurred the curiosity typical of that age and encouraged her to try trendy new substances and cocktails, to visit suggestive gambling dens for the infamy of it all or maybe to establish something resembling friendship with fellow okupas, members of the so-called "skwatter" class. For what it's worth, though, I've detected significant inconsistencies here, because after ranting about class equality and the importance of leading by example, most of these disheveled rebels would go home to their parents on weekends to eat and shower. Not to mention the fact that they were students at a private university paid for by the same adults whose bourgeois lifestyle they had come to regard as indecent. In any case, while her colleagues were debating a number of issues which seemed reasonable to her despite their apparent contradictions, Natalia became a vegetarian. This new diet allowed her to reconcile herself with rice.

For Natalia, the weekend usually started by going out to party on Friday night. And even when she stayed out till dawn, the next morning she'd grab her bicycle and hop on the train to L'Aldea, and as soon as she got off she would start pedaling toward Buda. Spending Saturdays and Sundays in the little El Pas shack helped her reconsider her standards, especially during the winter, huddled next to the fireplace, because her economical, ecological, semi-skwatter mentality convinced her not to waste any energy by plugging in the heater. Local workers and residents of the surrounding towns who had known her since she was a child assumed she was simply going through the typical period of urban rebelliousness that many rural kids living in Barcelona got caught up in, and they continued to regard her as they always had.

She also spent a lot of time drawing. There are several members of the family who appreciate sketching and painting; Natalia figures it's the landscape influencing them. The delta is so remarkably beautiful that it simply invites one to share this beauty with others, and one way to seize this charm is through art.

As time went by, Natalia's lines shed their realism. The contours of her figures grew more attenuated, as if leaning toward a certain abstraction. At some point, the young student began to paint mandalas. At the time she didn't realize her father was a Zen acolyte, but now she's amazed by the notion that at some point Mateo could have been meditating on the island while she was drawing mandalas, neither of them aware of what the other was doing. The island, the repetition, the loneliness, the mandalas. There is an almost atmospheric certainty that distinguishes each space, and it's enough to simply breathe it in for different minds to end up thinking in similar ways. What her father didn't share was a vegetarian diet . . . not even as a Buddhist. In that sense and others he professed a more casual faith, one more adapted to the Mediterranean, allowing him to circumvent certain rules and, for example, enjoy a good steak without a second thought. That was when Mateo began to relax. At least a bit. The limits of things began to dissolve like the margins of the delta itself, and although he was never going to shed certain moral burdens he'd acquired over the decades, he did manage to live better. Just a little bit better.

Meanwhile, Natalia struggled to internalize some semblance of coherency by giving up sirloins, fillets, frog legs, and eel, though she was shored up a bit by the solidarity of her sister Andrea, who joined the cause despite being an avowed carnivore. And Andrea's company went well beyond that, for when her sister left Logroño to move in with her in the bustling metropolis, Natalia found herself taken with a principle of responsibility that led to her pumping the brakes on her excesses. While she was still sporting dreadlocks and partying into the wee hours of the dawn, she began to judge certain hypocritical attitudes. The blatant contradictions evidenced by a number of her friends went from being background noise to an annoying nuisance. Why should she be making excuses for people not only deceiving themselves but also actively trying to deceive her, regardless of how close they might have been? Were friends like that even worth having? The Gallarts can be rough around the edges but their word is their bond, and she wasn't going to keep on stomaching this pile of good-natured nonsense being spouted, however convincingly, by a select few who had drunk the Kool-Aid, as if truth or reason were dependent on tone. That was the worst part: the tone of voice and the tendency to lecture, because they weren't just trying to hold on to a poor man's dream while living in obvious utopias. They were trying to seduce you into following them down a path which most would abandon before turning thirty, as many so-called "rebels" did in May 1968.

Human psychology: such a tiny world in and of itself. The doctor with the jet-black beard must have got almost as much of a kick from psychoanalyzing her father in Logroño as she did from reading on the porch of the El Pas shack, hearing the flap-flap of the flocks of glossy ibises as they flew overhead, silhouetted against Buda's splendid sky. The purity, the pristineness of these images are also part of her moral education, and in Buda any lie or strife is stripped bare for all to see, appearing intolerably artificial. Buda shows you a path, a possibility that often clashes with what a large part of society calls the "real world." Buda, though, is reality: one which can at times be so wild that it gives the sensation of being more real than any other, and what the island had begun to murmur to Natalia was that she should act in accordance with what she had learned there, that she should live for real. Old scenes to which she hadn't lent much importance or which she'd interpreted simply as fantastical episodes or anecdotes began to move her more now because of how much they spoke to the human soul, including hers. She established even more illuminating associations about how families and places can sway people, realizing that four of her cousins were educators or psychologists, humanists like her, and noting that her cousin Sofía in particular was part of an emergency response team whose duty was to inform families when a loved one had died in an accident. In other words, many of the grandchildren born into Buda's lineage had chosen educating and caring for people over managing the land. Occasions of ambition and generosity, of affection and contempt, danced in her head, one idea led to another, and, without knowing how, she found herself investigating Nazism, having been impressed by *The Diary of Anne Frank* and *A Bag of Marbles*, tracking down documentaries and films about the Holocaust, engrossed by images of concentration camps. Considering all that, what the hell did she have to complain about? She'd better be counting her lucky stars. Her father was stubborn, overbearing, and at times almost unbearable, but she could tell that he loved her and would protect her from any aggression.

Natalia remembered taking care of an owl with Mateo in the cohetera, a construction unique to the Ebro Delta which was used to both store and shoot off firecrackers and other rockets that would theoretically scare away birds and disperse hail-bearing clouds, both of which could devastate their crops. "An owl usually has five or six offspring," her father had told her. "But two or three, the weaker ones, are always going to be pecked to death and eaten. You must be strong if you want to keep going."

She also remembered nocturnal expeditions in search of an old, pregnant hedgehog. As time went by, she figured out it was just one of many excuses Mateo used to entertain his daughters while he was on patrol scaring away ducks, wonderfully playful little lies that wrap an already intriguing territory in a veil of adventure and mystery, one that should be treated with caution but not fear. Her father taught her how not to become paralyzed by her own fantasies, though she did find her way. Being as little as she was, Natalia was terrified of going to the lagoon because she believed it was infested with crocodiles. One afternoon, when four of her friends from school had come over to eat, Mateo proposed canoeing on the Gran Calaix. The children accepted. Natalia got on board with them.

"Do you see how calm you can be?" her father asked as they crossed the lagoon. And Natalia did calm down. She began to enjoy the coots and cormorants. She asked for the names of several other species. All of a sudden, the canoe shook violently, tossing everyone into the water. While Natalia was thrashing around, disoriented, Mateo waded over to her, laughing, gave her a hug with one arm while steadying the canoe with the other, and repeated: "You see? There's nothing here. I can even touch the bottom."

Real reality. There are no crocodiles in Gran Calaix. There are no actual skwatters in the Universitat Ramon Llull. There's no need to suffer more than necessary. Black magic happens in the delta. Specifically, that performed by Pedrito and Montse, one of the last couples to have lived in Buda and who inhabited the same little shack in El Pas that would, many years later, house Natalia. This is precisely why Natalia knows that magic exists and that, no matter how exotic it may seem, it's a much more real reality than those daydreams of her former college classmates, because magicians and believers carry her creed to its ultimate consequences.

When Mateo settled on the island and began to make his changes, not only did Pedrito and his son continue poaching despite the many warnings, they even threatened to kill him. One night, Mateo found a cross made from grains of rice under his bed. He doesn't believe in witchcraft, but for a while after that he slept with a shotgun next to his pillow. Tensions approached breaking point on the famous "Night of the Long Telephones," during which

Mateo snuck into the reedbeds with a camera, intent on capturing evidence of the son fishing that would be used to kick everyone off the island. At the time, Natalia and Andrea had recently settled down in Logroño, and their parents were still together. Since Mateo wanted to have someone on call in case things went south, or he needed backup or a witness, even just someone listening in, he deployed the long antenna of his primitive cell phone, dialed his wife's number, and whisper-relayed the details of his operation. He managed to get the shots he wanted, but he decided not to expel the poaching settlers and sorcerers. After all, despite those exigent circumstances, Pedrito and Montse had always been loyal. The family remained on the island until the father was diagnosed with dementia. As a parting gift, they trashed the interior of the house and tore out every plant and tree they could from the garden.

Real reality. Black magic in the delta. And, in that revisitation of what's real, Natalia had an inkling that humans might be able to eat meat while still vindicating noble causes and fighting for a better world. This was without dispute her most nourishing conclusion of the time after she'd discerned that many of the fake skwatters who doubled as environmentalists were urging that meat be eliminated from the diet. Natalia continued to share many of their ideals, though she challenged them with her memories of Buda, which included hunters who ate what they killed. It's true that, in the delta, a certain amount of genuine animal slaughtering occurs, not just a case here and there, but a handful of senseless fools couldn't ever stigmatize those who hunt well. It's just as possible to hunt well as to eat well. That's what Artur told her shortly after they met at a New Year's Eve party.

She liked him right away. A tall, solid boy with a lantern jaw who, amid all the confetti, streamers, and cigars, spoke to her without a hint of affectation, meeting her eyes with his. This guy isn't trying to hide anything, Natalia thought. They agreed to meet up a few days later. And then again. Natalia detected certain values in Artur which she'd long since forgotten. She was impressed by his innocence, or perhaps she should call it his honesty. Whatever the case, he was a young man as strapping as he was transparent, and who was constantly looking out for his people and respected his elders in a way she hadn't managed to respect anyone, at least not in the unwavering manner he had demonstrated. Artur granted his ancestors a reverence which they had earned for whatever reason, elevating them to that pedestal of ancient legends in which old folks shine as if they were idols. All of it seemed a bit naive to Natalia, perhaps because her elders were the ones who'd harmed and disappointed her on so many occasions that they'd never warrant such a prestigious ranking. Yet for that same reason she admired the love Artur radiated, love in general, which is another way of saying love for life, and if that hunk of a man enjoyed hunting, then who was she to try and change that? After all, she'd shot and killed animals herself. Her Uncle Gonzalo had taken it upon himself to introduce her early on to what he considered almost an art form.

Natalia could sense that Artur wasn't clear about what vegetarianism meant. He might not have even understood that someone could survive without eating meat, though he was willing to accept the possibility because, at the end of the day, there was his sweetheart: blond, lush, and radiant. Pure Gallart energy. When Natalia started going to Artur's house to eat, his mother always asked, "What am I supposed to do with her?" But everyone was quick to take in this little oddity who would remain a vegetarian even after getting married and becoming pregnant with Max. She was never tempted to eat meat to gain strength and get more nutrients associated with bloody foods, because Natalia's blood tests showed her to be in perfect health.

Artur would often go out with the shotgun and come back talking about the pack of hunting dogs that had been after roe deer or wild boars, about the effectiveness of this or that hunting dog. He showed her photos of dead ducks. Natalia wouldn't say that living with a hunter was what brought about the change in her diet, though. She was likely more influenced by the eco-posturing skwatters who made it possible for her to picture herself following their trashy purist vibe to the point where she'd become anchored in the role of hysterical vegan who humanizes animals. Luckily, she hadn't fallen into that trap, continuing to see animals as having different natures: something which, if she felt like it, she could gobble up without having any complexes about it. At the end of the day, she just felt like eating meat.

"It had to happen," Artur said.

"Stop it," Natalia replied. "I might eat a duck you shot once in a while, but you'll never catch me with a factory-farmed pork chop on my plate. And you know I'm not going to the grocery store for chickens pumped full of antibiotics."

"Welcome to the family."

No, Natalia doesn't think Artur was the decisive factor, but it's true that his tendencies as a hunter were a contributing factor in bringing her back to meat. Naturally Artur influences her: they're a couple. His effect on her can't be compared to what Karen has on Mateo, though, because Artur hasn't transformed Natalia, far from it, while her father . . . well, he's simply different. Over the past eight years he's gone from being a canonical conservative to breaking one rule after another. Sure, this more relaxed lifestyle is good for his general wellness, but on the other hand he's now delegating more control to Simona, a person with whom, regardless of her trustworthiness, you don't discuss diplomacy or details. At a time when both La Administración and the rest of the family are waiting to pounce on the slightest careless act, you can't leave the island in the hands of someone who, to be honest, doesn't give off the best of vibes. It's worth noting that the supervisor has always treated Mateo's daughter with the utmost respect, but there's something about her that makes Natalia uncomfortable. Also, certain things aren't working the way they should, and lately Dylan and Quim have been complaining about Simona more than usual. Natalia knows this because her father still gives her regular updates on the daily operations of life on the farm. Too regularly. She'd like a little less information, thank you very much, to avoid getting caught up in power struggles which, granted, she's already a part of, being a member of the family. These, though, are inherited struggles she's not entirely sure she wants to continue waging. Mateo blames all the island's problems on the Generalitat and the state (mostly the Generalitat), and Natalia believes he's found himself a comfortable little obsession, because attacking those pinnacles of abstraction known as institutions allows him to play the romantic role of a tiny guerrilla standing defenselessly against the tentacular forces of Evil.

"My father feeds off the Generalitat because it's not a person," Natalia once said, convinced that, ever since Mateo "bent the knee" to Karen, renouncing the man he used to be, he's replaced earthly confrontations against determined people with the epic of David against Goliath . . . only in this story it's David who ends up being defeated.

None of that matters. What's important is the epic itself, surrendering to Karen while these wars continue to absorb him, keeping him up at night despite, paradoxically enough, the protests of his partner, who's tired of seeing him constantly on his phone, because the physical distance from the island hasn't resulted in him taking fewer calls or visiting fewer offices. Mateo's objective is still to save Buda. He's aware this is a doomed effort, but he's willing to keep it safe and dry until the centenary in 2027, when someone, whoever it may be, will take over. Or so he says, because right now he can't even imagine himself being far from Buda. Natalia often feels as though the island matters more than anything else to her father. Perhaps because it's a war pitting him against old, detested rivals harboring too many deeply entrenched grudges, and he feels like his pride and dignity are at stake. Mateo's obsessive character will never allow him to give up the fight, even under the dulcet persuasions of dear Karen, who might not even be trying to dispel him from his fixations anymore, something to which Natalia fully admits. Karen assumes it's in the nature of masculinity to be always competing for something, often making a fuss. But having Mateo there, constantly bitching and moaning about fucking Buda, isn't pleasant in the least.

Natalia is sure Karen has, on more than one occasion, experienced a certain amount of rage against the island. The same rage she herself has felt. *Please, let the sea finally wash it all away.* This isn't an uncommon thought for Natalia, but when she comes back to visit Buda on a sunny afternoon, she finds herself once again taken with the island's beauty. She regrets having ever wished for its demise and wonders why everything has to be so damn complicated. She'd wager that Karen doesn't ask herself those kinds of questions, and in that sense she envies her. What a woman. She negotiates problems like a giant slalom skier, and in the end she gets what she wants, including her father accepting their common-law relationship. Mateo and Karen never married, but their civil union status will still protect them financially if things go wrong. I'd be applauding her if Mateo didn't tell her about every single dispute, she thinks; the two of them could have walked straight off the set of a soap opera. It makes Natalia sick to her stomach to find out about some of these personal matters that border on the extravagant, but that's how things are with the new Mateo and Karen. When Natalia finds herself thinking these things, she regrets these thoughts, feeling uncomfortable, and remembers when, early in the relationship,

Mateo assured her that—despite the heated blowups he and Karen might sometimes have—these sorts of rackets aren't just part of being in a relationship but also act as a pressure valve for releasing pent up tensions and clarifying issues. He also repeated to her that Karen was a good person.

Mateo can act however he pleases. Natalia figures she'll never understand how her father can mix ferocity and submissiveness with such ease, but it's up to her to decide with whom she associates in life. She's told Mateo that of course she wants to spend time with him but that he doesn't need to bring Karen along with him every time he visits. Everything in moderation, Dad, please, she says. I'm sure she doesn't care; it seems like nothing affects her, which is exactly the opposite of her father. Mateo could learn a thing or two from his Colombian companion. Natalia herself has done so, and is starting to study relaxation techniques. Since giving birth to Max, she's been aspiring to detach herself as much as possible from nonessential issues and is focusing on not letting herself get caught up in problems that belong to others. If I keep going down this path, she once thought, I might find myself consulting my father's Zen library.

"I've always been very involved in matters regarding Buda. I've experienced them on a deeply personal level," she said one day to Artur. "But that intensity is gone. I need to learn to not be so affected by Dad's issues."

Which is also why she settled in Els Reguers, the town where Artur's parents live, forty minutes from Sant Jaume: an ideal point for staying close to and yet far enough away from Mateo. The house Max has been growing up in for the first two years of his life is situated on the side of a mountain and has large windows allowing you to contemplate a majestic amphitheater with one end in the ports of Beceite and the other in the Montsià region. On clear days, you can see Peñíscola, your eyes sweeping across the plains of Campredó and Amposta before landing, most spectacularly, on the undivided delta. The view spans hundreds of kilometers in a grandiose panorama which Natalia tries not to associate with anything worrisome, though the vista does include Buda. She and Artur have been thinking about where he might find work now he's been laid off after three and a half years with a tractor company. Artur is an expert in these machines, and his knowledge is so valuable it shouldn't take him long to find another job. Still, though, Natalia asked Mateo the other day about how to file for unemployment benefits, to which her father answered: "I was thinking about bringing on some new staff. Planting begins soon, and I'll need someone for a few months. Do you think Artur would be interested?"

While some are looking for work, others like me are sleeping among the dunes, and it can be easy enough for us to despise one another. Years ago, back when I held a different notion of time and employment, I'd have been disgusted with myself, but this morning I slept like a baby. Dreaming is a unique job which, if you do it well, allows you to float calmly through life, like certain marine species with special support structures designed to keep them afloat. Among the experts in this art, plankton are particularly notable. Suffice it to say that, in Greek, their name means "wanderer."

Now temperatures are increasing, realities that were once wandering or otherwise camouflaged are becoming more clearly expressed. With the added heat, the cold water begins to sink, giving way to summer beings. Animals that for months seemed like plants begin to emerge. Jellyfish sprout from polyps, unfolding like umbrellas, and the surface waters are coated with living dust: millions of microscopic organisms absorbing the rays of a sun that suckles and fattens them and which will soon bring about an outbreak of a spring visible in the water itself.

On the river, there is a man who often stops his boat at the end of the La Pantena canal, where he takes out his rod and casts it. Yesterday he told me that he loves to fish without fishing: "Just imagine if I catch something."

That man with a plankton's disposition is happy whenever a storm slices through the long arm of sand that forms Trabucador beach, because that's when restorative fresh water enters the bay of La Ràpita. Those who look through a plankton's eye see the sea as an amusement park full of gifts, which is precisely why they can't believe how many people still ignore the underwater meadows lush with razor clams, pen shells, other mollusks, sea cucumbers, and sponges that spread across the sea floor. And they're not judged by their gastronomic potential but by the spectacle itself. Plankton people observe the sea as a place of leisure where we can feel different, and that's what may be scary to many: being truly different.

Take Joan Barberà, for example. When her grandfather, a fisher from La Ràpita, noticed how interested she was in water, he said to her: "Where are you going? To the sea, *tontot*?"

Joan's grandfather associated the sea with cold, inclement weather and the death of companions. With the trash can into which he tossed his Zumosol cartons. Joan's mother, who worked at a fish market, immediately told her to go look for a job. Maybe she'd like to be an electrician. Meanwhile, Joan went to school, and when class was over she'd go to the market to help her mother gather up the leftover fish. In her free time, she continued going down to the sea. She decided to major in psychology. When she started learning about behaviorism, she was hit by a wave of depression. If all human reactions are based on previous stimuli, and you don't know where most of those stimuli came from, how can you gain control over even a sliver of your life? If there are no heroes or killers but only products of their environment, what can you do to influence your own destiny? This vision of helplessness, of being condemned to the perpetual drift like any other plankton, left young Joan feeling desperate, perhaps because there was too much she wanted to control, until one day she visualized the world as a ball swinging back and forth. As she wondered how to stop it, the answer became clear: with a barrier. Put up a wall that modifies the situation. Introduce a new obstacle that lends value to your actions, which shows you can create change. And Joan decided her barrier would be the sea.

She decided to change the notions people harbor about the sea.

Impart a different way of perceiving that mysterious mass.

Since then, Joan has been teaching everything from tying knots to sailing a fixed course, refurbishing boats to make them seaworthy, and above all spreading the word about the virtues of neoprene: that second skin which makes it easier to understand the waves and fish by allowing us to immerse ourselves regardless of the season. Neoprene is the key that can open us up to an almost virgin wisdom of the sea and water, still so foreign to us.

The answer that granted Joan a sense of calmness is a single word: barrier.

Every alleged complication has a simple answer, regardless of how obfuscated it may be. And often it's the place that makes the decision for you: shortly after I arrived in La Pantena, a window popped up on my phone screen indicating that it couldn't be recharged due to excess humidity. The isolation, especially during nights and weekends, prompted me to keep the device with enough charge in case of emergency. Until the rice presented a solution. Every night I buried my phone in a soft bed of Bomba grains, and by dawn it was dry enough to accept a fresh jolt of electricity.

A delta is nothing more than a place where something arrives and everything else begins.

SALT

THE SALT CEDAR sheltering me in the dunes is surrounded by saltwort shrubs which I use to garnish salads. These two plants mark the reaches of salt that extend along the shore as far as the tide comes in, tracing irregular white silhouettes in the sand that mingle with seagull droppings.

The island's future depends on how far the salt manages to advance. Mateo's favorite willow received a saline overdose and no longer exists, while several poplars near La Pantena will succumb soon enough. Palm trees, however, stand up well against this war of attrition. Among the birds, black-winged stilts are capable of filtering salt through a gland connected to their nostrils, but the advancing sea will affect them too as their current rice supplies greatly reduce.

Salt has such a transformative effect on identity that it even forces name changes. When it expands, the lagoon will become an estuary, a salt marsh, or even a small sea. It will bid farewell to the cattails, the ducks, the ibises, even the Gallarts. A few years ago, La Administración made moves to accelerate the expropriation of Buda by naming the lagoon something else.

"At first," Mateo says, "they said these were beaches, and since they're clearly freshwater lagoons, we won. The state had twenty days to appeal the ruling, but that didn't matter—the bureaucrats filed their appeal almost three weeks past the deadline and the court still accepted it for processing. They're the ones in charge, so . . .

Anyway, they sent out a geologist to get his expert opinion, and he determined that the lagoon wasn't a lagoon after all."

He resolved to shadow this geologist, dissecting his struggles to justify the continued presence of salt, because it was clear to Mateo that the decision had been made before any test was carried out, and that the scientist would shamelessly ignore, for example, the fact that the fauna present in the area were lacustrine or that the predominant water was fresh.

"He submitted his report a year and a half after it was commissioned. A year and a half! That's criminal! Why did it take so long? The judge extended the deadline three times. In the end he declared that these were all salt marshes. We provided evidence that there's nothing to this and uncovered lots of inconsistencies. There was nothing this guy could point to, no way for him to defend his conclusion that it was a marsh. Instead of a deductive analysis, instead of looking for evidence to prove it was a salt marsh, he did an inductive one. In other words, he wanted Gran Calaix to be a salt marsh, so he managed to pull together an argument that would prove him right. An argument without any evidence."

A marsh is a seasonally flooded space that dries out if there's no rain. The delta has very low rainfall, so this could easily happen, but Gran Calaix is always inundated thanks to the network of canals and pumps supplying it with fresh water. Unable to cite temporary periods of drought, the geologist suggested it might be a salt marsh because storms would often overtop the sandy barriers and introduce seawater, but the defense countered by arguing that these storms were too infrequent to fill Gran Calaix with enough salt water to turn it into a marsh. The judge ruled that the geologist hadn't met his burden of proof, reproached him for his shoddy work, for wasting the court's time, and for failing to acknowledge his own evidence.

Nevertheless, it wasn't long before the state expropriated the lagoon regardless. Mateo's lawyer, Daniel Monclús, still remembers his astonishment and shock at the court ruling that decided to ignore the law so they could satisfy who knows what interests. When La Administración also relieved the expropriated parties of even their most basic legal rights to access the land, the attorney understood that his client was the target of someone so influential, so untouchable, that they were willing and able to break the rules to exact some sort of revenge. This ruling even prohibited property owners from hunting and fishing on that thinnest sheet of land. Fishing. A particularly crucial economic activity, considering hunting wasn't bringing in much of a profit (the family limited those sorts of invitations to friends and investors) and that a significant part of rice production was managed by tenant farmers. Indeed, fishing provided a significant amount of money used to maintain the island, second only to subsidies.

Gran Calaix went from being a lagoon to a salt marsh as easily as Pedro Fumadó becomes Lo Xarnego, "the Mongrel," or Josep Bertomeu becomes Polet, "the Cockerel," although sobriquets like these are more sincere because they reflect an actual essence. Other nicknames from around here include Cagay, Picapalles, Mosquit, or Brillante.

Perhaps prompted by the sinuous spaces in which they live, inhabitants of deltas have a proclivity for slipping between names and creating new ones in original and unexpected ways. In the Euphrates Delta, the writer Wilfred Thesiger met Muslims who went by Chilaib (Puppy), Bakur (Sow) or Khanzir (Hog), all of which came as a surprise considering that, in Islam, dogs and swine are considered impure animals. Jaraizi (Little Rat), Wawai (Jackal), and Barur (Excrement) were other names that roamed the boggy landscape, enjoined with the idea of warding off the evil eye cast by children whose siblings had died in infancy.

In any case, there is another option: the one chosen in 1990 by a former mayor of Camarles, in this very Ebro Delta, who replaced the nomenclature of the streets with numbers to do away with their Francoist names, or so he argued. His own name was Primitivo Forastero, though, so it's permissible to suspect another, perhaps more traumatic reason.

It's common for us to wonder how a name might influence us, to speculate whether Señora Fuentes will love the waterways or why Señor Blanco dresses in such bright colors. There are those who decide to change their names, while others transform themselves as if through inertia, as has happened with Gran Calaix, where the lagoon is, yes, now a salt marsh. The increased storm frequency has resulted in a buildup of the same salt a geologist once tried to imagine, and this name change heralds the end of rice in Buda, which already lost its sense of self when it lost the cattails, themselves also casualties of the salt.

That same, ever-changing meteorology has had an effect of its own on names. For years, storms were named using the letters of the Latin alphabet. But in 2005, tempestuous events became so widespread, taking on such differing forms, that even the Iberian Peninsula was greeted with its first hurricane since 1842 and the Latin alphabet ran out of letters, forcing scientists to turn to the Greek.

The climax of delta literature, its epic, longed-for setting, is the flood. The spectacle of an overflowing Ebro or the Mediterranean steamrolling its already tenderized coastlines has become a perverse fantasy currently fueled by the sense that it will soon become a reality. The fragility of this space, of any delta, invites us to bear this inevitability in mind. It's a universe as lonely as it is rigorously watched over. Here, the river's culmination invites thoughts of the ultimate end, making it an ideal place to saturate oneself with the life that still shimmers amidst this long-enduring death rattle.

From the Danube Delta, writer Claudio Magris notes that agony is measured and monitored "like no other moment in a lifetime." When he reflects on things ending, he wonders where deltas culminate, whether the Danube's surface spills across every one of its 4,300 square kilometers interlaced with channels, with forks and branches, with drainage basins. Magris suggests not answering. "To establish the mouth of the river," he writes, "it would not be proper to pursue squabbles such as exist in the case of the sources. Men, animals, and rivers should be allowed to die in peace, without ever being asked their names."

After a certain point, why ask? In death, the river is more than ever what it always has been, and perhaps that's enough for us to add to its name the word that bids it farewell. The Ebro Delta. Nothing more.

In Paquito's shack, the workers breakfast around the large table, talking about differing ways of cooking the various rice varieties. The most grown rice in Buda is known as Bomba. Cultivating it is a highly technical process, requiring greater attention than other varieties, but in exchange it demonstrates a higher tolerance for sandy, salty soils and, when plated after cooking, the individual grains don't clump and stick together as quickly. Of course, this means it commands a much higher price. Carmelo, a cook, claims Marisma is the ideal rice for paella.

"Well, for my wife it's J. Sendra."

Others talk of how they won a competition preparing rice with mantis prawns and blue crab over a wood fire, stopwatch in hand.

"I don't even bother looking at the time."

"Impossible!"

Other Buda options include the round-grained Guara and Xirio varieties. There is also much discussion regarding the amount of starch Gleva contains, about how Taiwanese long grain rice is sold. Right now, the market is booming for Marina, grown in Seville, where they're able to produce eleven thousand kilos per hectare; in the confines of the Ebro Delta, the maximum yield is eight thousand.

"But wouldn't eleven thousand be too labor-intensive?"

"If we could do that here, we'd already be doing it."

"The important thing is to turn a profit. The more you grow, the better."

Montsianell has a 68 percent yield: it's a phenomenon resistant to storms and pests alike due to a series of clonings and adaptations that have resulted in a bionic grain. Rice farmers are incessantly testing formulas for getting a return on their investments, so they also grow an organic strain imported from Italy: the transgenic Xirio, another seed for all soils that was first used to garnish salads or as a cheap option sold precooked. Now, though, given the increase in demand, its market value is the same as any other.

Xirio is designed to survive a chemical pesticide that often kills rice as well. But not this one. This grain, the result of mutations and experimentations, will endure whatever is thrown at it, saving farmers a lot of stress. The same with dry or upland rice. In the delta, this form of planting in dry soil was first tested in 2016 to combat the apple snails after promising results nearby in the Spanish city of Badajoz and as far away as Italy. Indeed, there were already farmers who wouldn't plant any other way. Among them was Fermí, a hired hand who's invited me to ride along with him on the tractor. There are two screens in the cab, each divided into various grids reporting on the speed of the machine, the distance between furrows, whether they are parallel or not, the height of the wheels, the steadiness of the seed's output . . .

"It's like being in a video game," I say.

"Exactly. I really like video games. All the ones I have are about wars and tractors."

The tractor rolls along, spreading the contents of a five-hundred-kilo bag. It will be an hour and a half before it needs to be loaded up again. Fermí takes his hands off the wheel and the tractor continues trundling straight ahead at 12.3 kilometers per hour.

"There are some fields it still recognizes from previous years," he says, referring to the tractor itself. "They're all stored in its memory, so it could do all this by itself. And the new ones ready for planting this year . . . I'll record them for next season."

"Could you let go and start, I don't know, scrolling through your phone?"

"These fields aren't very wide, but in the United States, where the farms are massive, they can simply program the machines and doze off. Maybe in Seville too. They have twenty-hectare fields there, while here the fields are just two or three. Anyway, I'd rather be driving the tractor myself, turning the corners, pulling back . . . none of this autopilot, snaking-back-and-forth stuff. Nah, I enjoy the machinery."

Fermí is a third-generation tractor operator. Here he drives a five-year-old John Deere, and is one of the first to test such a contraption: a forty-thousand-euro seeder which he calculates can spread grain across eighty hectares if operated twelve hours a day for a day and a half. Precise figures for high performance.

Simona is in favor of more dry planting. She likes the results, and it earns her a few weeks she'd normally spend flushing flamingos, but Mateo isn't convinced of the benefits. Since rice naturally grows in flooded fields, it continues to be planted the traditional way.

"If our grandparents saw us dry-planting rice, they'd think we were crazy," says Pol over breakfast.

His is a salami sandwich. Others have ordered mortadella, chorizo, and mass-produced pastries, along with bags of peanuts and the coffee Dylan prepares . . . with a splash of cognac.

Pol is one of the few who knows how to *birbar* (to hoe out weeds) and sow in the old style: walking backward in a crouch, methodically depositing rice seeds in the furrows from the sheaves of rice plants tied around his waist. He's an emphatic man who radiates strength when he speaks, and like the rest of the Mestre family he keeps the folkloric image alive. Though only so often, because he's not about to break his back with so much science and technology being available. The 450 people who once spent hours hunched over, weeding and sowing, have been replaced by two or three tractors which must now deal with new weeds; fifty years ago, it was enough to pull out the tiger nuts, millet, and scraggly, undergrown *bord* rice, but there are now seven or eight types of excrescent outgrowths: an argument many farmers use in favor of the continued spraying of herbicides.

Expectations are high this year. It's hot, there's plenty of water, and there's not much wind: ideal circumstances for rice to thrive in.

"It's like this rice has been urbanized. It's really nice," Fermí says in the John Deere cab.

Such an immensity of rice is the result of a failed nineteenth-century effort to connect Cantabria with the Mediterranean by digging countless canals which led to the desiccation of vast swaths of plains. A group of Englishmen thought they could take advantage of the situation by converting them into rice fields. This was back in 1859. The resulting crop even attracted farmers from Valencia, and the delta began to populate itself.

Rice production continued to grow over the next century, taking up so much space and requiring so much water that the plains of La Tancada also dried out. The Parc Natural was created in 1984 with the express purpose of doing something to protect the wetlands.

Despite prioritizing rural Catalonian farmhouses over hotels and curbing the expansion of the grain, this monoculture crop's dominance leads to the widespread use of tractors that crush thousands of tiny beings under their massive wheels. Environmentalists report an alarming decrease in the number of frogs and snakes, as well as the disappearance of turtles. Furthermore, they allege that the crop itself is unsustainable due to the amount of water it consumes, because it emits 8 percent of the methane entering the atmosphere, and because its production favors large landowners. They also invite us to take note of who's actually making a living from rice farming: fewer and fewer people, with more and more money.

"I hadn't set foot on Buda until I came here to plant," says Fermí. "It was like I'd found a space cut off from the rest of the world. Like things were different here. Now people recognize me. Sometimes I'm on the island in summer now, even if I don't have work."

"Mosquito season," I say.

"They don't bother me. I just lather up with some aloe vera or natural honey and that's it. Anyway, I don't really notice them anymore—I'm basically from the delta."

Finding unique ways of tolerating mosquitoes and salt is a defining trait not only among natives, but also among bulls. Up until the nineties, Buda was home to a herd of fighting bulls and fearless cows under the care of a herder named Tarranda. The herd of *bous* grazed in a fenced field on Sant Antoni, although an animal would occasionally slip away and reach the beach. Mateo remembers the first time he saw a number of hulking masses in the distance: at first he wasn't sure what they were, but as soon as he identified them as bulls, he started to scream as he and everyone with him ran into the surf.

When the authorities decided the animals were a disaster waiting to happen, the *bous* were banished from the delta and replaced with horses from Camargue, France. The image of a bull with a cattle egret perched on its back is, as the bird's name would indicate, more natural than an image of the same bird on the back of a horse. But times have changed, and if you want to catch a glimpse of an egret on a bull you'll have to head to Lo Moreno's pastures near L'Ampolla and L'Encanyissada. Or visit the velas, the plots of grazing land here, where the Bernabé family maintain their herd. At the head of this cattle dynasty sits Pablo Archer Bernabé, who just the other day was sitting next to my fireplace and talking with me about the issue, only to end up lending me his bike so I'd be able to move about the delta more speedily during the coming months.

Ah, that bike.

What a great little gift.

I told him Mateo had seen bulls in the sand on this beach. A rustic breed of animal grazing on rough terrain, capable of digesting the salty grass growing among the rocks, whose presence inspired the name of the family business, Ganaderías y Arroces de Buda, Garrobud Associats, alluding to the raising of hogs, goats, and *bous* on the island years ago. They were fighting bulls and fearless cows descended from the studs that came with a military detachment that had settled on the island. The herds of *bou* had the advantage over the flocks of sheep thanks to their sheer strength, useful when hauling and dragging plows and carts through the wetlands. Furthermore, the *bou* is the only farm animal which, if trapped in a swampy area, can escape from the mud unaided.

Tarranda was the last herder to freely graze bulls on the island. He lived in Villa Teresa, the house on the straight route connecting La Pantena with El Mas, which is now patrolled by a quartet of goats and whose facade features a fig and a formation of olive trees which served to separate the house from the bulls. Beyond that stretch are the swamps the animals once crossed, muddying the lagoon. When grass was scarce, Tarranda gave them salted fodder, but when that wasn't enough to sate their hunger, he'd drive them into the water, clinging to the neck of one of the bulls, and together they'd ford the river. The neighbors referred to Tarranda's house as Villa Torera. One day he drowned.

It's true that fighting hooves once splashed there among the eels, but today no one holds on to that image, because the current notion of the bull seems to admit no more history than what's being told by two small bands of people in conflict with one another and moulding the animal to suit their own purposes.

Pablo Archer has an artist friend who teaches postgraduates. One day he showed his master's students photos of a dauntless cow grazing in winter, though he presented it as a bull. Upon asking his students to adjectivize what they were seeing, he was hit with a barrage of prejudices tinged with politics and emotions, such as "Spain," "pain," and "picador," ignoring most of the animal's objectively natural attributes.

The reality now looming over Pablo Archer and his herd of purebred Navarras oozes an atavistic aggressiveness on the verge of ruining him, leaving him depressed and separated from his partner. He's now a man of consensus who shares many of Mateo's opinions. Both are heirs to historical traditions. Both find themselves navigating emblematic spaces which are under constant attack, though for differing reasons.

"The four spots that have supported biodiversity in the delta are those with wild cattle," Pablo said yesterday. "L'Encanyissada, La Tancada, Les Olles, and Buda."

The bulls' presence churns up the soil, spreads seeds, and prevents open plains from becoming dense wilderness. Bulls are such deltaic animals that inhabitants of the French Camargue have integrated them into wetlands to stave off desertification by combining the animals' presence with organic farming practices like crop rotation between rice, alfalfa, and chickpeas. Instead of the land being forced to accommodate a single seed, it's regenerated and produces stronger, varied fruits capable of surviving without the need for chemicals.

Wilfred Thesiger enjoyed seven years with the ever-dank buffalo that lived alongside the Ma'dan people of the Euphrates Delta the Sumerians built in what's said to be the first civilization in history. And he described the seasonal migrations of the North Arabian nomads in the Tigris basin. Buffalo and water seem to sit at the origins of the world as we understand it today.

"I loathed cars, aeroplanes, wireless, and television," Thesiger wrote. "In fact, most of our civilization's manifestations in the past fifty years was always happy, in Iraq or elsewhere, to share a smoke-filled hovel with a shepherd, his family and beasts. In such a household, everything was strange and different, their self-reliance put me at ease, and I was fascinated by the feeling of continuity with the past. I envied them a contentment rare in the world today and a mastery of skills, however simple, that I myself could never hope to attain."

I sensed a hint of Ma'dan in Pablo as he sat there by the fireplace, which means that, yesterday, I was Thesiger learning the value of the bull from a Sumerian successor.

"In the delta, symbolism has to be paid for twice over," Pablo said after recounting his first clashes with the pro- and anti-bullfighting sorts. He also mentioned an island in the delta populated only by bulls, and invited me to visit it one day with him.

The crackling fire and hissing logs are lulling me to sleep on a rainy Sunday as I'm reading a book. As symbols, it says, we need endings, we need goodbyes. I go out to the porch, where this morning the clutches of cats' claws that had tinged the entrance path with lilac have since retracted their blossoms. The afternoon has turned gray, bringing with it a north wind and rain that smells of mud. Two steps later and I'm starting to get soaked. Past the canal, the water machine-guns the river. Upon sensing me, a flock of coots scatters; immersed in the book's ideas still, which can be roughly summarized as *Sometimes you have to know how to bring it all to a close*, I'm not sure I see them.

A hundred meters from the tip of Sant Antoni, where river and sea meet, I switch off my eyes while continuing to walk. I hear the sound of waves, wind, and raindrops falling on my eyelids. I walk blindly along the empty coast listening to the waves. "We understand the world better when we tremble with it," said Édouard Glissant, so there is something to be understood now. In October I'll turn fifty, and I'm beginning to think about death in a rational way. I lost my fear of it a long time ago, and since then have paid it little if any attention, but at this symbolic crossroads, in these fading boundaries, death's inevitability reappears, and I realize I only fear her in others. There's nothing more normal than dying. Having lived is a reassurance, though I wish I'd lived longer. By the time I arrive back at La Pantena, the heels of my boots have acquired such an immense layer of mud that they raise me up like a drag queen.

EELS

PLANTING HAS CONTINUED intensely for ten days, and the fields in La Pirenaica are already cultivated. On a couple of nights, I could see the red lights of a tractor in the distance until after midnight, rushing through the final few hours before the floodgates upstream in Tortosa were opened. There have been days of radiant sun, little wind, and rising temperatures, which I've taken advantage of by enjoying breakfast and lunch on the porch, and which the first few mosquitoes have also enjoyed upon emerging from the reedbeds. On April 11, one stung my eyelid, and on more recent nights, their small clouds have begun to proliferate, fluttering around the white front door to La Pantena, attracted by the light from the entrance.

Yesterday, Dylan showed up with Artur. He announced that Mateo's son-in-law is starting work on the island and that the water is already flowing toward Buda. It will still be a couple of days before it arrives, because the island is the final stop on its journey after flooding the rice fields in the delta. Still, though, some landowners make a head start by collecting water from the canal, meaning some fields have already been inundated for days. I can see them when I leave Buda by bike. Between the road to Sant Jaume and the sea a checkered pattern unfolds, its squares alternating between the still-dry fields of brown and the reflective sheens known here, as well as around the Valencian Albufera, as Lo Lluent, "What Shines."

The nerve-racking season for the farmers begins, and the birds take to feast. The north wind, the blue crabs, the ducks, flamingos, sparrows, apple snails, and the nematodes . . . from now on, these and other potential threats will define daily life for Simona, Quim, and Dylan. Maybe Artur, too. The Peruvian wields a hoe, removing algae and seaweed from a canal where the accumulated vegetation both reeks and restricts the flow of water. When the new water arrives, it should flow quickly through the irrigation ditches like blood through the arteries of the body that is Buda.

While the rest of his colleagues are operating machinery, Dylan organizes, cleans, and otherwise tends to the fields with thick, broad hands that have spent over a dozen years on this land and which are the direct heirs of Pep's legacy. That's why, owing to another one of those legal entanglements, Dylan is the only member of the team with permission to fish. To fish for anything, that is, except eel. Eels were old Pep's specialty. The cabin/workshop next to La Pantena stores an endless number of fishing nets, gaffs, squid jigs, creels, rods, fillet knives, cutting boards for gutting the fish, and crab pots, but above all the gánguile or *bou*, a beautifully artistic trawling net used by seasoned fishers of yore. They've since passed the baton to a Peruvian migrant who, like me, is about to turn fifty, though he looks ten years my junior. Pep cared much more about the eels than the rice, because they were what fed him.

Eel was one of Buda's primary sources of income until the fishing ban solved the whole mess on the island. Later, a restricted license was granted to the La Pantena channel and to one sole individual who, Mateo decided, would be Dylan. With one condition: that he not fish for eel. Ever since then, only Dylan and his helper of choice can fish here.

Dylan, Pep, and eels are all survivors through confluence, capable of moving through and between at least two worlds. Pep was the only tenant farmer not evicted from Buda thanks to his skill at catching fish in a sea of rice. Dylan is an immigrant whose heels are firmly dug into the ground despite being surrounded by native tractor drivers who often are also the owners of extensive landholdings, and he slides from one language to another as if moving between fresh and salt water: an eel-like talent, one that consolidates his existence between oceans, rivers, and seas.

The eel is the most mysterious of all fish. It seems as though every single species is born of the hypersaline waters of the Sargasso Sea, and for reasons to do with the moon, eels undertake transoceanic journeys where they can swim as far as fifty kilometers a day at depths approaching a thousand meters to reach river mouths such as that of the Ebro. They can then stay in the same place for as many as fifty years—though there are some specimens that have reached the century mark—before returning to the Sargasso to die.

No one truly knows where the eels come from. In his impressive and pioneering *History of Animals,* Aristotle stated that "they originate in what are called the entrails of the earth." They were born from mud, suggesting spontaneous generation. The philosopher and scientist lived in Stagira, on Chalcidice, a peninsula north of the Aegean Sea with three large tongues of land, and frequent contact with that Mediterranean embayment seemed to favor his interest in aquatic fauna, specifically the mysterious eel. He dedicated a significant amount of time to observing and dissecting them.

Enigmas surrounding the fish have endured for centuries. Eels were once said to emerge from the gills of other fish, from morning dew, electrical disturbances, even thatched roofs. Stoic philosophers considered the eel a representation of the pneuma, the breath of life. The animal became a symbol of the mysterious origins of life. In 1653, Francesco Redi made the first reasoned critique of the idea that life could be generated from nothing, and the scientific community had mostly accepted that "omne vivum ex vivo," but even so, how eels reproduce remained unknown. Zoologists began to talk about the eel question, drawing researchers of all kinds to the topic for centuries, including a nineteen-year-old Sigmund Freud.

At the University of Vienna, Freud was a student of Carl Claus, a specialist in marine biology and an expert in crustaceans who taught zoology (among other subjects) to the young man. While Carlo Mondini claimed to have identified the eel's reproductive organs, no one else had been able to confirm these findings, and while some questioned his results, others dedicated themselves to finding evidence to support his contention that such an organ did exist. Which is why Claus sent his outstanding young student to a bare-bones laboratory in Trieste on a mission to finally find the fish's testicles.

Freud's investigations are reflected in the letters he wrote in Spanish to Eduard Silberstein, a friend he had made when they were both studying that language. "Recently, a zoologist from Trieste has found, as he says, the testes, that means the male eel," he wrote, "but has not given a precise description of those, because he seems not to know what a microscope is. He failed to offer an exact description of his find."

Having summarily equipped himself with said microscope, Freud began to dissect eel after eel in search of an obvious male specimen. Days passed, and nothing. Frustration began to take over the young student, who, alone in an unfamiliar city, became obsessed with locating microscopic gonads. After dissecting over four hundred eels, he failed to identify a single male, but he began to ask himself—like never before, and like few others ever would—questions about sexuality, and not only in regard to fish. Some time after that, he abandoned the pure natural sciences in favor of psychoanalysis. It's conceivable that eels may have been decisive when it came to the theories Freud developed about sex and sexuality which directly influenced twentieth-century thought.

Freud slipped from one discipline to another, always hooked on mysteries while cultivating a colorful personality that recalls the question posed by the artist and journalist Patrik Svensson: "What kind of person chooses to become an eel fisherman? What does the eel provide such a person with? A profession and an income, is the simple answer. But that's not the whole story. True, the eel has been an important source of food in large parts of Europe throughout history, but it has always been tricky. Difficult to catch, difficult to understand, enigmatic, and to many people simply unpleasant." Svensson's response is that these fishers tend to be proud and tenacious people who have often cultivated a sort of marginalization for themselves, increasing their hostility and distrust toward the majority and those in power.

Old Pep's nature stood in contrast to that of the surly folks Svensson described. As a grandfather he was kind, caring, and respectful, but when Dylan arrived, he refused to teach him how to fish. He took him on as an assistant, a young jack-of-all-trades who could maintain boats and gear, look after La Pantena, or haul nets, pots, or plates of fish, or whatever was needed—if he stayed far enough away from the water. Dylan understands. Simona treated him the same way. That's how it is when you sense a threat to your space. You see everyone as a danger, you figure you're about to be replaced, so you're not going to make things easy. "Pep was a little afraid of me," Dylan will often say. The old man had seen others fall, and regardless of how much Mateo assured him otherwise, the only real guarantee that he wouldn't be kicked off the island was that nobody else knew how to do what he did. The same policy Simona had. With one denying him tractors and the other fishing, this pair presents a vastly different mentality than what Dylan had known in Peru, where neighbors helped each other, even exchanging food. Well, Pep occasionally gave fish to Simona, to a friend, and especially to Dylan, who split it with his crew, but when the numbers were no longer adding up, the old man started to have his doubts. A good part of the catch was sold to Vicenta, the fishmonger from Sant Jaume. It wasn't hard to conclude that, if he continued to give the fish away to folks he knew in town, Vicenta would have fewer customers, so she'd buy less of his catch, and he certainly wasn't going to squander money. From then on, Pep ordered all leftover fish to be returned to the sea, even if dead. The old man's word was law on the island, and Dylan obeyed without question because he understood Pep's needs.

Dylan focuses on his tasks and earns his rewards. That's how it's always been. He came to the delta having been encouraged by his brother, who'd been working in the area for a year. He told him that if he flew to Europe he'd quickly find himself a job, and he was right: the day Dylan showed up, they hired him as a construction worker. Shortly after, he was called to Buda in August to bring in the harvest. Mateo suggested he stay through December, after which he offered him a permanent deal, but when Dylan's wife ran the numbers, she pointed out that it would be better for him to remain a freelancer if contract work paid less for the same type of work.

"I came here to work, and they're guaranteeing me work here," Dylan countered. "Either I stay with the farm, or we go back to Peru."

What he didn't agree to was settling in one of Buda's little houses. Accepting that part of the deal would have meant isolating himself from the outside world. The island would have become a prison and he'd have become a clone of old Pep, and that was out of the question. As much as he appreciates working on Buda, and although he says he doesn't keep track of his hours and takes care of the island as if it were his own, Dylan has a life outside of work. Besides, he's seen how Buda swallows those who surrender themselves to it. He's seen how it's engulfed Mateo, because its effect on his boss is overwhelming, owing to the hours and worries he's left on that land. Still, though, if it weren't for him this would be a jungle. Both for him and for Dylan. Simona, too. That much must be understood.

Despite all the backbiting and stupid shit she's done to him, she was also key when it came to cleaning up the reedbeds, the fallen tree trunks, the ironwork, the tiling in the abandoned houses.

Dylan enjoys a job where no two days are the same, and if he could get the supervisor off his back, this would be an ideal gig. How can one woman cause so much trouble? While Mateo blames the officials, though, the word around town is that the ban on fishing in La Pantena is because Simona, who's from Sant Jaume, wanted to sell the catch only to her own townsfolk, leaving out the fishers of La Cava, who had been the historical promoters of fishing in Buda. So when Europe began requiring the registration of licensed fishing operations, and with the La Cava brotherhood now managing that requirement, La Pantena was left off the list: the only exclusion on the entire delta.

In any case, they continued in their fishing ways on the island, oblivious to a prohibition nobody had told them about until, ten years later, an agent from SEPRONA, Spain's Nature Protection Service, who was making his rounds found Dylan fishing and issued him a warning. And how did Mateo react? Oh, he went off on his standard tirade about La Administración. Dylan doesn't deny that the bureaucrats against whom Mateo spends his entire life fighting played a part in the ban, but it would be nice if occasionally the boss entertained the notion that some of the dirty tricks were self-inflicted wounds, caused by Simona.

When Dylan arrived in the delta, he immediately noticed the deep-seated disagreements among neighbors, especially between those from Sant Jaume, on this side of the river, and those from La Cava, on the other bank. They say people from Sant Jaume don't like to work, that the streets are empty until well past nine in the morning, and that they're always looking for easy money, which is why they've always hunted and fished *de matuta*—by poaching, and indiscriminately at that.

"If folks from La Cava fished in Buda, they'd still be catching eels," a Cavero once told Dylan, remembering that Pep was from his town, and that Buda and the Migjorn rose from the sweat shed by these people rough around the edges but respectful of natural cycles, and that the Santjaumeros are so conscious of their lack of initiative that they didn't want the supremely modern bridge which now spans the banks of the Ebro to be built because they feared a Cavero invasion. That's the exact word they used: invasion. Now it turns out that they're the ones spending their days in La Cava's bars and shops, delighted with the rival bank's comforts.

Dylan settled in Sant Jaume, where he has friends, so this whole fracas amuses him. The Santjaumeros have their peculiarities, but there's no need to go beyond that. A dispute between neighboring towns is a familiar story across the globe. What you should do is pay attention to individuals, because Simona is a unique character and not exactly adored in her own Sant Jaume. She's fought with half the town, though via Buda, and she employs many of the townsfolk, buying them gasoline, tools, and giving them rice or fish which, incidentally, were often caught by Dylan and Quim. The supervisor has created a network of dependencies that protects her, but considering her personality and the enemies she's made, one day things will go off the rails, and who knows who'll help her? But while Mateo rules things here, Simona can rest easy. Dylan is surprised the boss is so dismissive of the complaints he and Quim have filed against Simona because Mateo is normally attentive to his employees' needs. Sometimes he even pays more attention to them than necessary, like when Pep refused to reinforce La Pantena with concrete.

"As long as I'm here in this world, that house won't be touched," the eelman said to Mateo.

And here stands La Pantena, still without concrete.

Mateo is respectful of his people. He's always made sure everyone is doing well, or at least as well as can be. Dylan is very appreciative that the boss was with him when he had to spend several days in the hospital after one of his testicles began to swell, eventually growing to the size of a pétanque ball; Mateo assured him the whole time that there was nothing to worry about, that nothing was more important than his recovery. Dylan spends so much time covered in mud that one would expect him to get even more infections than he does. There are deltas where people come in contact with the water and have worms slip underneath their skin and start laying eggs that cause everything from diarrhea to blood in the urine and even purulent sores from which the worms themselves will emerge. Freshwater mollusks can also cause these symptoms, so an apple snail might have been responsible for his inflamed testicle. And, as if that weren't enough, there are the diseases caused by the chemicals and waste runoff that enter the river and spread across the rice fields. But Dylan doesn't concern himself with such things. His body has adapted to all sorts of substances, and if one of his balls swells up occasionally, it will shrink back down to normal size eventually.

I'm woken by the blustering. There's a fig tree branch that scrapes frantically against the corrugated Uralite roof. At night it doesn't matter much because I can usually fall back asleep, but when it happens at dawn, I'm up early, like today. Through the window, in the depths of the darkened night, there's a little red dot that could be a bird-flushing vehicle. A resounding boom resounds across the fields. Gonzalo says Simona is intentionally setting up sound cannons near his house to make sure he's awake. The rice fields are dotted with reflective posts and scarecrows that can't be seen at this hour.

The walls and roof are attuned to each external nuance. The house expresses itself like a hypersensitive skin capable of perceiving every quiver, every gust of wind, every drop of water. It's a waterproof dermis that allows me to feel like an eel. A suit of armor equipped with sensors connected to my pores, to my nerves . . . because I am this structure. It's an extension of me. Oblivious to the news of the dense, external world that can only enter via TVs or phones. Regarding the latter, I dig out my own from the bed of rice in which I lay it to sleep every night. I could leave it disconnected but I want to talk with my family, follow my father's progress.

I check out a viral tweet that says *Coming back from the dead isn't free*. I hesitate between responding to the tweet or going out into the gale to see what the fields look like at dawn before the mosquitoes take over the world. Because they're there, eggs incubating, their hatching imminent. When the temperature in La Pantena is right, when waters from the rice fields, river, lagoon, canal, and sea converge with their respective vegetations, each meeting of the waters will produce a different mosquito.

The first rays of light are now clearing the lighthouse cupola as I go out on the porch. I force my way through the gale using the crown of my Siberian hat as a battering ram. Upon entering the reedy corridor extending before the sea, the wind weakens and the temperature increases in accordance with the spectrum of fuchsia, lilac, and mother-of-pearl that unfolds in the sky: the definition of warmth.

On the beach I move amidst feathers, shells, and a few fresh footprints, my eyes on the ground to avoid destroying families, especially those of the terns, who have begun to lay their eggs in the sand. The shells, along with the occasional fossil or other remnant, act as buttresses against the air, seeding the beach with sharp yet minimal ridges like a hardened wind.

The salt cedar on my dune is shiny and prickly with crystals. I duck down into it and the wind disappears. Curled like a ball, the bush around me is a swaying delight, as if performing a sensual dance.

I find the size of this disconnect unparalleled because I don't feel the suffocating effects of time. I sleep eight hours if a fig tree doesn't wake me. I work without any sort of stress. Knowledge settles like falling feathers, unexpectedly. I gather that this is living. Or it always has been, and I didn't know until now.

Coming back from the dead isn't free.

There may be some toll that awaits me.

Back at La Pantena, Dylan is on his knees by the canal, dropping a rope into the water to which a dead chicken has been tied. "Let us catch some crabs," he announces. "I'm setting the bait."

A few meters away, he sinks another chicken tied to the end of another rope. A swarm of blue crabs begins to crowd around the pale bodies visible beneath the surface of the water.

"Tomorrow I'll pull up the ropes and see how many we hooked."

In the distance, a tractor with extra deep tread on its tires sows the fields over a sheet of water.

"All good?" Dylan asks.

I show him the noisy fig tree.

"I'm sure Pep didn't plant it there," he says. "If it keeps growing like that it'll tear the foundation apart." The roots run directly against the slab. "A seed must have landed there, and since the old guy hasn't been around . . ."

"Could we cut back the branch that's rubbing against the roof?"

"I'll just grab a saw."

I sit on the edge of the canal watching the crabs devouring the chickens, but the water has grown too murky and all I can make out are the slowly oscillating shells. One crab has been cornered under the bridge. It's missing a claw. Three others approach and attack until the crab has been fully disarmed and is ready to be eaten, as the eels surely would have done. The blue crab has largely displaced the eel, but it's just as cannibalistic, though the first eel was thought to have been a vegetarian. A thirteenth-century Dominican monk said they loved peas. In 1930, French scientists placed a thousand elvers in a tank of water. They fed the baby eels daily, but after a year they were left with seventy-one animals which had tripled in size. Nothing remained of the others, not a skeletal trace. Three months later, after witnessing "daily instances of cannibalism," scientists recorded a single individual measuring just under a meter in length: a modest mark, considering that Pliny the Elder had reported ten-meter specimens in the Ganges.

The enigmas surrounding this fish lend it the sordid charm of das *Unheimliche*: the German concept that applies to something disturbing or even terrifying, inexplicable and yet close. Something we think we understand until it turns out to be completely different. Deceptively familiar. Uncanny. Atum, the creation god of Egyptian mythology, the father of all gods and pharaohs in Heliopolis, was associated with the eel: a human head culminating in an eel's body, thus symbolizing the union between positive and ill-fated forces.

Rachel Carson distilled this notion of a complete animal, describing the fish as a conscious and sensitive being capable of both reason and memory, of joy and suffering. Through science, the daughter of a homemaker and a traveling salesman humanized the eel by presenting it as another creature with which she felt a singular empathy, perhaps due to its marginalization and mystique. After getting married, Rachel's mother had given up her teaching career to educate her daughter. By taking her for long walks in the countryside, she sparked in her daughter a naturalistic interest. It's been said that Rachel was a lonely child without many friends, but that her outdoor life always made her feel safe and happy.

Though Carson didn't fish for eels, she connected with them the way Freud, Svensson, and Pep did: as strong, alternative, and supportive types when it came to animals that were overlooked or ignored for being strange, unpleasant, or ugly even when they've played key roles during decisive moments in the history of a nation. Consider the case of the *Mayflower*, the ship that, on November 11, 1620, docked off Cape Cod, where Henry Beston would reside many years later. She had set sail from England two months earlier with around a hundred and forty passengers on board, most of whom adhered to a strict Protestant doctrine. That winter, they anchored off a coast so arid and desolate they chose to wait for spring on board the ship. Food grew scarce, water became contaminated, and tuberculosis, pneumonia, and scurvy spread across the *Mayflower*. By spring, half the passengers and crew had died, and nobody knew how they were going to feed themselves. Until the appearance of Tisquantum, a member of the Patuxet tribe who had been captured by the English and sold into slavery in Spain only to escape and make his way to, yes, England, where he learned the language. Eventually, he managed to return to his homeland, and now he found himself with compatriots of his captors who were in real trouble. After learning of the situation, Tisquantum went down to the river, returning with a good supply of eels. Over the course of the next few days, he taught the travelers how to catch them, how to grow corn, where to find hunting grounds, and edible fruits and vegetables. Thus, eels are part of the earliest foundational history of the United States. As Svensson has written, "It would have made complete sense for the eel to have become an important figure in American mythology, a fat, shiny symbol of the promised land, the gift that sealed what was preordained. But that didn't happen. Perhaps because the eel's nature doesn't lend itself well to solemn symbolism. Perhaps because it soon became associated with the simple eating habits of the poor rather than with feast days. Perhaps also because the gift had come from a native man . . . For some reason, this gift from God to the early pilgrims has been all but erased from the grand narrative. The story of the colonization of North America is full of myths and legends, but the story of the eel isn't one of them. On Thanksgiving, Americans eat turkey, not eel, and other animals—buffalo, eagles, horses—have been the ones to shoulder the symbolic weight of the patriotic narrative of the United States of America."

Dylan will occasionally eat rice and eel *en suc* from the big glass bowl he uses as a lunchbox. The delta's gastronomy has a reliable, resilient mainstay in the eel. It can be prepared smoked or fried, grilled or marinated in a sauce of garlic, parsley, guindilla peppers, and tomatoes that has been livened up with crabmeat. Another of the delta's signature dishes is the chapadillo de anguila, so named because the animal is cut into slices that are dusted with paprika and hung to dry before being grilled over a flame or seared in a pan. What all preparations have in common, according to local legend, is that, to be as delicious as possible, they must be prepared from a fresh kill, like the fighting bulls turned into sandwiches right outside the gates of certain plazas de toros.

In any case, eel dishes are on the decline, because fewer and fewer are being caught. Once there were so many elvers that they were fed to hogs and derided as "poor man's noodles," but since the 1950s, the numbers of elvers and thus eels themselves have suffered a disturbing decline due to overfishing and their extreme sensitivity to toxic substances.

The few eels that manage to escape the delta's nets, chemicals, and barbecues swim toward the Strait of Gibraltar, searching for the Atlantic so they can return to the Sargasso Sea, and only then do they complete their metamorphosis with flair, taking on a silvery color. The eel can alter its life cycle while waiting for this time. It can delay the development of its sexual organs and prolong its own existence, as if hibernating, waiting for the chance to return to the lone place from which eels emerge. When that day comes, then they dress themselves up. In silver. The color of their shroud.

Who knows when Dylan will return with the saw. I hop on the bike to leave Buda for the first time in several days and, as I pedal through the shade of the eucalyptus trees leading to El Sifó, I notice a tingling sensation on my face. There are no clouds in the sky nor drops of rain on my glasses or the ground. It's the mosquitoes. They're here.

When I return, Dylan has cut down the fig tree from the bottom: the stump is almost level with the ground. There are no half measures on the island.

The next morning, Dylan hauls up the two ropes from which he dangled the chicken in the canal. A few bare bones emerge without a trace of meat, and there are no crabs in sight. Feathers are floating in the water, but not many. "Wow," he says. "I thought it would work as bait. We'll have to go with the cages."

Quim makes quick strides toward the toolshed; Dylan follows, and the two of them emerge with a large rectangular iron cage into which they place two more dead chickens. They lash the corners of the trap to La Pantena's pilings and sink it almost completely.

The next day, Quim and Dylan arrive in a pickup with Artur. Dozens of crabs have packed themselves inside the cage; most are submerged, though others crawl over the bodies of their fellow crustaceans, peeking out of the water. Artur helps to haul up the cage and dump the crabs into a steel drum. Dylan sets two chairs on either side of the drum, two wicker baskets on the ground, puts on a pair of thick gloves, and sits down on a stool. Quim opens a package of small straps and takes a seat inches from Dylan, who grabs a crab from behind and lifts it up. The animal snips the air with its enormous pincers. Dylan grabs the left one, closes it, and offers it to Quim, who in two deft movements tightens a strap around the claw, preventing it from opening again. The dance is then repeated with the right one.

"If you don't tie 'em, they won't buy 'em," Dylan says as he tosses the crab into the males' basket. The other is for the females. The males of the species are larger, the blueness of their claws is more intense, and their underbellies feature a rather phallic engraving. Artur and I stand by, watching as they band the claws. Dylan tosses a specimen missing a leg onto the porch. "They don't buy the crippled ones. You want some for rice?"

The lame crab makes a disoriented run across the concrete, though in the opposite direction from the canal.

"Alright, your turn," Quim says to Artur, after having cinched a few.

Artur jokes about maybe losing a finger. Among the various jobs he's had, one was selling crabs. The fisher who caught them would sometimes stick a pencil between the pincers so he could show his customers how the crab could snap it. Artur hesitates before taking his place on the stool. He immediately gets the hang of it, cinching crabs at a good pace while mentioning that Mateo has offered to keep him on as part of the team, this team, for a few more months. And that he'll accept. His father-in-law has promised he'll be behind the wheel of a tractor again, and he's excited about that. When he was a kid, his *iaio*—his grandfather—would carry him up into the cab of one of those massive vehicles, sit him on his lap, and say: drive. So he brings a few years of experience operating heavy machinery, but he also spent six months maintaining a slurry pit. In Buda, from what he's seeing, he'll be able to do a little bit of everything. Simona can be a bit of a ballbuster, a *torracollons*, as they say in Catalan. The other day, she got into it with Artur when he asked her to flush the ducks two nights in a row instead of alternating assignments, but, hey, the place is great and Natalia likes that he's supporting the family farm.

"So what are you doing all night long out there in the rice fields?" I ask.

"Just driving the truck up and down the rows. You flash your high beams. If you see a flock of ducks, you honk at them."

"All night long?"

"You've no idea how many kilometers we blow through," says Quim. "But then again, there are those who take the occasional nap . . . and some who doze off completely."

"How can you tell if someone's done their job?" I ask, because I still struggle to tell the difference between one rice field and another.

"You look for feathers on the ground," Dylan says. "And, if the birds were there, the soil will be torn up."

"But lately I've been scaring them off pretty good, right?" Artur says with a grin.

"For me, sometimes it's even relaxing," says Quim, tying a claw. "I crank up the speakers in the trailer and blast some industrial music. Hell yeaaah! One year I came here on a Saturday afternoon—not at night, no, in the middle of the afternoon!—and people were driving around blasting music."

Dylan takes his eyes off the crab he's holding and turns to Artur. The rookie says don't worry, he's not a rat and he's not going to run to Mateo and snitch on the other workers and their private lives. Dylan and Quim believe the kid, though they do expect he'll tell Natalia at least some of what he'll be witnessing while working on the island. And if she knows, they figure Mateo will find out eventually as well.

Quim has to head out to repair a tractor. He could use Artur's help, but there are still dozens of crabs left to tie up.

"I can do it," I say.

The three of them look at me.

"No, we'd better not, in case you-know-who shows up and tells us we ought to be doing it ourselves."

"But it'll save you some time, right?"

Artur looks at his fellow crew members, knowing full well he can't make the call. Quim and Dylan look at one other. The Peruvian nods toward the chair currently occupied by Artur. "Come on," he says. "Let's see if you can finish with all your fingers."

The claws are intimidating due to their size and the strong, sharp, protective spikes that extend from the shell, but Dylan holds the crabs so securely and calmly it's contagious. As soon as I get the hang of the mechanics involved in roping the pincers and cinching them, we begin to chat, almost forgetting—Dylan more than me—about the enormous crabs in our hands.

"How are you doing in the house?" he asks.

"Good," I reply.

"*Moooolt bé*," he says approvingly. "May it last."

WIND

STRENGTH AND STEADINESS

NOW THE FIELDS ARE FLOODED, satellite images confuse Buda with the sea. From that high up, all you can see is expansive blue. There are no fine lines of land separating the square fields I bike past on my way to Trabucador, so I don't exist. I want to see the condition of the short sandbar that the storms always tear down and regenerate. They do this with the help of trucks, yes, but also because the ocean currents favor depositing sand on that strip of coastline.

The wind blows fresh, tempered by a sun that grows stronger as the morning progresses. After fourteen kilometers of zigzagging through rice fields, I arrive at the Eucaliptos housing development, one of the ones the sea will flood. It exhibits the typical signs of winter abandonment, with neglected gardens, heavily pruned palms covered in dried leaves, and signs advertising apartments for sale . . . something not unusual at all. A group of bikers decked out in all the gear of a Hells Angels gang roar their scintillating chrome artifacts a few meters from the beach while I continue pedaling on the hard-packed sand, saturated with white streaks, into which thousands of arthropods will sink their heads to suck salt.

It's prohibited to access Trabucador beach by automotive means. Several people cluster near the checkpoint which prevents the passage of motorized vehicles, the majority of which are parked on the stretch of coastline facing the bay, with La Ràpita in the background. It's an immense, diaphanous space with some horses here, a few flamingos there, kids flying kites while taking selfies, others taking a dip while life jackets hang on a nearby wooden fence. A restaurant has also recently opened. The sylvan space I visited six years ago has become a postcard. The sandbar is slimmer than it was, but its length is the same. Hundreds of people are heading for the salt marsh as if on a pilgrimage. I turn around and head back to Buda.

Natural disasters, especially imminent ones, are a primary concern. Geographic agony is growing more profitable by the day. Now, more than ever, we want to be there to witness the final breaths of a landscape, and we want to do so en masse. I myself am here in Buda to certify one.

Among the different types of fatalistic voyeurism, there is a recent trend of going to a beautiful place in the delta, contemplating the dusk, and then applauding when the sun finally sinks below the horizon as if it were the culmination of an opera. I saw the same thing happening in a desert in Rajasthan, so it must be a new, widespread practice on our planet. A touristic practice. One in which people gather to pay homage to the sun and its beauty while demonstrating solidarity with the dying place, to which they offer their ovations like tears. Some, though, especially delta natives like the artist Jaume Vidal, whom I've seen splitting crabs with a machete, believe the applause lacks any real substance, rendering it nothing more than a pose, a public display of affection. It was in this spirit that, at the site of one of these crepuscular ovations, Jaume nailed up a sign that read:

YOUR APPLAUSE WILL NOT SAVE THE EBRO DELTA

It's easy to cheer for something, but current times require more than two hours' commitment. The wind carries away applause, and if it's as blustery as here, the claps fade away more quickly than ever. What a wind it is. Earlier it was blowing steadily, but I didn't notice it because it was on my back. When I cross through a corridor of eucalyptus trees, the trunks creak like old hinges while the tops whisper and hiss. When I go out into the rice fields, the conditions increase to an almost blizzard-like state. I pedal slowly, hunched over the handlebars. The tractors with the extra-deep treads have ground to a halt. You can't work when the *dalt* blows, say the rice farmers. Making progress is an ordeal. It takes me two hours to cover ten kilometers and, although I'm sweaty and spent by the time I reach the porch, I need to take some time to stretch the cramped muscles in my abdomen, which are already sore. I walk to my dune through violently warped reeds. Waves are visible in the flooded fields.

The air is inhabited by aerial plankton and an infinite number of insects, including spiders, like the ones once captured at nearly five thousand meters above sea level. "The winds possess rare virtues, and are usually quite personal," a character says in *Southeaster*, a novel written by Haraldo Conti, an aficionado of a different delta.

The Levant, an easterly wind, blows counter to the earth's rotation, bringing rain. The *dalt* staves off work but also tames the sea. The westerly Ponente winds favor the mosquitoes. The Gregale will devastate this beach if it rages hard enough. Headwinds are what inspire me the most. However, since their influence depends upon a relative position, and now I'm tired, I've hunkered down on the dune next to a fly who's missing a wing and rolls along on the sand.

A fly's lifespan is around a month, and while I don't remember Henry Beston having written about them, the one word the American uses more than any other in his book is "fleeting." In this realm, losing a wing will certainly accelerate that sense. Sofía, the daughter of my neighbor Gonzalo, knows a lot about the subject.

Sofía visited her father a few weeks ago with her partner, Muriel. When Gonzalo went to Barcelona for a few days, they were there alone. I now know the two girls met while working in an emergency room. Muriel was Sofía's supervisor, and both were part of a first-response team tasked with caring for abused women, passengers in traffic accidents, and families of victims of suicide and other forms of sudden death. Which is to say they were—and Sofía continues to be—the kind of people who knock on strangers' doors to inform them about the loss of a loved one.

"You're delivering the worst news that could ever happen to a family. You see, in the fraction of a second, how their lives change," Muriel said after having collected shells on the beach to make a necklace. Discovering Buda through Muriel's eyes is making Sofía fall in love all over again with the island, an enjoyment she'd all but given up on because it was tied to issues she preferred to forget.

"I'm also starting to want this thanks to my father's insistence," said Sofía, who admires how quickly Muriel has adapted to Buda. Muriel wakes up at dawn, around five or six, lights the fire, and keeps looking at the flames until she falls asleep again.

"I give thanks to the flora and fauna for allowing me to spend time among them," said Muriel with humor. She is clear on her feelings about the delta. "Being here reminds me of what I don't want back there," she continued, alluding to the city. "The noise, the superficiality of it all, the insane speed at which everything moves . . . Is this house too small? No, it's just big enough. There's comfort in opening this door"—we were at Gonzalo's house—"and stepping out into the night to look at the stars." The delta sky has a distinctly African clarity to it.

If they spend hours in Barcelona doing nothing, they both feel guilty for having wasted a day.

Here, however, *nothing* doesn't exist.

The idea, the word *nothing*.

It doesn't exist here, because everything has meaning.

Because you don't march to the same beat as others.

Fast, slow, and fleeting all depend, like the wind, on your viewpoint.

This dune will vanish soon. They've already told us as much. There will be days or years of counting down, though no exact date to point to. There are those who hold on to the hope that it will last many more years, even decades. That everything will remain the same. Not me. Not anymore. I prefer to look beyond my own lifespan, to worry about my children and any children they may have, so it gives me no comfort that disaster may strike long after I'm gone. It worries me all the same. There was a time when suffering was for me primarily self-centered, but now, when things are bleakest, is when I truly perceive the suffering of this world I love. Perhaps that's what it means to mature. Once you have your own answers, you devote yourself to helping others find theirs.

Back at La Pantena, the pain in my abdomen has grown worse, forcing me to walk even more like a hunchback. Among the reeds, a butterfly gleams brightly. The hurricane-force winds seem as if they could rip it apart, but butterflies are much stronger animals than their bodies suggest. Maybe that's why Mateo appreciates them so much. His collection of lepidopterans includes roughly five thousand specimens, and he's on record as the first person to have documented the presence of a monarch butterfly in Catalonia.

He caught it on the opposite side of the canal bridge with a fishing net Pep had lent him, and as he did, he could sense his heart racing. Those not attuned to such passions often assume he's exaggerating, which is why he's often hesitant to talk openly about his hobby, but in this case it wasn't an overstatement. His heart was revving even higher than normal, because although he's an excitable man, there's something about butterflies he finds almost overwhelming. He can sense them regardless of where he is: the first monarch he saw in the delta was while he was driving. He'd just left work in L'Ampolla when, while taking the off-ramp toward Deltebre, he looked at the ground and noticed a tiger-striped butterfly on the shoulder of the highway. It can't be, he thought. That butterfly doesn't exist here. Mateo pulled over awkwardly, got out, and . . . yes, it was a monarch. A dead one, so he took it, drove to his house, moistened it, and prepared to dissect it, though without thinking to report his discovery. However, years later, when there was an unusual hatching of monarchs in the delta, he went to an expert with the Parc Natural whom he'd consulted previously about butterflies and told him that, whether he believed him or not, he'd seen a *Danaus plexippus* run over on the road five years earlier. He hadn't notified any officials because he believed it must have escaped from a butterfly farm someone had brought from the United States.

"No," the expert replied. "There is an endemic population in the Canary Islands. Any monarchs you find here have come from there."

Mateo enjoys imagining thousands of butterflies, guided by their solar compasses and knowledge of air currents, migrating thousands of kilometers from Mexico to Canada. Their deceptive fragility fascinates him, and whenever he gets the chance he'll go on at length about the charms of *Danaus plexippus* or *D. chrysippus*, their names pronounced in Latin because he's not interested in "common" or "household" names. Nature must be respected, even in speech, and many of these modern environmental defenders don't even know the names of what they're defending, which reveals a lot about these people. Mateo continues to be the first to note the presence of *Chrysippus* each year because he maintains the will and the drive to contribute alternative knowledge to what's being acquired by the institutions that are quickly beginning to disappoint him, even including SEO BirdLife, the Spanish Ornithological Society, Spain's primary bird conservation charity. Look at how closely he once aligned himself with them: by the time he was ten, Mateo was already a bird aficionado. He became an SEO youth partner, drawn in by the allure of Salvador Maluquer and all the ornithologists who came to Buda for bird-watching and who taught him how to see and listen. But when SEO people, aligned with those from the Parc Natural, began to impose ways of doing things that completely disregarded his family, treating them as if they hadn't been there for over half a century, his sense of disbelief mixed with his helplessness at seeing how his father and other family members were forced to submit to decisions he often considered arbitrary and unfair. And when the rage finally reached a tipping point, he canceled his membership, shaking his head at how the SEO thought they could govern these complex spaces from bases in Barcelona or Madrid. When it comes to activism, it's still important to coordinate campaigns with big cities, yes, but you must also execute on the ground, where new developments and unexpected incidents can only be resolved by those who know what's really going on. The city can't think like the country, always with its damn theories that are often completely out of touch with reality. And Mateo knows what he's talking about, because he's tried both places, and after studying veterinary medicine in Valencia, he decided he'd never live in a major city again. They're unbearable. Barcelona? Don't get him started. By his second day he was already feeling suffocated by the concentration of everything, by the noise of it all. The shouting was what bothered him in particular. At most, he'd consider spending a certain amount of time in a more manageable city like Logroño. And he was able to settle down for a bit in Zaragoza, which was halfway between everything. But anything bigger than that? No way. Butterflies, rice, eels, prawns . . . All these require a gentle touch and attention to detail: a treatment that can only be prescribed in daily doses, as evidenced by how well Bomba is doing here today, and by the delta's success thirty years ago in cultivating prawns, sea bass, and sea bream, having placed L'Ametlla de Mar at the forefront of Spanish aquaculture, on par with Cádiz. Because, yes, he has raised prawns in Buda.

How did he do it? Well, he first confirmed for himself that all aquaculture at that time was devoted to mussels or trout, neglecting native Mediterranean species to such an extent that prawn cultivation had become a lost art. He'd seen chickens and bulls raised, and during his military service he'd fed and inseminated dairy cows and wiped out tuberculosis in herds of hogs. It couldn't be that difficult to apply similar techniques at sea. He marked off the lagoons with fine netting, and introduced the fry and fed them, as human beings have done with livestock for ten thousand years, only his thing was going to be "aquastock." Why not? The blue crab was confounding rice farmers, and he needed a challenge. He's never been about productivity for productivity's sake. His aim is to learn and enjoy, not to sleepwalk his way through the same repetitive tasks, which is why, when the company he was working with in L'Ametlla decided not to incorporate one of the new breeding methods he had proposed, he implemented it himself in Buda.

First, Mateo created a fry nursery, but the initial prawns he introduced were unsuccessful. He supplied the crustaceans with hormones and the resulting eggs embryonated in incubators, but shortly after the larvae appeared, they died. He fed them with phytoplankton, with rotifers, with other special foodstuffs, yet every attempt proved ineffective. Ninety-eight percent of the stock didn't make it.

Then he looked at how Norwegians industrially raise sea bass and salmon in the sea, and he traveled to San Diego and Hawaii to visit shrimp farms, concluding (among other things) that it was advisable to oxygenate the water via pumps to rejuvenate the air and stave off massive poisonings. It's so simple it's impressive, Mateo told himself. All he needed was the will to do it. And the ability, sure, and he was willing *and* able. So he bought prawns from the Sea of Japan and fed them with a special blend that included a high-quality protein that cost him an arm and a leg—which was fine, because the fish farm took off. The eggs embryonated in large tanks into which the premium feed was poured, and when the animals grew big enough, they were transported to larger pools to fully develop.

Mateo is occasionally surprised by the versatility he was capable of at twenty. By the way he was able to combine his passion for butterflies with his veterinary medicine and Buddhism studies. Although in reality everything feeds back into itself, because if butterflies represent life lived freely and studying involves dedicated, methodical work, Buddhism was, for seven years, the common denominator that helped him reconcile both worlds. Buddhists know how to listen to the wind. Few things are more relaxing than one's prayer flags. If there's one thing Buda isn't lacking, it's wind. And when Mateo returned to the island on a break from veterinary school, he came filled with questions. Being in contact with people his age who had developed a critical spirit, even with regards to religion, had forced him to look inwardly from a different angle. And to accept that he needed to understand more about himself, to shake off the emasculating religious education that had turned him into a meek, mild boy who addressed his problems through prayer (prayer!) and followed his marching orders, whatever they were. "Everything I've ever learned is of no use to me now," he declared. "What have I been doing all this time?"

He'd enjoyed veterinary school: he found it pleasantly distracting, and it could even become his future, but if he wanted to move forward as an individual, he was going to have to hitch himself to something stronger, something he genuinely believed in. He didn't want to go through life feeling everything raw and uncut: he needed to connect spiritually with something luminous, something that would bring him closer to the nuances of his own feelings, allowing him to understand them, to understand himself through the same order of magnitude by which he understood butterflies and eels. The Opus Dei doctrine had left him disappointed, but there was still something substantial, and therefore useful, in religion. Something capable of guiding thought and action. The issue, then, was to determine which religion best suited his own personal nature, and so he began to study different ones.

He became a regular customer at a couple of esoteric bookstores in Barcelona, where, in addition to soaking up countercultural titles in which Alan Watts or Krishnamurti proposed rebelling against conventions by articulating their own wisdom that followed the teachings of ancient Indigenous peoples, he spent hours poring over the section dedicated to religions. His spiritual letdown encouraged him to put some distance between himself and the more familiar religions, so right from the outset he rejected any investigation into Judaism, Christianity, and Islam, opting instead to delve into Eastern monotheisms.

It was many years later that Natalia would find the religious titles on her father's shelves and be amazed by the number of books on Hinduism, Taoism, and especially Zen Buddhism: the creed that would end up seducing the twenty-year-old Mateo. He liked the idea of having to pass tests to achieve a form of happiness. Buddhists aren't concerned with becoming big and powerful, rubbing shoulders with the elite, or controlling anyone. It's all much more intimate, more personal. You're accountable to your own self, spectators are unnecessary. There are no confessionals, no absolution bestowed by chaste gentlemen. No, it's you, there, with your history. You are the one most responsible for your actions, for your thoughts. And to dig deeper into these thoughts, he began to meditate.

Since Mateo lived alone in Pas's shack, nobody interrupted him when he settled down in front of a white wall and performed the physical and spiritual exercises that undoubtedly strengthened his mind and his muscles. He complied scrupulously with Zen mantras, with one exception: the consumption of meat. We come from where we come from, a duck is a duck, a prawn is (needless to say) a prawn, and, well, it's not necessarily a good idea to become an extremist in any creed, right? he thought.

He'll never thank Buddhist meditation enough for the flash of lucidity that brought him back to Christianity. He's not entirely sure how to explain the epiphany: it was a light, a revealing lightning bolt in the antediluvian style, a certainty that told him to give up Buddhism because his God was Christian, even if He didn't resemble the one the Opus Dei priests had described. Mateo is convinced his bad experience in Opus Dei led him to Buddhism, which is what eventually awakened him . . . with a paradox. Because, through getting to know himself, he realized that it wasn't within his grasp to go back and redo things. That guilt has a limit, and that no matter how much you try and calculate and bend over backward to please someone or achieve a goal, the resolution won't always be the one you'd hoped for. You are simply in His hands. Buddhism freed him from guilt—what a relief!—and reconciled him with his God, at once old and renewed. And he turned back to Christ the way Natalia returned to meat. Ever since then, he's taken delight in the Catholic faith. Every morning he attends eight o'clock Mass at the church of Sant Jaume or Sant Miquel in La Cava, and he's begun to think about building a hermitage near La Pantena. The chapel will include a confessional, altar, and kneeler, creating a sacred space, and while nobody can say whether such a shrine would be worthy of a pilgrimage, he's uncovered a perfectly acceptable, mostly unknown reason that could potentially attract thousands of people. The young clergyman from Sant Jaume tells the story of two girls, related to Ramoneta, who saw the Virgin near La Pantena. One of the girls has since died and the other is in her eighties, but their story has lived on in the clergy, and now in Mateo as well. Granted, people have seen virgins in many other places, and every one of these little towns has milked that trick as best it can. But the Buda virgin stands out among the crowd because, as legend has it, she was pink, like a flamingo. When he thinks of the Virgin, Mateo says he sees only advantages, which is why the idea of honoring her excites him in a way few things have in recent memory. "I do want to build a little chapel," he said the other day, "to mark that something important happened in La Pantena. Because I'm a believer, but also because it would be such an amazing attraction. Just imagine: Buda's pink virgin."

Mateo believes pilgrims could be a way to safeguard the island for the family, the formula by which religious faith could end up attracting both people's attention and their money, something which would strengthen Buda's position when it came to bargaining with politicians. Years ago, his ingenuity encouraged him to design a shuttle train that would loop around the island transporting small groups of tourists who'd finance some of Buda's expenses, but his father and other family members didn't have such a clear vision of the project. Especially Gabriel, the most imposing of the uncles. If the Gallarts have a reputation for inspiring trepidation in others, Gabriel was the most intimidating of all. Perhaps it's because the family has always respected the preponderance of the firstborn. As the eldest, Gabriel dedicated himself to redeeming his privilege without compassion, crowned by a glower that lent him an even more disturbing presence.

The adults in the family had their doubts about that little shuttle train, but Mateo believes it was Gabriel who shut down the project when he found out his nephew was intending to take suspicious initiatives on the island which he wanted to govern, which is why he told him to get out of Buda and do his thing somewhere else.

His uncle didn't have any concrete arguments to present, nor did the officials who have put one obstacle after another between him and his hunting and fishing, in addition to their expropriation of the lagoon and ignoring his request to build dikes and his plans for a shuttle train. Having these things would mean officially endorsing the family's permanence on the island for who knows how many years, when for some time now the final objective has been to put an end to Gallart & Co. as soon as possible.

Very well then. If there's no shuttle train, there'll be no prawns or sea bass. And if he can't have those, he'll still have Arroz del Faro: a brand conceived to avoid dependency on others. Why deal with third parties if you can grow and sell your own rice? The fewer intermediaries there are, the fewer permissions you have to obtain and favors to ask from people who are either disinclined to offer them or will charge you God knows how much for them. Managing one's own production is a source of pride. Each package is the culmination of decades of work, confirming that all this relentless drive has amounted to something, that rice from the island of Buda is capable of standing up to the punishing winds that lash and flatten the grasses and, these days, even the gales that bring butterflies from afar.

Ever since identifying that first monarch, Mateo has taken annual note of their arrival. He's not the type to summit a peak only to bid it farewell. His role is to support, to maintain, because that's what he does: preserve the legacy of his grandparents, take care of his daughters, the butterflies, the ducks and flamingos and all those people who, paradoxically enough, are also able to enjoy the prawns, rice, fish, and ducks he provides. That's why he's anxious today. There's so much to look after, and no God to relieve him of the anxiety washing over him as he watches the stalks of rice shaking electrically at the mercy of these hurricane winds. Every year he steadies himself, preparing to control his nerves. He convinces himself that this will be the season he learns how to control his paranoia. And all the while he's encouraged by Karen. As much of a spark plug as she is, it's amazing to see her soothing effect on him. But when sowing time comes—thwap!—the insomnia, the bad moods, the doubts about whether he should have planted so many hectares dry or whether the few fertilizers Simona bought will be as good as the supervisor said they'd be . . . all those things spring back into the foreground. And among all that anguish, the wind is by far the worst. Because the wind is there, it's there right now, manifesting itself with bellowing booms that empty the streets and shake the houses to their foundations, and when that happens you know the rice is in danger. Even if you wanted to let your mind wander into other fields of thought, you can't, because the wind is always there. Ever audible. There's no way to escape it. That fucking delta wind, forcing him to think about the old folks hunkered down in their barracks, about what all those people must have endured throughout the years. A piece of flashing was once ripped from the roof of La Pantena during a gale, hitting Ramoneta in the head. Luckily only a bit of blood was lost on that occasion, but there have been others where people were in danger of being swept out to sea, like the night Quim and Dylan were trapped on a rowboat out on the Gran Calaix. They found themselves pinned against a floating mat of reeds, and despite the torque they threw into the oars, bending them in their rowlocks, they couldn't free themselves from the muddy pile of mire. These are two big guys, toughened by the daily toils of farm work and capable of acts of strength, but the wind was overpowering, keeping them imprisoned in that cage of reeds and brush until an even more violent gust capsized their vessel. The virulence of the wind immediately righted the boat, the men hoisted themselves up and in, and only then, soaked to the bones, were they able to maneuver themselves to the center of the lagoon.

As with the Tramontane in Empordà and the Saharan sirocco, the winds here in this delta are unlike any others. The openness makes them massive, granting them kilometers of unencumbered space through which to run with a strength and perseverance that strikes at the souls of many people, forcing them to bow in acceptance of their great powerlessness and, at times, to their raving madness.

Back at La Pantena, the pain in my abdomen is so sharp I can't tell whether it's a muscle cramp or some gastric disorder. I go to bed without any dinner, curl in the fetal position as the wind pummels the corrugated fiber cement roofing and whistles through the one small window I leave ajar every night in the living room to vent the smoke. It's the weekend, Gonzalo has left for Barcelona, and I'm alone on the island. If the Big One were to make landfall today, the bike would have to be left behind owing to both the wind and the pain. The alternate route is to make a run for the lagoon's embankment and follow it toward El Mas. Either that or find a way to lash myself to the roof of La Pantena. I could also call Mateo or Simona, but cell phone coverage all but disappears on windy days, and even when you have a connection, it's near impossible to decipher messages. When I've needed to talk with someone or write an email on those days, I've had to resort to the Wi-Fi at El Mas. Now it's empty and I don't have a key to the old farmhouse. To anything, really.

GLORIA

I WAKE TO FIND THE PAIN HAS SUBSIDED. Although my muscles are sore, I'm able to walk without a problem. The wind has died down a bit too. The birds have come to feed in the fields, but they're also tolerating my presence much more now, and if I'm careful, I can observe them for some time with the naked eye.

The day is so gray it's grown quiet. Everything moves with an autumnal calm, though it's spring that's about to arrive. In the clutch of reeds before the sea, I take notes, which seem to me as fresh and drenched and light as the landscape itself. I don't even have to think. There is no preparation, no intention, no premeditation. The prey I hunt is the sentence, and I track it with a flow so natural that, elsewhere, I'd have thought it automatic.

The lighthouse stands there, clearly outlined, like a colossus. Behind it, in the offing, an imposing range of clouds begins to gather, as if they were mountains emerging from the sea. Storms are brewing everywhere.

Once back at home, I start a fire. It's raining six ways to Sunday. It's precisely when you're contemplating the grand scheme of things that your own insignificance begins to emerge. Storms remind us of who we are, of our relative size and influence. From what I've been told, experiencing a Gloria-type gale firsthand will quickly help you figure out what your true priorities are.

The week before the cyclone, Mateo had participated in a televised panel where he warned that no one was paying attention to climate change, and that as a result everyone would pay the consequences. He was dismissed as a pessimist, a scaremonger, all the usual things, while the weather service was forecasting the arrival of a big Levant: news that excited Marc Masià. No matter how strong the winds get, the delta isn't a place where big waves develop, and surfers like Marc usually head up to the Cantabrian Sea, where they break out their boards (Marc makes his own by hand)—except when a good Levant is seething and swelling, bringing waves up to five meters high, which sow terror among rice farmers like his father, with whom he must have had plenty of arguments about the wind. Marc lives in an inverted world. He gets his information like everyone else, he checks the forecast on TV or online, and he's interested in the same thing as his family and neighbors: the strength of the wind. But when they announced that the storm could be an eight on the Beaufort scale, Marc's response was "That's perfect!" while his father's was "You're crazy. You don't understand how much damage that can do."

To Marc, the wind force that presents a problem to his father represents an opportunity to take advantage of, and when he sees the predicted intensity level, he's not thinking about falling trees or driverless cars being blown down the road. No, he's thinking about finally having some rideable waves, of Hawaiians practicing the art of *he'e nalu*, wave sliding. Which is why, although the Directorate-General for Civil Protection and Emergencies had ordered people to remain indoors, Marc called his friends and started waxing up his board.

By that point, Gonzalo and Teresa had also checked the forecasts. Faced with impending winds topping out at more than a hundred kilometers per hour, they boarded the next ferry leaving the island. Gonzalo didn't want anyone to have to come rescue him. Besides, what would happen if, for whatever reason, one of them got sick? Who'd be able to help them? And, most of all, when?

Pep said that the most dangerous wind for La Pantena is the Gregale, blowing from the northeast, because it could cause the river to jump its banks. If he had been alive when Gloria began to intensify, he might not have been overly alarmed, since it was an easterly wind. Ramoneta and Pep had experienced great storms of their own in the past. The last of them had made landfall at night, also in the form of violent wind and rain. Pep had called Simona, telling her the sea had jumped.

The supervisor was able to reach the island by ferry at three in the morning. The road to La Pantena was still crossable, and she was able to drive there. The older couple had sheltered themselves in the workshop filled with paddles and gánguiles. Simona dropped them off at El Mas before returning to Sant Jaume. Yes, it was quite the storm. The old folks had experienced something similar. This one was back when Buda wasn't as well equipped as today. You could suddenly find yourself in the dining room in chest-deep water, swimming through a swarm of rats which, as Ramon del Cadell knows, could be eaten, because in those days they didn't spray the rice with chemical pesticides and the animals were healthy.

Dylan remembers one of the floods where the water reached his knees, though it wasn't the same as with Gloria, because that storm hit during the day and the river didn't overflow. The colossal damage wrought by a Gloria-type storm blowing in from the east defied logic and plunged Buda into chaos.

The day after the storm made landfall, Dylan and Quim went out to evaluate the situation while its remnants continued to dismantle the delta. Overflow from the river had flooded large plots of grazing land. The two men attempted to remove debris, cleaning up what they could, but the wind was still excessive—branches could break, and a fragile-looking tree was leaning at a treacherous angle—and so they left.

In Els Reguers, Artur, Natalia, and their in-laws, who had all gone out to eat, couldn't peel their eyes away from the windows facing the sea. For the first time in the many months the couple had been living in that town, they could make out white crests in the vastness of blue. If they could see foam from over fifty kilometers away, it meant that the waves themselves were gigantic. "How crazy is that?" Natalia exclaimed. "That can't be the sea."

They had canceled their trip to Albarracín scheduled for that weekend. The meteorologists were predicting snow in the mountains, and while those mountains were in inland Spain, surely that forecast was in some way related to what they were witnessing from their living room.

"The horses," Natalia said in a hushed tone. Then she thought of the donkeys on the island, and with that came an unusual, almost unnatural wave of distress. Overcome by a growing, almost overwhelming rage against the deaf ears the entire community had been turning to her father's warnings for years, she felt a powerful need to get back down to Buda. She'd even grown tired of Mateo's incessant data-spewing and sometimes had her own doubts about whether he could be right about everything. Now, though, they had their answer.

Whitecaps visible from fifty kilometers away.

There was a time she had thought leaving Buda would be more painful for the family than seeing the island flooded. But the real possibility that it was going to happen, that it *was* happening, sent a shiver through her.

What Natalia and Artur couldn't see from the window were the four surfboards cresting the waves, heading out to sea, looking to set up two kilometers off the coast in search of the perfect spot to catch waves and project themselves like torpedoes. Because Marc

Masià and his three friends are windsurfers. They prefer the vertiginous speeds a sail gives them to immersing themselves in a macrotunnel of water. They love performing simultaneous acrobatic moves, transforming themselves into a miniature school of flying fish-men abstracted from the all-too-human world. While Marc was practicing his pirouettes against the storm, he didn't even think that, right then, his father was more concerned about the destruction Gloria would bring to his fields than about the destruction of his son, which, depending on how you look at it, indicated the rice farmer's level of confidence in the kid's talent.

When Quim and Dylan returned to Buda on Tuesday, the inundation was absolute. The sea had encroached three kilometers into the island, and the waves weren't merely lapping against the base of the cohetera as if it were a cliff, but they had also reached as far as El Mas. A tractor parked in the middle of a flooded field looked like an island. When the two men entered the field to try and remove the piece of equipment, they felt as if they were walking out to sea.

Mateo had asked them to keep him informed, minute by minute, about the state of the island. Quim shot videos of the waves splashing against the palm trees and the walls of the farmhouse, he snapped photos of some of the more than twenty fallen century-old trees, of the shacks with their roofs blown half off, the broken doors, the flooded rooms, the Corona cabin that had been completely destroyed . . . and he sent them all to his boss, who in turn forwarded them to Natalia, who passed them along to her cousins through the family group chat.

When the storm had passed, Buda was submerged. At first, nobody could access the island in conventional vehicles. The workers arrived on a barge from El Sifó to evaluate the damage and begin to repair what they could. They immediately found Natalia's donkeys and horses in the corral next to El Mas, but Dylan grew concerned when he couldn't locate the herd of other horses anywhere near the Parc Natural. After searching for over two hours, there was still no sign of them. Since Buda had been cut off from the mainland and the animals were free to range and even enter private property, it was possible they had sought out higher ground near the sea. The only way to navigate the flooded road was by tractor, so the men started up the one with the highest axle and rolled out on the amphibious vehicle.

"There they are!" Dylan yelled.

Fifty horses huddled together on a high section of the embankment in front of Nil's shack next to the fig tree. Dylan felt relief tinged with sadness at seeing them helpless. But the worst was over. The animals were well fed and the waters would recede soon, so it wouldn't be long before they were able to escape.

Natalia was struck by the indifference with which most of the people in Sant Jaume and the delta regarded that disaster. They didn't think it was that big of a deal. But if it had been, and if one of the casualties went by the name of Simona, then fine, she thought. Fuck her the way she'd fucked over so many others.

There was more talk in the surrounding towns about the damage incurred on the other shore. The flooding in Bombita, the Los Vascos restaurant, La Marquesa beach, and Punta del Fangar, where the waves had destroyed the tuna farm, flinging hundreds of fish against the coast. When the waters receded, the beach was littered with all sorts of fish, tuna most of all, as well as assorted garbage, which included everything from the usual bottles, cans, and tires to an inflatable doll.

Pol Mestre had undergone surgery to repair a hernia back in December. His recovery period should have been two full months, but he wasn't about to sit idly by in the devastating wake of the storm that had left his brother and in-laws' coastal property half buried. So he went out on the beach to shovel away the sand from where it needed to be removed. In La Marquesa, he came upon eleven asphyxiated tuna and plenty of television cameras. "You see that tuna?" he said to his sister-in-law, nodding at a massive specimen. "If I were my normal self, and all these cameras weren't around, that tuna would already be on its way to my plate."

Hours before the beach turned into a circus, Quim and Dylan had carted off a huge tuna in a wheelbarrow. They skillfully avoided a group of people with meat cleavers and carving knives who, unable to carry off the entire two-hundred-kilogram fishes, hacked off large hunks of flesh before returning to their homes. When the police finally arrived, they cordoned off the beach, bringing an end to the robbery. Over the next few days, several neighbors claimed that anything spit out by the sea immediately entered the public domain, and that they had a right to dispose of the scattered animals, but all they really did was stand by and watch as a good number of fish rotted in the sand.

"Such a tuna massacre," thought David Pallarès, lost in the images being broadcast to his hotel room in Lisbon. He was spending the holidays there with Carla Bonet, his partner and Parc Natural colleague. Carla and David had witnessed the occasional environmental catastrophe, but this was *apocalyptic*. That was the only word to adequately describe the carnage. They wouldn't soon forget the images of dismembered tuna and the splintered wooden mussel traps. Nor the panic that washed over them when they feared the storm could have damaged their house. When they returned, days later, they found the basement flooded and the yard sunken.

David and Carla didn't think about Mateo, or not specifically, and Mateo wasn't exactly thinking about them either. But he did think about all the Parc officials, the farmers, the fishers, the neighbors, and every other person who had been ignoring him for years. The Budero felt an avalanche of contradictory feelings crashing down on him, though the prevailing one was, without doubt, the joy of seeing his prediction come true. The losses were going to be significant, and Garrobud Associats didn't have adequate insurance coverage—paying a little less up front almost always turns out to be expensive in the end. But it was January, the harvest had been months ago, and the fields were barren. Despite being the storm's primary victim, he appreciated the self-satisfaction of seeing his worst fears come to fruition.

Mateo sees Gloria as an unwanted event that, deep down, he had been longing for. The detonation that separated the before from the after. Because while tuna and palm and eucalyptus trees were still strewn across the beaches, dozens of journalists were wanting to interview him, giving him an opportunity to repeat what he'd been proclaiming for the past twenty years. This time, though, he had a more powerful bullhorn than ever, and images of the shattered delta to back it up.

What was odd about it was the general oddness of the whole situation. Son of a fucking bitch! As if he hadn't said it all a thousand times before. Because if Mateo's sure of anything, it's that everything he says will be clearly understood. The post-Gloria days saw dozens of cameras and microphones pointed at him, but it was Natalia who was upset. The attention, to her, seemed insufficient and limited only to the region around the delta. The disaster received some coverage in Barcelona, yes. It was noted with the detached aloofness commonly directed toward that remote place where poor, unfortunate souls are always having to rebuild their lives. As if there, in the big city, and in an infinite number of smaller towns, they still didn't grasp that the havoc wreaked on Buda or La Marquesa foreboded what was about to happen on the coast of Catalonia, the coast of Spain, and coastlines around the world. So many people, even right there in the delta, had no idea what was coming. Luckily, Natalia had learned something from her parents' separation, from the documentaries about Nazism, from the family infighting, and from the many disappointments. She couldn't lay her finger on it, but she had learned something that freed her from that damn pain in the gut that had plagued her as a child during those tense times. Plus, as an adult, she had the knowledge and tools to combat that anxiety. She wasn't going to get sick to her stomach because she felt powerless or because she couldn't understand other people's nonsense. No. Now she had a new magic potion to turn to: action.

Natalia had dabbled in the world of social media, having managed the family business's Facebook account. After Gloria, she devoted her personal accounts to bombarding her Friends (capitalized on the platform) with images of the devastation. Let them demonstrate to what extent they were actually Friends. She became obsessed with this. She couldn't fathom such pervasive indifference in the face of collective catastrophe. She therefore understood better than ever the fervency with which her father clamored for the attention which no one seemed willing to pay him. Because after those first couple of weeks of whimpering and whining, everything seemed to have reverted to the way it always had been, with the usual intransigents arguing that Mateo had taken an inappropriate, even rude tone in defending his thesis. Which was fine. Maybe they had a point. Diplomacy wasn't the Gallarts' greatest virtue. But what her father said was true! Did tone now matter more than content?

In 2005, Hurricane Katrina devastated the Mississippi Delta, killing 1,836 people in Louisiana. It's been estimated that the 1970 Bhola cyclone resulted in half a million—half a million!—deaths in Bangladesh, making it the most devastating storm of the twentieth century. The Pakistani government's handling of getting aid to the victims caused such deep-seated unrest that war was declared, something which resulted in the creation of the People's Republic of Bangladesh in the Ganges-Brahmaputra Delta. In places like this, a storm can change a government.

Bangladesh and Louisiana are experiencing the most rapid coastal regressions on earth. They're also located in hurricane zones, they have considerable population density, and flooding is a risk as frequent as it is serious.

Gloria was categorized as a full-on gale, with winds reaching level ten on the Beaufort scale, having been clocked at 102 kilometers per hour. That doesn't seem like much when compared with the 240 kph winds of Bhola or the 280 of Katrina, but as modest as it may seem, it took the lives of at least thirteen people in Spain, with four more going missing, and was a significantly motivating factor in establishing the Taula d'Acords, which has since gone on to pressure La Administración to take action in the Ebro Delta.

"I want to become stronger, along with all of Gloria's victims," Mateo told me three afternoons ago during a conversation on the porch. "They used to see me as an owner. Now, though, we're all suffering equally. They understand what I was trying to tell them. The delta is a government issue. The wetlands are too."

In Spain, wetlands like Doñana, Empordà, and the Ebro Delta are deteriorating rapidly. Across the globe, wetlands are disappearing at a rate three times faster than forests. Half the planet's wetlands have disappeared over the course of the past century. Meanwhile, government management and stewardship agencies have done little more than contemplate the decline, as if ignorant that these spaces can sink over fifty times more CO_2 than tropical forests: an essential value in the fight against climate change.

Water politics and diplomacy are going to be even more crucial in the years to come. The future will depend on local alliances, because if your neighbor doesn't support you in your efforts, it'll all be for naught. One of Gloria's positive legacies was to iron out all the rough edges simultaneously, getting habitual opponents to agree that "defending the delta is, for those who live here, something more urgent than defending its beauty," as Joan Todó has written. La Taula del Sénia, a commonwealth of municipalities totaling nearly one hundred thousand people, drew up a plan of action and submitted it to La Administración, emphasizing the urgent need to apply it as quickly as possible. Yet they've been waiting for over a year for the approval (let alone execution) of any of the proposals.

"You have to carry on," Mateo says, addressing La Taula. "Either we stick together, or we'd better start saying goodbye. We've got a problem: when a neighbor isn't doing well, everyone else is happy, and that turns us all into targets in a shooting gallery. We have to change this. We have to start thinking of the delta as a federal matter, because the state is trying to take it away from us. They've abused us, plundered us, and tricked us, and not realized that if they let the Sagrada Familia collapse—because the delta is a natural basilica—no one will want to protect the neighborhood where it once stood. What efforts will they make to defend the neighborhood knowing that the history of our most emblematic symbol has ended? Nobody. We'll all be gone. And I'll be the first to go, because I'm from Barcelona, though I think I'll move to Terra Alta so I can forget about this . . . this nightmare. But you? You're all from here. What will you do? Where will you go?"

Luzia Galioto, who was born in Portugal, listens to Mateo's tirade before La Taula, feigning indifference. She tries not to erupt despite vehemently disagreeing with many of his points, especially since La

Taula is close to reaching terms with her organization, SEO BirdLife. Ah, the patience it takes . . . because, after all, Buda cannot last. No matter how many dikes Mateo builds, how much sand he moves, how long can he hold out? Everyone knows, himself included, that their fate has been cast. But until a couple more Glorias hit, she'll have to continue putting up with short harangues from this *siñor* of the delta who knows as much about biology as she knows about soccer. And now it turns out that, thanks to this most recent storm, he's gaining allies who support the construction of several allegedly protective breakwaters that would cost the public coffers a fortune and which would likely be torn down by the sea in a matter of days. They want to reclaim the landscape using a calculator, telling it what's best for it. As if the land needed any education from us. The earth has its own long history of education, and what the delta needs is sediment. How much clearer could that be?

She's indeed a biologist, and from Setúbal, having grown up in the Sado estuary. She's caught sardines by hand in São Teotónio, where her mother was born. She's familiar with tides that can rise as high as three meters, so she doesn't buy amateur theorists intent on preserving their own little beach bars come hell or high water. Nowadays it's all but impossible to justify having a rice field on the seafront, even though my *iaio* had one of his own. What's most important is the common good, and anyone who can't understand that will have it as bad or worse than Mateo. Can't he see this?

At the Reserva Natural de Mur Fort, Luzia works to show how nature conservancy and economic activity can coexist, but only if the current model is changed. For example, in Mur Fort, they've converted rice fields into natural areas with ponds, reedbeds, coastal grasslands, and an ornithological observatory people can visit for free. And they still produce their own organic rice, largely thanks to the help of volunteer conservationists who come from across Europe.

Young people are key. Look no further than Luzia as an example of this. She came to the delta at twenty-one through the Erasmus program, an EU student exchange service, to expand her studies in biology. She liked the place so much that, as soon as she defended her thesis in Portugal, she returned to settle in the region. She's spent twenty-six of her forty-seven years speaking Catalan so perfectly that everyone tells her it sounds like she's from around there. And she is. After spending more than half her life in the delta, the space is now hers. Here she's experienced the deserted beaches before the stampedes of tourists, seen bright blue scarab beetles for the first time, stopped her car in front of a snake that raised its head in defiance . . . and what she hopes is that such scenes aren't lost, either in memory or reality. The delta still excites her after all these years, and she's going to continue defending it so other locals are similarly moved, because ultimately that's what life is about: the emotions that move us.

When she looks back over the major events of the past three decades, she remembers shedding tears of joy the day she watched the telephone poles in La Tancada. Only she and her colleagues knew what it had taken to get that accomplished. But even more significant than that—to this day, she still shivers at the thought of it—she treasures the day in 2016 when she boarded a small wooden boat and made her way out into the middle of the Ebro. Hours earlier, one hundred tons of sediment had been injected into the river to certify whether it would slide, unhindered, downstream. A preliminary test to see whether, in the future, if the floodgates of some dam were to be opened and the sediment came pouring out, the technique would truly work, torrentially speaking. Luzia spotted the brown water approaching from upstream. She watched as the churning flow of clumps approached her. And then the muddy gush was enveloping and overtaking the tiny vessel: the culmination of years of bureaucratic battles inoculating her with a lash of pure emotion that gave her goosebumps and brought forth tears.

The test went well, but after that, La Administración didn't do much. The pilot would remain a success frozen in time, as it is to this day, after Gloria and then Filomena this past January, when it seems like the experts have gotten down to work, conducting studies to determine the best source and destination for the tons of sediment they will need to release from the dams in order to add sufficient volume to the delta without destabilizing either the riverbed or the river itself. It turns out that everything has to do with scientific and political timing, as Luzia says, specifically using the English word *timing*. The timing must be right, because there are those so anxious they can't bear waiting for their turn, fearing that the sea will swallow up their rice fields in the meantime. It's always the same. Always about patience. Which is exactly what they don't have, what they've never had.

But let's see what happens, because there are hydroelectric companies who support the construction of a large-scale breakwater in Punta de la Banya, a place that has never mattered to them before. Now, thanks to the alarms Gloria set off, someone is willing to shell out a few million euros, and suddenly people are interested in building breakwaters which they're pitching as a "guarantee of sustainability." The language used by these modern thieves is disgusting. Well, actually, what's disgusting is the way these thieves make use of expressions that until recently were green cultural heritage, and how they distort the true meaning of their messaging by including references to nature in their speeches. They manipulate everything. Like that graphic promoted by wind companies in response to those protesting the number of birds killed each year by their windmills. Studies on wind farms show that cats are the primary cause of bird deaths in Spain, while wind turbines are at the bottom of the list. That's it. But they leave out the information that these turbines mainly kill birds of prey, many of which are threatened or even endangered species. Cats kill passerine birds, and there are tons of those. And Luzia is with SEO BirdLife, of all things! Or do the engineers also know more about birds than she does?

Science is a marvel we use in a perverse way, putting engineering solutions ahead of natural logic, allowing us to carry out environmental destruction in the confidence that we will always invent a solution to fix it later. Without realizing we're in the midst of a great climate emergency, and that the Marshall Islands and Kiribati are already paying for the shortcomings of Western countries. Yes, the Marshall Islands in the central Pacific. And Kiribati, an island nation in Micronesia, whose president has been buying land in Fiji, where he hopes to move his compatriots. He's aware that, soon enough, the archipelagos on which they live today will no longer exist. Sure, at first only isolated and low-income, developing lands will be sunk, but we're next. If the planet's average temperature continues to rise while much of the Arctic melts, exposing permafrost and releasing massive amounts of carbon stored for millennia, a series of sudden shifts will be unleashed as early as 2030 and will transform the face of the earth. What has already been announced with certainty is that, by 2040, 250,000,000 people will not have access to water due, among other things, to extreme droughts. Meanwhile, by 2050, in a cruel paradox, 200,000,000 people will have become climate refugees, many having been displaced by rising sea levels. Are we as a species aware of what all of this is going to catalyze? Of the homeless pariahs who will be wandering the globe? Of the coming wars fought over water?

Luzia doesn't have any children. She believes the earth doesn't need any more offspring, and she mourns the ways in which her nieces and nephews are going to suffer or be angered. Because if they happen to take after their aunt, they'll be plenty angry and frustrated with the infinite stupidity of the species to which they belong. Since humanity recently learned how to turn to science to solve a problem as massive as a global pandemic, now would be a good time to rely on that same science as a healing agent. Listening to scientists can help. But no. All people want from their experts are cutting-edge technologies that continue accelerating the world's capitalist progress. Spaceships which will ferry away the privileged few when they can no longer exist on earth. But when those same meticulous scientists warn that, since 1970, more than 90 percent of the world's large fish have died off, or that the 1998 Yangtze River floodings were largely due to the systematic elimination of wetlands throughout the river's basin, then their opinions aren't valid. Assuming they're not completely disparaged from the outset, they're countered with "but this" and "what about that?"

This is why the world has already reverted to how it operated before COVID-19, why it's making the same tired mistakes, why it has yet again demoted science to a subset of technology, as if science itself were limited to mere technique. If this continues, technology's high-water mark (so to speak) will be to have prospered so effectively that it can capture the incredible speed of our extinction. Soon enough, there will be nobody at all to watch some transmitter broadcasting images on repeat of how we disappeared.

"This all affects me personally. I know I'll end up somewhere outside the delta. I'd like to get back to Portugal. Anyway, if you told me that my death could make everything right, I'd sacrifice myself. I'd die for that," Luzia says one resplendent morning.

And, with that statement, I find myself doubting her for the first time. I have little faith in the ethics of martyrdom in twenty-first-century developed countries.

Later on, Luzia acknowledges that she agrees with Mateo on at least one issue: the need to save the wetlands.

Environmental disputes often have sociopolitical roots. It's taken for granted that landowners and other proprietors, the gentlemen known here as *siñors*, tend to have a more laissez-faire attitude when it comes to caring for their property. Less affluent yet more educated people assume a more extreme environmentalist stance. Throughout history, we have assumed it was the *siñor* who hunted, fished, or sprayed DDT without regard for its effects on the surrounding populations.

During his stay in the Euphrates Delta, Wilfred Thesiger pointed to the distance separating the sheikhs from the rest of the people, citing Saddam Hussein as the epitome of abuse. "As I soon realized, Saddam was extremely unpopular," Thesiger wrote. "He was overbearing and tyrannical, and his temper when roused was ungovernable. The villagers complained that he made full use of his position to enrich himself, but any of them would have done the same. They admitted his generosity, admired his strength of character and were also amused by his sense of humor, which could be outrageous."

Thesiger offers an impressive analysis of this relationship:

> In general the official class, and the intelligentsia of the towns, were hostile to the sheikhs, envying their wealth, and being anxious to destroy their political power. When they talked glibly of confiscating the sheikh's land and distributing it among the peasants, they overlooked the fact that Iraq did not possess an Irrigation Service capable of taking their place. The larger sheikhs of Amara Province were usually extortionate and tyrannical, but most of them, like Majid, were first-rate farmers, with a knowledge of their estates acquired since childhood. The best felt a love for the land that went deeper than self-interest. If they were replaced, officials, brought perhaps from Baghdad or Mosul,

> would take years to acquire the same local knowledge, even if they could be induced to remain. The success or failure of the harvest would not affect them personally, and inevitably they would be tempted to grant water, not to the farmer who needed it most, but to the one who would pay most for it.

In other words, Thesiger accepts the bosses' abuses while recognizing their refined understanding of nature. And since he doesn't see anyone more capable of taking care of the land than these bosses, he proposes forgetting about the ignorant fixers from the city and entrusts the future of the collective to individuals as unpleasant as they are equipped to apply ancient techniques that will allow the ecosystem to survive.

The distance separating the *siñors* from the farmers in the Ebro Delta isn't as expansive as the one between the sheikhs and the Iraqi peasants of the Euphrates, but the parallel is there. Now, though, everything is moving faster and, most of all, becoming more confusing. Mateo struggles to maintain his solemnity in this new world, so different from that of his parents, where the *siñor* was a sheikh. Where time passed slowly. Or when time passed in real time, because who knows what today's clocks now show. Every person should lend to their life the rhythm that best suits their character. But the environment is an influencing factor, and the current environment is dizzyingly off-kilter, possessed of an unnatural speed that brings about anxiety, confusion, and which is reflected in the delta with its concentrated number of criminals, drug addicts, and people with suicidal tendencies and other mental health issues. Mateo might easily be one of them: his head isn't always situated squarely atop his shoulders. Insomnia, stress, anxiety, violent outbursts. Perhaps it's due to this new certainty that wealth is no longer enough. Lampedusa and the leopardine Don Fabrizio are history, so now we must negotiate much harder, and we must do so with individuals who are often obsessed with exacting some sort of exaggerated benefit as vengeance for what their ancestors suffered. Money helps, but it doesn't have the durability it had during centuries past. These vertiginous modern times are themselves a constant threat to any empire, and it's exhausting to keep Buda, the family, and the brand of rice afloat. Then again, maybe the two are the same thing, brands, because that's what shields and flags have become: logos and brands.

What's curious is that, one day, when Mateo had squirreled away a few minutes for thorough self-reflection, like in his Zen days, he realized he wasn't sure whether he continues unto the breach because he's driven by some ember of the love he's always felt for Buda, or if it's by inertia, by a sense of pride in maintaining traditions. He finds himself fearing that his drive is due to the latter. And if that's the case, he should retire to Terra Alta with Karen and make way for the younger folks or those who still feel the intensity of emotion. The question then becomes: is there anyone left who feels it more than him? Perhaps that's also a part of a declining tradition: the feeling of roots. The force that allows you to perceive the wonder in and the damage to an environment you wear on your skin and in your heart, and to react to any need before anyone else or file a complaint without fear of retaliation—can they do any more than they already have?—stating that, after a little over a year since Gloria struck, not a single action has been taken, although the Taula d'Acords has finally managed to present a Plan de Protección for the delta that has even been endorsed by the most darned of environmentalists. Surely the sheikhs did not, and do not, have such problems.

La Administración's latest excuse for prolonging the delay is that experts must carry out preliminary tests using sediment from the Ribarroja dam. Mateo knows these tests cost a fortune and that the final analysis will take who knows how long to complete. That means they're going to spend a lot of money on study after study, and that nothing will be done until the sea floods the land they want. These are the ones concerned about climate change who'll march in Barcelona to protect the Llobregat Delta, but here they let us drown. Climate change depends on who holds the purse strings to the grant money. Those who previously didn't want to release anything are now rallying around the sediment, which is where the money is. Funny: when the subsidy changes, they change.

SAND

THE SUN IS ALREADY SHINING when I open the small bedroom window. I watch the birds in the rice field through the mosquito netting, which is better than any hunting blind. As it approaches the glass, a yellow wagtail detects something strange and takes flight, alerting the eight glossy ibises lined up in the last cultivated furrow, who also take off. It's been said that nobody truly knows a bird until they see it aloft, but you might add that it can be known even better when it flees in the instant of fear.

After the storm, there are more crustaceans than ever in the aisle of dead crabs. At first light I can still see some birds pecking away at the claws and carcasses. A log that rested comfortably on the shore for months now floats in the water like a resurrected wreck. The saltwort shrubs and salt cedars are still there, along with some wood covered in moss that smells like damp furniture. Beyond the vegetation, a couple of meters from the water, the morning shore is adorned with a skirting of dead jellyfish. There are hundreds of them, each the size of a fist, spilled out like transparent blue glitter shining in their gelatinous packaging. They extend across the beach, invoking ancestral words: nobility, ode, eternal. Infinite, honor, gratitude. Stillness. It seems incredible that this is Europe, let alone the Mediterranean. The stillness comes steeped with a sense of that ancient sea.

I lie down on my mother dune, where the first flowering buds are starting to appear. Eventually they'll be lilac in color, although the bush still appears bluish green, with several branches the color of toasted honey. Perhaps they've finally succumbed to the salt. For now, though, the last salt cedar tree holds firm, visited by a brigade of red-headed ants and me.

Researcher Juan José Kasper Zubillaga has written extensively about sands, detailing the difference between beach and desert dunes. Basically, when it comes to the beach, the sea is the primary influence, whereas storms and other meteorological activity impact dunes in the desert. The most exciting thing about Kasper Zubillaga is to imagine him focusing on what seems like nothing, enabling him to obtain results that have encouraged him to collect sand the way Mateo collects butterflies, and to create a "sanditarium." Kasper dedicates thousands of hours to observing how millions of insignificant particles can move in unison until he uncovers the meaning of a reality that exists and yet manages to escape most of us.

His obsession is reminiscent of that of Vaughan Cornish, the wave aficionado who sold his house and reinvented himself as the pathfinding geographer who created kumatology, the scientific study of waves (κύμα is Greek for wave). As Cornish perceived affinities between atypical elements, he nurtured an alternative view that began to tie things together, and I quote the writer Robert Macfarlane: "the movement of steam quitting a chimney, the arrangement of water-weed tresses in a stream, the way fallen leaves drift before the wind, the composition of quicksand, the rippled cloud effect called 'mackerel' sky, the body-shapes of fish and cetaceans, the wings of birds, and the cahots or undulating tracks that were made by the procession of sledges or carriages or snow or mud." And upon detecting that the friction between the waves and the sand created fantastically unique shapes, he was captivated by the inventive obstacle sand presented to water. Cornish studied the sandy waves and ridges that formed around the marram grasses that reinforce this delta and give rise to the dunes, which themselves are as distinct as the rocks, minerals, shells, and other particles that compose them.

Kasper and Cornish discovered in the dunes a place where they could happily live parallel lives, and their vision invites us to find enchantment in what for centuries many judged as a sort of emptiness.

I spend hours looking at water and sand.

Maps pay no heed to the horizon, possibly because they don't owe it anything.

There are moments when vision becomes cloudy, losing spatial awareness. Time also appears different. It's all distilled into a color that refines the senses. I have a deep sensation of what's happening as my countenance is sucked into the immense monochromatic tunnel, fluctuating between blue and brown.

When I sit up in the afternoon, I feel a healthy sensation of oblivion.

Quim seems more relaxed by the day. Today, while out rambling along the beach, he said that when he was even younger he'd bring his hookups to Buda for a *piulada*: the native equivalent of getting laid. Until now, Quim had limited himself to brief answers to my questions, ceding the floor to Dylan, and when Simona appeared, he shrank himself down even smaller, obedient to every order. Although it's not quite the same thing, that hulking man subjugating himself to someone else's wishes recalls the story of El Boga, who lived in the Paraná Delta, an hour outside Buenos Aires. When the old fisher to whom he was subservient passed away, El Boga adapted to his new, solitary life by building a small boat and accepting the intermittent company of Cabecita, a caring neighbor with a learning disability, and her dog. El Boga internalized the cadence of the delta, surviving in silence. Dozing off among the reeds. With the everlasting hope of one day catching a golden dorado whose scales shone and shine as if promising something. One day he helped rescue an injured man who, once he recovered, became a sort of a chief or boss, and while El Boga considered himself a free man who could have changed things at any time, for some reason he chose to continue obeying the wishes of this new leader.

Quim reminds me of El Boga, because his obedience is misplaced. And the passing of time El Boga experienced between the old man's death and the appearance of the wounded man makes me think about the waiting. Had El Boga been expecting the arrival of further orders? Nature writers Sylvain Tesson and Peter Matthiessen waited for the snow leopard in temperatures that sunk to forty below. Residents of Ordesa dubbed biologist Juan Seijas "a waiting rock" because of the stillness he maintained for more than a thousand hours spent on the lookout for the Pyrenean ibexes he intended to count. Lieutenant Giovanni Drogo was stationed for years in a fort prepared to turn back an invasion from barbarians who never arrived: an experience with an ending identical to that of Vladimir and Estragon, though they waited for Godot. People who wait for animals, invaders, bosses, gods. I'm waiting for an element, which is why I ask myself the same question every day: when will the water arrive?

What happened to Drogo and Estragon won't happen to me, because the water is going to arrive. My golden dorado is the storm. Yesterday's one left me with a bit of damage and a lot of firewood, but also the final page in Haroldo Conti's story of El Boga.

As the years have passed, it has become known that El Boga actually existed, that he may even have been referred to by that name, and that Conti simply breathed new life into him by deploying his own knowledge of the delta region he had settled into in 1949. The Argentine writer rented a cabin along the shores of the Gambados tributary of the Paraná River and began exploring the region's waterways. He joined a rowing club. In 1954 he bought the cabin, along with a boat he intended to name after his daughter, Alejandra. In 1962 he published *Southeaster*, in which he tells the story of El Boga and his delta, one of the most literary deltas on the planet. This is where dissidents, outlaws, bohemians, intellectuals, and millionaires have for decades sought refuge from the expansive nearby metropolis of Buenos Aires. Haroldo Conti represented a space neither grassland nor jungle nor forest nor urban, but rather a marginal space of names as illustrative as Hombrecito, La Rubia, or Cabecita, one in which many powerful emotions were stirred by boats. He was kidnapped by soldiers serving dictator Jorge Rafael Videla who, two weeks later, summarily announced the writer's death. To this day, his remains have never been found.

Rodolfo Walsh was a good friend of Conti, whom he occasionally visited at the cabin. Walsh also explored and wrote about the delta and its surrounding tributaries, noting that he'd been bitten by mosquitoes while floating down the Tigre and Corrientes rivers and near Mercedes, but not on the Iberá wetlands. It's thanks to him that we know the *Pygocentrus palometa*, the red-bellied piranha, whose ability to sever a finger is on par with that of the blue crab. It can attack you if you're still, while it holds back if it senses movement. And he met Bernardino Díaz, a gaucho who slept on reed mats, who was guided by the shadows cast by sticks and stars, and who forgot everything when he realized he'd gotten lost. And by erasing from his mind all that had confused him, he was then able to reorient himself. Bernardino was living proof that it's important to pause every so often and trust that you're heading in the right direction.

Intuition matters. "It seems like there's a path," Walsh said. Despite the dictatorship, and the profound risks he took that put his own life in jeopardy, his intuition told him that following the path meant writing about the "plundering illiterates" caught up in the frenzy of "accumulating land, riches, and provincial aristocracy." The military disappeared him. But, today, Walsh is Walsh.

Domingo Faustino Sarmiento was the first to write about the Tigre Delta. He also had a home there, as did Manuel Mujica Lainez, Juan Carlos Moretti, and Leopoldo Lugones, who killed himself with whiskey and cyanide at the El Tropezón inn, which stood close to the river whose waters he had once described as "lion-colored." Roberto Arlt's ashes were scattered across the river whose name pays homage to none other than Sarmiento himself.

However, going beyond their tragic endings and their relationships with the delta, there comes a point where these writers and their characters, whether real or fictional, encounter people from various countries. Such is the influence the river holds over them. "They don't exactly love the river, but they can't live without it," is how Conti summarized it. That's how it is. I've come to understand that during my time in Buda, where I might be the only person looking seaward. Everyone else is faithful to the river. While they may accept the meeting of waters as the sole or the eels do, denizens of the delta were raised on river tales, and that's what channels their imagination, into which they pour their legends, their dreams, the memories they might have aspired to. Local fantasies flow easily down the Ebro, and while they may overflow sometimes, everyone knows they're under control.

The issue, or perhaps the problem, is the sea, into which the fresh waters of the river spill out, exposing them to the salt and moods of the waves and forcing them to consider existential questions. The delta marks the end of the riverbed's dreamy monotony, of its familiar current, and instead proposes more constant pulsations that might inspire thoughts of dams and dredges. This wild immensity, impossible to tame, invites us to flip the roles of the two spaces, because what if the river were fiction while the sea were reality?

In Guaraní, Paraná means "similar to the sea."

This afternoon I need to connect to El Mas's Wi-Fi to hold a virtual meeting. I got distracted at the beach and I'm twenty minutes past the time I gave Simona, but, well, Dylan and Quim finish work at eight every day. Following protocol, I call the supervisor to tell her I'm running behind. She replies that she's already left with the keys, that she's in the car just outside Sant Jaume.

"What about Quim and Dylan?"

"They're gone too."

I fall silent. She adds that, since I hadn't shown up, she figured I wasn't going to.

The day I met her she told me I should call her for any "out of the ordinary" movements I might want to make around the island, and since then I've scrupulously complied with her wish by asking permission to cross the two spectacular kilometers of the Parc Natural, letting her know every time someone is coming to see me—after having been read the riot act twice for not doing so—in addition to answering her questions about whether I've seen a particular car pass by, about the alternating on and off status of the generator next to the canal, about whether I heard any strange noises the other night. While respecting her schedule, I keep her up to date on everything she wants to know, but today, when I'm a few minutes late, she can't call me or leave me the keys somewhere? I tell her all of this in fewer words and a polite tone that nonetheless reflects my annoyance.

Simona goes ballistic.

She spouts off about how she has too much work to be wasting time on my stories. That her job isn't to be taking care of me. But fine, she's turned the car around and is heading back to the island. "I'll leave the keys at the door!"

Click.

I call her again.

When she picks up, I say, hoping she'll do the opposite, that there's no need for her to come all the way back. I speak softly, remembering Quim's look of intimidation when he talks to her, but Simona goes right back to her rant, which is reaching a crescendo, telling me to stop busting her balls—yes, that's what she said—before finishing: "Don't fuck with me, okay? Don't be fucking with me, because you've no idea what I'm capable of."

Simona has been able to go from scaring off ducks in Buda to being the boss's right-hand woman, earning so much influence that some see her as a somewhat ambiguous *minisiñora*. The secret of her success lies in her tireless surveillance of the island, in the network of Santjaumeros that allows her to negotiate almost everything with the locals—and in another set of things she won't reveal because "a closed mouth catches no flies." One of her methods is not letting the staff get too bigheaded, too high and mighty, which is why she spends the day in the car, ripping up and down the island, as Buda is big and requires nonstop movement. When you're not buying gas or phytosanitary products, you're looking for spare parts for a car or tractor, repairing a pump, taking fish to market, preparing duck blinds, fishing cages, maintaining power lines . . . Buda is never-ending. Beyond that, all I can say is that when you complete a task, you should keep on talking about it, especially with outsiders. You have to know how to clear your head, *xeik*, unlike Mateo, who, now everything's freshly planted, returns to his usual, anxious behavior. It's head-scratching. Just let him up and take the pills, because this is no way to live. Or come down here to clear algae and seaweed from the canals, which is more relaxing than it looks. Or do some reconnaissance around the island to take some of the burden off the supervisor's shoulders. Simona has learned the benefits of pausing to breathe in some fresh air, which is why she now goes home every day for lunch. If nobody holds her up, at one o'clock she'll leave Buda for Sant Jaume, and she won't return until four. Three hours during which she can disconnect and build up some strength for when she has to work more overtime than a clock, whether it's leading a hunting party at dawn, supervising planting, or rushing out on a Sunday because an intruder, or perhaps even the sea, has snuck their way onto the island.

There are those who tell Simona she's lucky to be working in Buda, but with her it's not about luck. It's hard for the staff to chalk it up to effort or intelligence, considering the weight envy can carry. Good luck, they say. You must play your cards right—close to your chest when needed, tipping your hand if necessary—though everything works better when you play things tight. She's been squeezed hard, really hard, and look where she is now. Walking around like she never stole Communion wafers as a kid. Like a dyke, like a butch woman—why doesn't she let her hair grow out, they ask. And she's not forgotten her time as a novice in a convent, either. It didn't help her confront the cowards who bullied her, but it did steel her, harden her like a stone. So take a good look now, you smart-asses. Where are you now, and where is she? Let's see if you've figured out that Mateo appreciates her because she knows how to drive and defend the island's best interests like a true owner, and because his supervisor's advice helps keep the farm prosperous. Dry planting or new seeds or pesticides may not always work as expected, but attempts must be made. Mateo appreciates this, because if it's progress you want, you must try new things. Not like Manuel Bosch, the supervisor who came before her and who didn't last long once Mateo arrived on the scene. There was a lot of history, a lot of origins and roots, a lot of you can't touch this or change that, but the guy had the island in shambles. Do you want to live in the now, or anchored in the previous century? If you want to move forward, you must bet on the new. Some will be annoyed, but others will be happy about it because their time will have finally come. Life is about making progress, keeping up with the times, being modern, *xeik*. Then, the offended parties come to you, asking along with a whole lot of nonsense how she can do this to them after many years, because their *iaios* broke their backs on this land. Who do they think they're talking to? As if she's never seen worn-out *iaios* and miserable families before. The reason she's committed to progress is precisely because she doesn't want to see these stories repeated. That's why she asked Mateo for the 4x4 adorned with Buda's crest. An impressive vehicle that doubles as a declaration of intent: prospering into the future.

Besides, it was a strategic decision. All modesty aside, it was a great one, because we all know money begets more money. Driving a nice car through the towns in the delta generates interest in your business, enticing people to sell you phytosanitary products, gasoline, even their own mother . . . because there are some who'd be willing to do that. Oh, you can bet they would. Don't come to Simona talking about drugs, poverty, and trash, because she knows what all that's about. She's seen it all around here with her own eyes. Everything and anything.

But the Mensurado delta hasn't. And right at the mouth of the river is West Point, the largest shantytown in the Liberian capital of Monrovia, where drugs and poverty find a kind of grotesque expression in the form of dumping tons of waste and detritus next to the sea. Bulwarks of garbage that cover nearly every square inch of ground, or whatever else is down there, make up the first line of . . . the sea? The dwellings are so close together, you often have to turn sideways to pass between them. It's a labyrinth of substandard housing units, largely submersible during the rainy season, when the river overflows its banks and the sea encroaches the land, aquatically walling in the settlement.

Authorities plan to build a massive wall in the next year to protect coastal shantytowns. But, given what we've seen, the government's word amounts to another type of garbage, leaving West Point's inhabitants to trust only in the sand and their own hands when it comes to dealing with the sea, even if only temporarily. The Monrovians take advantage of all sorts of waste, from bottles to barrels, tires, containers of any kind. They pack them with sand and even feces to fashion a kind of stratum that extends across the surface of the water, expanding the inhabitable area. It's a city in flux, because when seas are low, locals build, and when they rise, the shantytown disappears. Local inhabitants have grown accustomed to their comings and goings as if part of a natural migration.

There are people capable of living on a foundation of trash, and there are others who are not, like Matthieu Duperrex, who has explored deltas from the Rhône to the Mississippi. In Louisiana, he visited the St. John the Baptist Parish, the unofficial capital of Cancer Alley. This led him to wonder why there are people in the world who have no qualms about poisoning deltas as well as those who have accepted life amid such contaminated filth. Until 2019, most of us weren't aware of the statistics, but now we know that the risk of dying from cancer in Destrehan is eight hundred times higher than the American average.

That the earth has been perforated by approximately one million oil wells.

That there is a map of New Orleans drawn in 1878 by a civil engineer on which the swampy areas unfit for building are clearly marked. Structures were nevertheless put up, and these correspond exactly to the neighborhoods flooded by Hurricane Katrina.

That, in 1988, New Jersey's Passaic River basin was hit with a "syringe tide" of needles and other medical waste contaminated with HIV-positive blood originating from the Fresh Kills landfill in Staten Island, considered for years the largest in the world. To this day, many of the hypodermic needles that reached Jersey's shore remain there, sealed under layers of clay and concrete.

We now have this sort of information.

And naturally we accept it.

Today, these new ways of living in these outskirts, in these deltas, intrigue Duperrex in much the same way that naturalist Henry David Thoreau was intrigued by Walden Pond in 1845. In the Rhône, humans have learned to read the chromatic gradients of the sky based on industrial fumes, and they can distinguish Shell's dusky twilight from that of Total, EveRé, or ArcelorMittal. Which is precisely why Duperrex dreams of following in Thoreau's footsteps and building a cabin where he can live a wild life amidst cordoned-off highly industrial spaces and reflect on a new ethos of nature.

Foundations of garbage and branded sunsets have forged a new, conceited way of thinking that delights in how it's able to transform the world while despising what it once was. Which is why, when modern Western engineers found centuries-old canals, reservoirs, and dams in Asian and American lands, they attributed these architectural achievements to European invaders, convinced the Indigenous mind would never have been able to conceive of such perfect constructions.

In Anatolia, a dam has been discovered that was designed 3,250 years ago. It incorporates the same techniques as modern ones, the only difference being that the Hittites used clay instead of concrete. There are Syrian, Mesopotamian, and Iranian dams that have been in operation for more than 1,500 years. The oldest in the world is Marib, which has been operating in Yemen for over two millennia: an age similar to the Qattinah, in Syria. Most modern dams, though, tend to last about a hundred years or so due to poor design or planned obsolescence. The companies managing them must submit regular reports on their status, but as is often the case—take the Mequinenza dam which impounds the Ebro as an example—it's all but impossible to look at the data. If they're in violation of safety regulations, they could well be endangering populations who live downstream. In coming years, many Spanish dams will reach their expiration date, forcing them to be eliminated or restored. Regardless, the country will have to thoroughly review the relationships many of its territories have established with water.

While humans are capable of living among mounds of garbage, toxic fumes, and cracked dams, the dung beetle lifts 1,141 times its own body weight because it remains strong and healthy. No wonder Duperrex has said he has more hope in the dung beetle than in his own race.

The dung beetle does incredible things with the sand of the deserts and dunes he inhabits, but he needs unmarred skies so he can guide his enormous ball of manure. Scientists have proven that dung beetles are guided by the glow of the Milky Way and other starry firmaments. The ball serves as food—he likes nothing more than herbivore feces—and he will climb up high when the sand he's walking on gets too hot. He knows the sands like few others, always looking for the right angle so his ball rolls more easily through those immensities of grains less than two millimeters in size: the metallic, mineral, and organic microremains that sometimes, though not often, once made up a human body. Before the dynasties, the Egyptians buried people in the sand, and now there are ecological funeral homes offering urns fashioned from sand that dissolve shortly after having been placed in water.

The dung beetle's life expectancy is about a year, so a modern dam should last for a hundred beetles. Natural accounting encourages us to weigh other things up. Which weighs more, a dung beetle's ball or a supervisor's balls? What is the beetle capable of? What about Simona?

Yesterday I saw two dung beetles fighting three meters from my dune. One had grabbed the other, who was now on his back, legs kicking away, trying unsuccessfully to right himself, as his rival's little legs were wrapped across his thorax, leaving him completely immobilized. I watched them for half an hour, during which the scene didn't change. I went to Galatxo, came back, and the twin combatants were in the same clinch. I figured the captured beetle would end up dying. I lay down on the dune to daydream for a bit and when I got back up, an hour later, the two of them were gone.

Artur grabs a fuet like a stick and bites into it without removing the sausage's casing. Dylan takes a swig of Fanta, having listened to my story of yesterday's encounter with Simona. Quim finishes his last bite of breakfast, lights a cigarette, and says, "She's like that." He exhales a lungful of smoke. "Mateo's got your back. But you still gotta be careful." It's the first time he's engaged in a politically complicated topic with me.

Over the next few days, Quim's the one who initiates conversations about all sorts of things, as if, after I opened up about Simona, he's now able to see me as someone trusted. He's spent the past seven years in Buda, confirming that the sinuousness isn't limited to the wetlands alone, and he always moves with caution. Though caution isn't exactly his forte. He'd prefer to go straight ahead, but he doesn't want to overdo it either, especially if he wants to keep his job. Then again, he's been doubting for the past few months whether he can continue putting up with Simona. He's had it up to here. He enjoys operating the tractor, but that fucking Simona . . . when she starts bossing him around . . . and the yelling, especially the yelling . . . When Simona screams at him, Quim stares back at the supervisor with a face full of fear. What Simona doesn't realize is that Quim is scared of himself, of what he could do to her, and that that's the face he makes while restraining himself. It's something he's learned after a long journey that began when, as a pupil, he set a live rooster on fire in the schoolyard. He was suspended for a week. It turned out well for him, because he was able to sign up for work in the rice fields and make some money. For the next few years, whenever planting or harvesting time approached, Quim would cause a ruckus at school, get suspended, and go earn a few bucks. It all turned out okay; when he's about to cross a line now, he's aware of what he's doing and can stop himself in time. Even more so now he's a father.

Because there's this party thing. Like many other people from the delta, he's done everything and then some. It was during one of those nights when he was mixing everything and measuring nothing that he was stopped at a sobriety checkpoint on his way home. He was hit with a €1,500 fine, after which he said to himself, "Damn, man, this is it!" After that, he says, he stopped using. He's a man of his word. He no longer sets roosters on fire, doesn't do drugs—so he says—and no longer practices kickboxing. He spent two years training only to discover that he can't even be compliant and abide by the rules of sports because, while sparring with one of his partners, he got so fired up that, damn, *xeik*, he didn't just want to hit the other guy but knock him out. So he gave it up.

Now, he's forged a great relationship with Artur. He's Mateo's son-in-law, after all. And he's a decent guy, being the fan of tractors he is. Artur was amazed when Quim told him that, at ten, he started collecting replicas of rice-farming equipment. He bought them with the little bit of money his parents gave him in return for helping them pick olives, and to this day his collection continues to grow. They're 1:32 scale miniatures by the most expensive brand, Wiking, known for their ultrarealistic tractors. They're the best, and therefore the most expensive, but that being said . . . Quim has all his little machines perfectly organized in a single display case: 150 in all. At one point, the number totaled roughly four hundred wonders that ranged from Fendts to Cases and Massey Fergusons, but when the baby arrived he had to make more space at home, so he reduced his collection.

The showcase tells the delta's recent history through equipment Quim knows inside and out. As strange as it may seem, it calms him down and helps him to dream. Whenever he looks at a John Deere, or especially a CLAAS, he imagines himself behind the wheel of the actual machine, harvesting a massive field without fretting or obsessing over anything, without feeling the burning desire to tighten his fist and smash it into someone's face.

Simona has done many things to Quim, many of which were serious. Dylan shares with him the cogency of never having had a boss . . . like her. And be careful, he says: her daughter will come at you from behind. You'll see. An eleven-year-old brat who gets away with whatever she wants in Buda. The other day, the little punk hopped on the tractor with Quim and started telling him she had to drive, calling him an *atontat*: the Catalan equivalent of a dumbass.

"Get down from here right now," Quim answered. He's lit roosters on fire, but never has he ever called an elder an *atontat*. Fuck. How did we ever get to this point?

We'll see whether Artur's presence helps Simona pump the brakes a bit, though he's doubtful. Simona sees herself as a true leader, one unused to making concessions. In any case, it's good to have Artur and a writer around these days, unless that girl starts to feel uncomfortable, like she's being watched. But hey, let her get a taste of her own medicine. And *moooolt bé* if the bully starts threatening the newcomers. Perfect. Let her keep messing with Artur and the writer, because they don't answer to anyone. They're free to talk about anything that happens, without fear—or with significantly less fear—of reprisals. Quim will occasionally speak up, but most of the time he remains silent. His position isn't exactly an advantageous one, and he knows how the money gets slung around here. He also knows to let time run its course. That we all will face our day of reckoning. That all hogs end up at the slaughterhouse.

Every morning, Dylan, Quim, and Artur spend a couple hours binding crab claws on La Pantena's porch. Sometimes I chip in and help. Once I learned how to encircle the claw and cinch the zip tie in two swift movements, Quim taught me how to lash them with elastic bands and tie a triple knot. It's faster, cheaper, and equally effective. The crabs are always held tight by Dylan, who plucks them from the basket as if they were snails, closes the pincers tightly, and holds them, suspended, until we bind them. On rare occasions, a crab will catch hold of his glove. Dylan shakes his hand, freeing himself from its grip, and, unharmed, redirects the conversation to the comment that this is the best time to sell crabmeat. There aren't many others in the fishing industry catching them right now, and they're worth around nine euros apiece: a good price.

The rice grows, turning green as we repeat these mornings, gathered around a basket of crabs. Someone remarks that storks here in the delta used to number in the hundreds; another asks what a writer's life is like. Then they go off to tend to the canals, the tractors, the tool kits, or to paint a house, and I either hop on my bike or walk out toward the sea. Today I dragged myself up to the highest point on the beach: a four-meter dune whose height will depend on the next strong wind. It's close to the mouth of the river, and from that vantage point its flow can be seen with renewed majesty. I can just make out the water sparkling toward the north, and the plains seem even flatter, stretching out until they reach the foot of the mountains, where a herd of intrepid, free-range cattle have begun their seasonal migration toward the pastures of Bajo Maestrazgo, where they'll spend the summer.

Mere hours before the 2004 tsunami, thousands of Indonesian buffalo began retreating from the coast in search of higher ground that couldn't be reached by the impending wave. Pablo Archer Bernabé's bulls in the delta are at sea level, though most came from the northern part of the peninsula. When faced with an imminent change in weather, they jump, run, and kick, but when they sensed the imminent arrival of Gloria, they all crowded together at the meadow gate, seeking refuge in the corrals.

Pablo has invited me to visit his stockyard, so one morning I tell Simona that someone in a pickup truck will be looking for me. For the first time in many weeks, I'll be more than twenty kilometers away from the island.

We soon turn off the main road, traveling now along dirt paths mainly used by cyclists. To access the pastures where the bulls graze, which around here are known as velas (sails) owing to their triangular shape and the maritime nature of life in the delta, Pablo unhooks a chain prohibiting unauthorized vehicles from entering. We're surrounded by greenery and water, from irrigation channels to the massive Circunvalación drainage system. The enormous L'Encanyissada lagoon sits nearby, though it's hidden by the tall-grass. The bulls raise their necks. They're spread out, grazing next to the corral currently being built. It's a large structure of wood planks and raised, steel-reinforced bridges that allow you to move from one bullpen to the next. The work may be unfinished, but it's already used to manage the livestock. Pablo greets the herd with short, musical shouts as we pass through two gates before entering the cordoned-off pasture in the truck.

Slowly, we drive across the pasture with the windows down. Pablo introduces me to Marinera, Naranjita, Niñata, Limonero, Galga ("because of her composition"), Perla ("the best we have"), Diablilla, Amapola, Pintoret, Voladora, Flequi ("because of the bangs"), to Melosa and his daughter Mimosa. In doing so, Pablo points to the kinship between them, reminiscing over moments spent with each animal or memories shared by his *iaio*. His grandfather used to hitch the tamest member of the herd to the front door of the olive oil mill, across from the restaurant, back when the delta was still an even more distant south.

We park the truck inside the corral and unload bales of feed, because the grass in this pasture is no longer enough to sustain the entire herd. Pablo wants to keep the *bous* here for a few more days before moving them to one of the other two pastures owned by the Bernabés. He slings a sack of feed over his shoulder and leaves the corral, spreading forty kilos of peas and twenty kilos of rice along with some fortified mineral blocks across the field. The bulls follow him like the children from Hamelin. He returns to the truck with an empty sack. Now we must distribute the bales around the corral.

"Don't stray too far from the truck, and keep an eye on any that might get close to you. There are a couple you can't trust one bit."

The fighting bulls and fearless cows begin to enter the corral a couple meters from where I'm standing with the passenger door ajar. I hesitate, unsure whether I should unload the bales from the bed of the truck or remain close to the door. Pablo begins tossing bales into the feeding troughs while calling out to the animals with either greetings or complaints. When he slips into the maze of pens, I'm left alone, surrounded by several bulls. Glued to the pickup's chassis.

My eyes are focused on three animals that seem a little too calm, as if they're more interested in the feed still in the truck than what Pablo is currently dispensing. I grab two bales and ease myself as far away from those static bulls as I can, right up against the fence panels, which I could quickly clamber if the need arose.

The bulls remain quiet.

Pablo reappears, grunts of exasperation in his voice. He walks calmly, maintaining his distance. A number of animals have lowered their heads, munching on blocks of feed when we return to the truck and depart the corral.

"I've never understood the people who say 'no bulls,'" he mutters as he closes the gate. "What does 'no bulls' even mean? Who says that? Have they ever stopped to look at one? To really look at it, at the animal? I don't understand how bulls have become so politicized. I guess there's a few people out there with an inferiority complex using them as if they were red flags."

The prejudices and demagoguery swarming around this animal irritate Pablo as much as he finds it stimulating to live in this delta: a geographical intersection that can help us to understand many things . . . if you *want* to understand them. Because to do that, you must review history. And who cares about the past in a world that orbits around the latest fashion crazes and breaking news, with rituals all but forgotten. Now, if you want to pray for something in church, instead of lighting a candle you insert money and an LED bulb lights up. And so it goes.

History of the bull. That's something that should be taught in schools. At least people would know there have been some twelve hundred head of cattle here since 1870. Many came down from Aragón, taking advantage of the canalization of both the left and right riverbanks, and over the years both animals and people from as far away as Teruel, from northern Castellón, and from southern Tarragona have gathered: the people from Maestrazgo, who basically share a way of looking at the world without fear of mixing. What were people from Maestrazgo before they arrived? Valencian, Aragonese, Catalan? The place might not be densely populated, but what an identity it has.

Maybe it is because of his *iaio*, who endeared him to the bull by tying the creature to the family, that Pablo takes the *bou*'s plight personally. He feels obliged to defend the animal as one of his own. With all due respect to his *iaio*, though, the son of the *besiaio* has lent his full name to the cattle ranch. When it comes to the people of the delta, they're the Soneca-Bernabés, having dubbed their *besiaio* Soneca after hearing him speak with the depth of the philosopher Seneca. Since everyone's name here is tweaked, they settled on Soneca.

Pablo remembers sitting on his *iaio*'s lap at five years old, watching the cattle being tended to.

At ten, he was going around with a sugar cube in hand so he could feed it to Estrellito.

At fourteen, he was herding wild *bous*.

And etched in his mind is the memory of the day he was caught standing between a bull and his father. The bull started to charge him. As soon as Pablo's father realized, he started running toward his son from the opposite side, waving a stick to scare off the bull. But the animal was far ahead of him. Pablo remembers the dark mass coming at a gallop, horns angled toward him. Getting ever closer. No more than a meter before impact, the bull pulled up, stooped in a bow, and leaped toward the ravine off to the side, kicking up a large cloud of dust before continuing down the slope. Pablo will never know why that happened, he doesn't believe in gods or miracles, but something caused it. He remembers feeling his hair standing on end. And then, now safe, he began to run. "Ever since that moment, I was hooked on *bous*," he says to me in the van.

It's the adrenaline, the exceptionally vivid experience of coming face to face with imminent death which serves as an emotional injection, that gives meaning to existence. Before the aborted attack, he was considering becoming a veterinarian or a forester, but from that day forward all he wanted was to have bulls nearby. He devoted himself to tagging calves' ears, he participated in the slaughtering of hogs and *bous*, attended events at the Plaza de Toros de La Ribera . . . all the while paying more attention to his *iaio*, who encouraged him to become a bullfighter, and less to his father, with whom he wasn't getting along and who had envisioned a different path for Pablo. Then, though, the government made significant changes to bullfighting regulations. Many old-time practices were now illegal, and Pablo had to readjust both his moves and his goals.

No, it certainly hasn't been easy for him. He's a twenty-first-century bull lover, which means he knows what it is to recycle yourself, to adapt to modern times, to negotiate with people who want to put an end to your way of life—and even with thieves. Negotiating with thieves is his specialty. Just ask the octogenarian who once stole a cow from the family herd. At eighteen, Pablo had hiked up the side of a mountain in search of a pregnant cow with hope of locating a few other animals who seemed to have dispersed themselves across the slopes, and lo and behold, he finds one of the family's cows grazing along with the old man's herd. Pablo goes right up to the old man and threatens to report him for rustling livestock that belonged to the Bernabés. Then, as he's about to walk away, Pablo adds, "But maybe we could come to some sort of agreement. We'll leave twenty cows and a docile bull here for a few days to gather up the rest of our cattle on the mountain, and I won't call you out."

The old man accepts. Two months later, the Bernabés collect eight wild *bous*, four cows, and two calves from his land.

Seeing how Pablo resolved the matter himself, his elders delegated a certain amount of responsibility to him. And then more.

Three years later, when the ranch was infected with brucellosis and the family had been served with an order to sacrifice 337 animals, his *iaio* and his father told him, his brother, and two other herdsmen to take the animals to the slaughterhouse.

Three hundred and thirty-seven lives. The punch to the family's collective gut was devastating. While financial compensation cushioned the blow, the Bernabés had to rebuild an entire ranch not only by selectively purchasing young animals who met the criteria of the fighting bulls they wanted to raise, but also by trusting that the increasingly restrictive laws wouldn't end up forcing them to give it all up because of growing public animosity toward any event featuring bulls.

Pablo sees a lot of hypocrisy swirling around the fighting bull. All he asks is that they be treated the same as the dogs who compete in CaniCross. If abuse is the concern, then it should be applied equally across the board, right? In any case, it surprises him that nobody's willing to sit at a table and have a sound, balanced discussion of the topic. Hasn't anyone noticed that the French have debated the issue enough to have found middle ground? Of course not. Here, there's so much animosity that everyone ends up radicalized, and suddenly, in "a *bous* country like Catalonia" (not his words but those of the director of the Museo de Historia de Amposta, a place not unlike the delta, where, years ago, castellers featured prominently in the running of the bulls because they were fit enough to keep just ahead of the horns, and where many separatists like his mother defended bullfighting), a lot of people are now demonizing his most revered animal. And there you have it.

Pablo turned to the media to denounce the flak being received by any festival that dared to feature fighting bulls, and to denounce the hypocrisy of certain politicians not content with simply divesting them of the water and its sediment but imposing upon them nuclear power plants which the politicians themselves don't want anywhere near their metropolis . . . And, on top of that, they're trying to steal their *bous*. All thieves. The lot of them. Worse than the old man on the mountain.

He said all this on local TV program *Banda Ampla*, boosting his self-esteem. While the anti-bullfighting crowd rallied against this new incarnation of Evil that Pablo represented, there were many more who interpreted his words as a call for unity in the region, leading some to consider him, at least for a few months, the delta's own Che Guevara, a new sort of regional liberator.

Pablo is aware of how engrossed he is in all things bull-related. He's also aware that, when he first started dating Xènia, she was very accommodating when it came to his passion. Now she's grown a bit weary of the monotonous theme over the years, more so now they've become parents, though she's willing to shoulder the burden, mostly because she knows the history. But Xènia's getting tired. Having overcome the hellish depression that knocked him "out on the canvas," from which he might never have gotten up, Pablo is asking her to hold on for a little bit longer now things are finally starting to roll again.

Sometimes misfortunes will build upon one another, forming what seems like an insurmountable wave. After rebuilding their cattle ranch, the Bernabés found tourism a good source of income. Every month they'd orchestrate a spectacular show for groups of Russian visitors. They welcomed guests with an appetizer of cured meats and sangria before sitting them down to watch a test of bravery—a pass of the cape here, a muletazo there—with the bull in the corral while the Slavs continued their meal with salad, paella, and an ice cream dessert. Between that, the local festivals, and government subsidies, the Bernabés felt that a peaceful, prosperous future was within their grasp, until a 2012 law came into effect prohibiting animal shows and dooming the business to failure. After his *iaio* presided over the Asociación de Ganaderías de Lidia de Tarragona, he became a participating member, working to elevate livestock farming through contracts and laws, changing parts of the Museo de Historia de Amposta. And although even local politicians, starting with the mayors, acknowledged that you were hard-pressed to find anyone in the delta who didn't consider the bulls and their bloodless festivals part of the region's soul, all of a sudden they turned off the tap.

Pablo wasn't yet thirty; he didn't have the strength to start up the business again. Since none of his siblings were willing to take over for him, he watched as five generations' worth of legacy was extinguished, taking him away with it. Yes, he had worked in pizzerias and was a solid cook, but suddenly he found himself working for the first time as an employee, hired by the city to kill apple snails. What kind of a life was that? His grandfather had died in 2009, and not being able to honor his memory was dragging Pablo down like a sinking ship. Depression crept into the marriage. He started going to couples therapy with Xènia. Well, they actually shared a psychologist, but each attended sessions individually, without seeing any results. On October 20, 2013, they separated.

He woke up each morning lost in a colossal void, lacking any plan or objective for that day, for that year, for his life. He doesn't remember what was running through his head back then. Those days lurk in his memory underneath a thick veil of sorrow, though the occasional phrase or idea sneaks in like a flash of light projected from the mouth of the psychologist to whom he's never stopped turning. Yes, it's odd to put it this way, but that mouth of hers sent out beams like a lighthouse, allowing even his innermost thoughts to be seen. A number of friends convinced him that this woman was almost magical in the way she was able to exorcise ghosts. He wouldn't call it magic, but after a session with her, he came away feeling calmer, feeling as though he was moving toward something. Yes, it was vague, diffuse, and nameless, but as with everything that keeps us moving forward, it was a form of hope. Every week, Pablo sat in that office in La Ràpita to let go of whatever he was carrying around inside him—that's how he still describes it to this day, "letting go of what I had inside me"—until he finally realized that what was oppressing and disturbing him the most was the silence. He didn't know how to process it, how to handle it. Which is why, when he broke down that barrier on the psychologist's couch, the words finally came together, flowing like water released from a dynamited dam, projecting themselves with the cumulative force of the months, years, and decades of repression.

More than anything, his therapist taught him to control himself, to gauge situations and respond as impartially as possible. She told him it might be a good idea to separate himself a bit, to observe the bulls with a certain perspective and see what happened from there.

Pablo left his sessions with the sorceress feeling so comforted that he wanted to apply her advice immediately. But a spirit can't transform itself overnight, so he began by trying to picture a better life for himself. The separation from Xènia allowed him to see himself as more or less alone. But the bulls were still there. They weren't serving him with divorce papers. If anything, he was the one who should be leaving them. He was so sad and tired that thinking about any sort of future at all was too much of a challenge. Even so, he still tried to think about himself without having a herd of bulls nearby.

He couldn't.

Every time he managed to envision a potential new future for himself, the *bou* would appear. Always a *bou*, emerging with such clarity and insistence that, as Pablo garnered the strength to identify valid ideas and organize them mentally according to a particular meaning, and despite the litany of misery and obstacles he'd undoubtedly continue to face, he decided that he'd be working with *bous* for the rest of his life. And that it wouldn't be incompatible with looking after other domestic spaces, with managing time in the same way as he was learning to manage silence, though perhaps both are the same. But the best part of it all? To do this, he realized he had a plan.

During the more calamitous years, he had articulated a coherent and, he believed, contemporary discourse on the value the *bous* brought to the delta, and now he had to popularize it by promoting concrete actions. He was going to turn the whole story around by presenting the animal as a point of intersection. Of encounters. Of dialogue. He could do this.

"The bull was my shelter when the cold was coming from inside myself," he says, years later, to anyone who's willing to listen. In certain ways, the lyrical influence of his mother, Rosa Maria Bernabé, a woman with a degree in Catalan and Spanish philology and law, can be detected.

If the bull had been his driving force to live, now it would be the driving force behind his reformation. Survival takes place through adaptation, and his life and that of his family's bulls depended on his ability to understand the new, bullish context and act accordingly. If he came out ahead, his bulls would too. Without the Bernabés, a place once occupied by twenty-five thousand head of cattle would be reduced to whatever specimens the Lo Morenos had. And who knew how long that herd would last, because Lo Moreno's son didn't have the intuitiveness or devotion of his father. There was no telling whether he'd want to maintain the family business once the patriarch had gone. No, the Bernabés weren't about to leave Lo Moreno on their own.

This is why, whenever Pablo sees Mateo's vehemence in TV interviews or when they're both attending Parc Natural meetings, he's upset that the rice farmer doesn't moderate the tone used in his presentations. If he were more cautious and deliberate, he'd be more enticing to more people, including a few politicians. But even if he doesn't share Mateo's manner of speech, Pablo empathizes with that man who's fighting for what he wants, for his land, for his family. Against all comers, if necessary. He reminds him a little bit of his grandfather.

Of course, Pablo does realize things don't work that way anymore, and that if you want your opponents to at least consider your proposals, you must be kind.

Pablo doesn't smile easily. He'd rather have his words be what gratify the listener, that the person with whom he's communicating understand that he's experienced understanding, joy, and resistance, but most of all that he's willing to fight for something that will benefit both parties. He prefers to hint at ways and opportunities to find enjoyment while sharing delightful, almost epic tales collected during his years of tending to fields and animals and which function as indelible fables, creating something of an intimate bond with the listener.

Mateo has a knack for sifting through parables, great phrases, and illustrative examples, but he's never quite able to hold back the lash of resentment that his listeners find unforgivable. He constructs buildings with a solid foundation which he then dynamites himself. And he gets increasingly explosive, because the sea is going to swallow half of Buda. When nobody reacts, he gets angry at their ignorance. Pablo feels like recommending Mateo to his psychologist, like telling him, *Mateo, it's the best money I ever spent in my life. I tip my cap to that woman for what she's done for me, for the miracles she's performed*. But he's not that confident.

Xènia comes from a long line of rice growers, so in her home they know what it's like to endure all sorts of suffering, whether the weather or cattle grubs and apple snails. And they don't even want to imagine the agony that would come from bearing witness to the volatilization of their family heritage. In that sense, it's easy to put yourself in Mateo's shoes and conclude that the only possible solution for Buda—if there even is one—lies in dialogue, in winning over others through evocative arguments. That's the theory. The reality, though, is that others will only be susceptible to persuasion if they like you, if you can offer something that interests them, or if you scare them. And Mateo doesn't meet any of these requirements. Meanwhile, for example, the Maghrebis continue proliferating, having confirmed that rice is stretched to breaking point and prospering instead through the harvesting of parsley and cilantro. They now offer something truly appealing.

When it comes to Pablo Archer, his parsley has been his (relative) neutrality. In his literal return to the ring, he paid careful attention to the opening up of public calls for livestock grants and subsidies, managing to win a few of these. And thanks to meticulous work and diplomatic efforts, when the management of the Illa dels Bous came up for debate, several head honchos thought of him.

So now Pablo is also the administrator of an island, though his role is the opposite of Mateo's because the Illa dels Bous is wild, producing nothing of use to humans because it belongs to La Administración. And since it lies in the delta, the possibility of flooding isn't even in the forecast for the near future. Still, though, it's an island someone must take care of, and this improbable parallelism helps further reinforce his affinity with Mateo.

"You'll have to come with me one of these days," Pablo says. "La Illa is an experience."

Pablo moved back in with Xènia on October 20, 2014, exactly one year after their separation. He assured her that he loved her more than he loved the bulls . . . or at least enough to cut back on the time he spent on the island and in the corrals. And that he had clearer ideas and the ability to prioritize. Xènia looked at him with her ambiguous eyes, which Pablo had always found equal parts attractive and terrifying. Very well, she replied. But I've also learned a thing or two, and at home we're going to share the work.

Since then, Pablo has been in charge of the kitchen. Which means everything from braising the meat for the dinner stew to cleaning the dishes and wiping down the glass-ceramic stovetop, while Xènia focuses on the laundry and other household details.

The most radical change, however, has been at work, because Pablo now devotes his mornings to crushing apple snails. And thanks to that he's shored up enough of a financial cushion that he's been able to dispense with the extra income he received from showing his *bous* at town festivals, while allowing him to take a chance on eco-friendly cattle ranching, betting on European funds aimed at promoting new uses for livestock.

"I like fairs and festivals. I'd be more than happy showing off the bulls there. Doing more of that sort of thing. But you gotta live."

In any case, he's not about to let the bull's new public image remain in the hands of some inexperienced if well-intentioned people who frequently don't know what they're talking about. As politicians and intellectuals are fond of repeating, we must construct a narrative. We can't allow others to build it for us. If there's one thing that's clear to Pablo after all the holy hell they've given him, it's that either you write the story yourself or they'll write it about you. The laws obey the existing narrative, so if you allow worthless people to control that, your world—*the* world—might come crashing down. This is precisely why he is promoting an initiative to reclaim the *lligallos*, the paths which historically were used by nomadic cattle. Talking about the *lligallos* will make it easier to talk about the sheep, the goats, and the bulls and cows that have played a key role in transforming the delta through preserving its biodiversity, dispersing seeds, keeping the grasses under control, and connecting some towns with others. Pablo aspires to design a *lligallo* trade route: a local version of the Silk Road, though instead of wild horses and camels, the protagonists here in the delta will be bulls. Initiatives like this are seeing much success in France, and it seems as though here the conditions are finally ripe for planting them. Pablo is unifying several diverse groups, all of whom see the animal's value as much more than the simple labels many have given it. The issue, of course, is time.

Let's be honest, though: Xènia isn't taking it well. She blames Pablo for having succumbed to his old tendencies, for putting the bulls ahead of her and the kids on his list of priorities. And she doesn't know how the money is being managed, since there never seems to be anything extra for taking a vacation, for taking a break, even a little getaway to a movie or a concert, lest anything mess with the damn daily routines at the corral. Because more than anything he wants his mother and siblings to see him as perpetuating the Bernabé legacy. If he has two quarters to rub together, his first thought is to reinvest them in the bulls. She can't live like this. That's what she's telling him. And yet he still presses her to wait it out. The Illa has garnered them some good publicity, and soon enough they'll receive the permits certifying their work as organic; the *lligallos* are going to be fleshed out, the new corral will be finished within the next few months. And once that whole operation has finally settled into place, they'll have an infinitely more peaceful life. Xènia just has to be patient a little longer. Put herself in his shoes. After all, according to Mateo, the bulls arrived in the delta before rice ever did. This is a pitched battle, one in which each side must defend their space. It's not about negotiating for something; rather, it's that a sizable number of their neighbors are looking to wipe them out. Xènia has seen Pablo sink to his lowest point, but now she's witnessing a resurgence that's on the verge of culminating. If only she can hold on a little longer. Please, Xènia, a little bit longer.

LAND

UNCERTAINTY

THE TEMPERATURE HAS ALREADY gone up high enough to where Dylan has replaced his green overalls with pants and short sleeves. "This is the first time since starting here in Buda that I've come to work without overalls. I just thought, if I'm more comfortable this way, then why not?"

There are fewer and fewer crabs, and most of the ducks have left La Pantena, but dozens of pennants and scarecrows remain stuck in the fields while intermittent sound cannon blasts reverberate in the background. The number of black-winged stilts and western swamphens has dropped by half over the past several days, and the lagoon overlooking the Migjorn is dry.

The harvest is expected to be good, because when the rice flowers were in bloom, it wasn't too hot, preventing fleas from appearing. Now, the grains have taken shape and the danger seems behind us. Since the wind has also been gentle, almost no plants have been blown flat. As soon as the stalks of rice are laden enough with grains that some begin to droop across others, a single gust of wind could knock down an entire field, one plant dragging down the next like dominoes. For the time being, though, the weather is ideal for the plants to remain upright. And for the mosquitoes, which have taken over the world. While they emerge en masse at dusk, during the day it's best not to go near shade or get two meters away from a rice field.

Mateo, Dylan, and company say they don't get bitten, and if they do, they don't even notice. After so many years, their blood simply accepts the mosquitoes' toxic saliva as a familiar substance. In that regard, they're a bit like El Boga, who suggested separating oneself from mosquitoes simply by not thinking about them. Literary characters can indulge in these turns of phrase while I slather myself in aloe vera and sticky creams that, whether by touch or by smell, should drive away these maddening nuisances. Gonzalo and Teresa light scented candles and incense sticks.

To more fully enjoy the sunsets, I waited months for summer's arrival, but I hadn't counted on the mosquitoes, which have initiated me into the underbelly of night in the delta, where winter calls while summer closes in. I find the cold March winds more tolerable than these clouds of insects that force me to go about with long sleeves and a hood, constantly waving a hand in front of my face. Long before nightfall, La Pantena's white front door becomes plastered with mosquitoes to the point where they form a kind of lining. To prevent them from slipping into the house, I dash in, slamming the door behind me, limiting ventilation to the drafty chimney and screened windows.

In exchange for having lost elements of the night, I've gained an appreciation for spiders. Now I want them close by. In the bedroom I sleep with two large, long-legged specimens—*Pholcus phalangioides*, as Mateo would specify—that have woven impressive webs. In the rest of the house, three other spiders have strategically spread silk in various corners, trapping dozens of mosquitoes. I wish I had more. I'm happy every time I see one. It's comforting to know I'm being protected by this animal that I'd once scare off or crush underfoot.

If the spider is my indoor ally, when I'm outside I revere the dragonfly. What a revelation. I was unaware of almost everything about this Anisopteran insect that has colonized rice fields and reedbeds. Once the heat ticked up, the first were bound to come. One here, one there. Then, one day, hundreds or maybe thousands were buzzing in the clutch of reeds leading to the sea. Slender, long-bodied insects circulating around me at high speed. Their sheer quantity was intimidating. Hundreds of animals roughly the size of your pinkie finger, buzzing their front and back wings at the same time—they're the only insect capable of this—surrounding me in all three dimensions, creating a living bubble, and yet not one of them ever came into contact with me. After a few more walks through their passageway, I was able to confirm that the dragonflies would always move aside at the last possible instant, and ever since then, I've enjoyed marveling at the dense mat of insects fanning out before me like the biblical waters before Moses.

I've also never been bitten by a mosquito while passing through a clutch of reeds. That's precisely why there are so many dragonflies here, gorging themselves on their prey of choice. The delta is their ideal buffet. Since they'll often hover in stillness, suspended in the air like a hummingbird, I'll occasionally stop and examine them face to face. Right now I'm in a dragonfly bubble, surrounded by four-colored specimens. Most are red and as big as your index finger. Others are blue with a greenish metallic sheen like the common bluebottle. And then there are the smallest ones of all, which have nearly transparent bodies and whose wings are invisible because of the incredible speed at which they vibrate, giving the insects the appearance of translucent, levitating sticks or magical beings. That's how they hunt: mesmerizing mosquitoes (and bees, flies, butterflies, and moths, but I'm primarily interested in their mosquito work) by creating a hypnotizing optical illusion. The movement of the dragonfly's wings is invisible to the mosquito, so even as it notices something strange, it relaxes enough for the static, semitransparent stick to strike and devour it. The dragonfly symbolizes good luck in the universe of feng shui: that Chinese philosophical system which harmonizes the relationship between the visible and the invisible, teaching ways of living better in both spaces. It helps us to discover unexpected allies like the spider or the dragonfly, and to appreciate the good fortune, such as mine, of having both nearby.

It's important to be aware of how perceptions change depending on the calendar. Passing through dragonfly-occupied airspace is a pleasure on summer afternoons. The dune, on the other hand, no longer serves as winter shelter, being now exposed to the sun. So I've relocated my summer office to the last bank of the river, some thirty meters from the miniature breakwater where the fresh and salt waters merge.

Around four thirty, with a blue scarf encircling my head, I lay out the towel, adjust my sunglasses, and read. Five fishing boats are out on the water, floating far away from one another. A couple of launches have anchored next to the beach while their occupants take a dip. Sometimes, a sightseeing boat putters down the middle of the river with speakers amplifying the guide's explanations: "We've arrived at the mouth of the delta. Out there, the Mediterranean."

I remove my scarf, my glasses, and little by little I ease my way into water warmer than the sea. I swim straight toward the opposite bank, and suddenly I find myself in the center of the river, near where the boats filled with tourists come and project like torpedoes toward the sea. The same thing happened the first time I went for a swim in the river: you have to pay attention, because the current quickly picks up steam the closer you get to the center of the channel, so I start stroking hard back toward my bank. The going is harder than it was before, because the current is roiling. A hint of nervousness creeps into my veins and I swim a bit harder now, though without giving it my all, saving my energy in case things get ugly. I'm closing in on the sand, and soon enough I find my footing . . . even if it's on tiptoes.

I start swimming again. This time horizontal with the shoreline, and with all my senses alert.

The river flows this way and that, yet ever toward the sea, requiring extra attention if you want to maintain a specific course or stay in a safe space. I swim against the current for some time without moving forward: apparently the strength of my body is identical to that of the water flowing in reverse. I summon the strength to pick up the pace and slowly make my way up a stretch of the river.

Every afternoon, I make like an eel, which is how I've come to understand that, if you want to surmount obstacles, if you want to swim upstream, you don't need strength but rather perseverance, calmness, and the ability to seek out the most accessible point of flow. The river's drag is constant, so if you stop, you're gone. If you slacken, you're gone. And if you get lost, it's all the same. Continuous movement, stubbornness, and attention are the secrets of the salmon and the eel. I can almost intuit what it might be like to be a fish.

No matter how little sediment is being transported by the river, the mouth is always murky. The collision between the currents churns up the bottom, mixing minerals and organisms, creating a dark soup that negates diving with a view but invites the imagination to wander. When I dive into the great brown, I care even less about being as short-sighted as Henry Beston. It's utterly impossible to see anything. Shadows of differing sizes crisscross one another at an indeterminate distance without me being able to identify any of them. The disorientation is ideal. I get a deep feeling of the water's temperature, which alternates between waves of cold and swimming pool-like warmth. The motor of a distant boat sounds as though it were no more than ten meters away. At the core of this crossroads, everything is ambiguous and calm: an unstable paradise where I swim blindly, joyfully, completely at the mercy of the underworld. The thing that almost brushed past my leg might have been El Boga's golden dorado.

Down here, I forget to breathe. I forget about the weight of my own body, which moves effortlessly through a compact space lacking any fissures or finery. It's like being inside a color. It's strange, because the more I expose myself to the elements, the less I worry about my body, which has become a simple tool for collecting thoughts. It's strange, also, because I'm putting myself through a physically demanding time here and yet it never feels exhausting. No matter how much I walk or swim or pedal, I always feel as though I can do more. Tension has left my body and I can no longer gauge my own strength, which is now expressed in a way previously unknown to me. I eel my way through the great brown, immersed in a lightness that seems like weakness yet is quite the opposite. I've never felt so ethereal, so feather-like. So happily vulnerable to an adoptive space. A hundred seagulls line the shore, the water dragging them toward the sea like a drifting ship. Maybe it's possible to live like this, to live in luscious, unstable paradises as we are. And to live well. Just maybe.

Karen Pineda has managed to do so. She knows the delta is even more sensual in the summer, even though Mateo doesn't like swimming, making it all but impossible for him to flash those beautiful, toned mountain climber's legs of his. Sure, the Ebrencs may be lacking a bit in sass and zest, but she's able to live here peacefully, something few truly appreciate. Her priority is living. There are those who apparently aren't aware of what it means to live. And it's not that Karen is smarter or more mature than anyone else, but she was born with tuberculosis, and everyone had given her up as dead when her father, his knees buckling, began the ten-kilometer walk from Bucaramanga to Girón to ask the virgin to save his little daughter. Yet here she is, the miracle girl paired with a man from the delta who'll take her to the doctor at the slightest hint of poor health. A man who buys her perfumes and creams and who's a grouch on occasion, but who's also someone who knows how to enjoy things. All she needs to do is convince him to leave Buda for good.

Occasionally Mateo will reproach her, claiming she doesn't understand how the island can have too much sentimental value to walk away from. Ha! If there's anything Karen learned from Colombia, it's the importance of letting go of what is near and dear to you so you might live better. When they talk about standing up and fighting for what's right, it makes her want to tell her story from start to finish, beginning with how she helped her father sell lottery tickets and ending with the advice she has to offer Mateo in hope of getting him out from under all the many problems the island is causing him . . . or that he thinks it's causing him. Because, to a certain extent, we tend to find the problems we seek. You're not going to strike it rich every day, fine, but with every experience you're left with something that will help you keep moving forward. For example, her father sold lottery tickets but never won anything, never hit on a single number. But he also never cheated his way to a win, never took advantage of a business others were liquidating through scams and racketeering. From that Karen concluded that, even if luck wasn't favoring her family, she should be respected, especially in the poorest areas of rural Colombia, where scheming and hustling were so normal that even her brother smuggled whiskey and chocolate made from the finest cacao through jungles controlled by guerrillas. Now that's risk, that's poverty, that's courage. That's where she comes from. Getting pregnant at nineteen by some wonderful guy named Rodolfo is a serious problem if you're not married . . . So much so that, to ensure her father and uncles didn't kill the boy, they fled to her mother-in-law's house in the country and eloped.

The hardest thing about that time was not being able to take the police entrance exam. All her uncles were members of the force, and she'd looked up to them ever since she was little, but to enlist you have to be single and child-free. She considered lying on the application, though quickly ruled that out, figuring it was no way to start a career in such a profession. It was almost better that way, because when Rodolfo took a job at an after-hours pool hall, he started drinking heavily, and it could have easily been herself slapping handcuffs on him some day. They split up, and Karen's mother-in-law helped raise the baby.

Then came another idyll: the impossibility of getting anywhere in Colombia, the proposal from her brother-in-law who had emigrated to Spain to work in L'Ampolla, the realization that, in Europe, she might rekindle her wishful thinking, and the painful farewell to her daughter and her mother-in-law . . . the person who had helped her more than any other in her life.

In L'Ampolla she soon found work as a server and began a relationship with Damián, the father of her second child. There, she felt as though she'd finally made it. She had a home in a small town seemingly tailored to her needs, she slept with the windows and doors open without fearing for her safety, and her wages were such that she was sending money back to her mother-in-law until she had enough to come to Spain, daughter in tow. Until one day when she returned home to find Damián in a situation so embarrassing it gives her the shivers. Well then. Just when she thought she was finally free from paramilitary groups and narcotraffickers, she found herself with . . . with . . . Well, she doesn't even want to think about that image, that damn scene there in the living room.

"I'd rather survive on bread and water than stay in this house," Karen said.

Karen qualified for public housing, and settled into an apartment on New Year's Eve of 2008. That year, people were talking about a major crisis which apparently was affecting everyone, but for her it represented the beginning of a new day of true autonomy and, therefore, simple freedom. To put it in perspective, it was the equivalent of Mateo's Zen period. Instead of reading Buddhist tomes, Karen was taking care of older people and cleaning homes, and that was when she felt empowered, like she was finally taking charge of her present situation. That's when she started working at El Mas. Like her other colleagues, she did a little bit of everything, and she didn't think too highly of her boss. She may have even scared him a bit. This man was caught somewhere between serious and shy, and he basically ruled through the use of buzzwords. It was as if he were a little ogre engrossed in the island; every time he opened his mouth the word Buda came out, and a rant about how it was under constant attack from politicians, how it was a natural wonder, and so on and so forth. Sure, Buda is fine, it's pretty enough, but wow. Karen comes from the Amazon rainforest, from the most colorful of flora, where there are farms so vast they can't be harvested in a single day, so she's found the island disappointing. Before setting foot on it for the first time, it was described to her as an immense region of pastures and animals, so she imagined cattle, and she's a fan of farm-fresh milk, but the day she arrived on the island she discovered there wasn't a cow to be found. Only rice. And the ogre. Not that it mattered much to her, because she liked El Mas and her colleagues as well, especially Susi, with whom she joked and laughed a lot while they cooked and cleaned. And Dylan was very kind, offering to fix anything that broke down, bring a cord of wood for the fire, even explaining everything from how they built the hunting *joques*—stands built along the edge of the lagoon with wooden slats and thatched palm roofs—to how much a kilo of eels goes for at the market. What they didn't talk about was Mateo. Nobody knew much about the boss. They all figured he was either married or involved with someone on the outside, because he was constantly traveling to Logroño. They joked about whether he'd ever had something with Simona, since they were always seeing them together, because no matter how settled the supervisor seemed, no matter how asexual she may have appeared, flesh is flesh, and stranger things have happened. In any case, he knew more about them than they did about him, particularly Karen, whom he'd occasionally ask questions. One day, Mateo strolled into the kitchen, and after the standard preamble asked her how many children she had.

"You have all these questions for me, and I still don't know anything about you," Karen responded.

Considering the magnitude of the island and its uniqueness in the delta, she was surprised that, after fourteen years, she'd hardly heard any chatter about either Mateo or his family.

"What do you want to know?"

"Whether you're married, divorced, or what?" Mateo looked at her like a little ogre caught in the headlights. After a brief silence, the boss changed the topic.

Susi was so certain Mateo had been paying special attention to Karen that, on the boss's birthday, she suggested she do something a little "mischievous." Karen's ears pricked up: she sent Mateo a birthday greeting on WhatsApp, but also encouraged him to figure out who the sender was, since he didn't have her number saved in his phone. The ensuing game lasted several days, during which Mateo guessed so many names he must have thought himself an expert womanizer. He was finally able to identify the culprit when, in one of the messages, Karen used the word *cariño*. Nobody in the delta, especially the Gallarts, would have used that term akin to "honey" or "darling." They got a good laugh out of how long the mystery had gone on, they flirted jokily, and then, one afternoon, when Karen was out for a walk with her daughter, they ran into one another on a town street. He was eating a piece of sponge cake and offered a bite to the girl. A small slice of cake, but such gestures say a lot about the people, their generosity, and even their intentions . . . which became even clearer to Karen when one day she saw Mateo walk into the bar where she worked part-time. He was carrying a laptop and wearing hiking boots and shorts that showed off those legs she liked so much.

"What are you doing here?" Karen asked.

"Just a little bit of work."

"Work? No, you're here to see me."

As Mateo is apt to say, the romance between Beauty and the Beast takes off there. They started by meeting clandestinely every day at dusk on the riverbank because Mateo didn't want word to get out that they were mixing work and pleasure. The river to which Karen had gone many times to cry after her separation from Damián, to curse her bad luck with men or the loneliness and effort involved in raising two children in a country not her own, growing ever more concerned about how she'd ever be able to face the future, was the same one now offering her deliciously intimate moments with a man who had not only taken a serious interest in her but was also offering her a salary. Maybe that was the winning lottery ticket. Getting involved with the boss might not be the most prudent thing to do, might not be the most lucrative of payouts, but she had grown fond of the little ogre and his island. Mateo seemed like a decent man of stout beliefs, and not only had he been smart enough to figure out where Karen lived, he also brought her bunches of grapes and other little gifts without ever going overboard. He was always griping about something, sure, that's how he is, but when he was with her, he seemed to grumble less about the world, wanting instead to dedicate himself to her happiness. Feeling that desire excited her—how can I put this?—in every sense of the term. There aren't too many men out there wanting to make you happy in life but who also know how to separate themselves. Because there's always the risk of keeping too much distance.

Despite their obvious attraction, their interests were so varied that they planned a day trip so each would have their needs met. In the morning they went on an excursion into the mountains, and in the afternoon they went to the theater to see a movie of her choice. They had dinner at a restaurant in La Ràpita whose menu should appeal to both of them, though Karen found it a bit too elegant. By this point, they had each gleaned key information about one another. Mateo knew that the way to Karen's heart was through her stomach, which is why, before heading for the restaurant, he told her: "You might not fall in love with me tonight, but you'll fall in love with the place we're going."

And Karen had been told Mateo had an apartment in Cala Nova. "Tell him to show it to you," Susana had encouraged her.

Despite the servers' excessive attentiveness, dinner went as well as the day had gone. Karen told him about the older folks she was caring for, and about how surprised she was by the care afforded to the older population in Spain, or at least in the delta. There it seemed (and, to her, still seems) that many children are so self-centered that they tend to look after their aging parents based on how they might benefit from them. She also told him that she appreciated the respect Mateo had shown her, because many men will look at a divorcée and immediately assume she's about to spread her legs.

"And you?" she asked her boss. "What's going on? You live alone like a scared puppy."

"So do you."

"Well, I have my daughters. And I've always got people around me."

Mateo talked with her about her separation and about the island. And while it was sensitive information, Karen isn't the sort of person who dwells on nostalgia and pain. Besides, she had something else on her mind.

"Show me your apartment in Cala Nova."

Sometimes one has to be a bit bold, especially when dealing with overly polite men. They brought chilled cava and grapes back to the apartment; Mateo associated them with pleasure. Each has their own devotions, and Karen respects most of them, but his dislike of kissing on the lips . . . Well, that kind of primness is how you turn into a little old ogre.

"I'll show you one of my kisses," Karen told him. She brought her lips close to those of the man who had practiced Zen Buddhism, knew how to raise prawns, collected lepidopterans, and kept a snake as a pet on the expansive island which he oversaw, but who, in all honesty, had never been kissed like this. It was such a . . . different sort of kiss. From some other place. Something new, a breath of fresh air that somehow got Mateo moving, maybe even got him to shed his skin. In any case, it increased the charm.

Some say that, ever since Mateo has been with Karen, he's seemed like a different man. Not when he talks about Buda; no, when it comes to that topic he's still the same as he's always been. But with other issues he seems more relaxed, less stern, more willing to adjust his stance. He himself slipped Karen one of those apparently conclusive lines: "You've gotten me out of the swamp."

The romance also gave rise to some overelaborate situations, like the way Susi and her companions started referring to her as "señora." She told them to stop kidding around, but since reconciling her work and love lives didn't seem sustainable, she bid farewell to Buda. Nowadays, she almost never sets foot on the island. It's her partner's job now, and that's that. There comes a point where boundaries need to be established when certain things are better left unmixed.

Since then, Karen has focused on caring for older people, two of whom she's grown so close with that she carries photos of them in her purse. But she's still in tune with daily life on the island . . . with Mateo, it couldn't be any other way. Buda is there, always present, in such an invasive way that it weighs heavily on the head and the health of her dear little ogre. Karen doesn't deny that Mateo is in the right with his claims and complaints, because—in addition to the stories he's told her, which often sound incredulous yet have been legally confirmed by attorneys—she's gone to meetings with him and seen people acting exactly as he's described. Like that time she was out with an arm injury, so she attended one such event and saw it all with crystalline clarity. She had no standing there, no vested interest. To get through the morning event, she simply kept quiet. What she did was sit and study every single person there. She watched how they moved, how they exchanged looks with one another. And as she was leaving, she said to Mateo: "Don't you see it? They're all playing you. Nobody is going to lift a finger to help Buda or the delta, cariño. Not even the Taula d'Acords. I don't have any confidence in any of them. It's all a bunch of blah blah blah."

Karen ended up just as outraged as Mateo was, having seen with her own eyes the posturing that made her think of deeply secretive, cloak-and-dagger operations like guerrillas and the Mafia. The proof that there's no solution. Because the interests of the people involved outweigh all the good intentions in the world. Now she's seen things as they truly are, she looks back and is astonished at how deeply naive she was when she arrived in the delta and how prudent she's become. But guerrilla tactics and Mafia-style dealings aren't identical in their approach. It's one thing to go out and cause harm in broad daylight, and something entirely different to commit evil acts in the shadows. They're so different that, there in a European delta, she felt ingenuous. The problem is that if you get involved in that story, if you see the faces of the people whose hands are dirty, it's all over. You can't go back, you can't ignore it. Not only are these people causing harm, but they're also getting away with it, and you can't ignore this. There are so many scams it makes you sick, honestly, and if for whatever reason you get the idea you can fix something, then you get yourself caught up in looking for solutions you're not going to find, because if Mateo hasn't already found them . . . The delta has completely consumed Mateo, extracting everything else from him, which is why he's often on the phone during dinner, why he's not walking with her so often, having surrendered himself to a mournful monotony whose consequences are tachycardia, muscle spasms, diabetes, not to mention those inordinate outbursts, the heated fits of rage that all but bring him to his knees. He was once a stout mountaineer, and now he barely even goes hiking. The one thing he never misses is Mass, because if he misses it he'll die, but also because he's a bit like her, praying for help, and help is always needed. But prayers aren't solving Buda's problems: its problems are getting worse.

The other day, an environmentalist snuck her way onto the island. When they caught her, she said she was there to conduct a census. So why hadn't she asked permission to access Buda? She sped off, burning rubber, and Simona had to chase her down in search of explanations. That led to a major argument, which wasn't much of a surprise, considering that this particular environmentalist harbors a particular hatred for Buda. She's always boycotting whatever Mateo proposes, and she's also on the supervisor's most-wanted list. It doesn't take much to set Mateo off, and if you put an intrusive environmentalist in front of him . . . Well, Simona isn't going to play the role of peacemaker in that story. Absolutely not.

Karen thinks Mateo's decision to hire Artur was a good one for Buda. Lately, Quim and Dylan have been complaining more about Simona, and while Artur is still learning the ropes, having Mateo's son-in-law on the farm must ease the supervisor's anxieties a bit. Karen appreciates the sheer amount of work Simona has on her shoulders, but her nature comes across as excessive in a place where excess is the norm. Plus, she can't take even a mild rebuke. She's lucky Mateo not only has patience in spades, but also is the type of person who turns one cheek and then the other. Maybe that's why he keeps Simona around: so she can express authority in a more emphatic way and defend the property by chasing you off with her truck when necessary. Karen is used to displays of masculinity and even appreciates some of them, especially when they come from a woman—her aspirations of being a cop may have influenced her appreciation for brusqueness—but she finds this woman's exhibitions overwhelming. And she doesn't want so much resentment and ill will infecting her little ogre, who already has enough to deal with between coastal regression and mafiosos. And to think that, all joking aside, she seriously found herself wondering whether he'd ever hooked up with Simona. She even hinted at the possibility once: how did that go for you? It was an open-ended question, but the look on Karen's face gave her away and Mateo burst out laughing so hard he almost choked.

As if tensions weren't running high enough, a couple of Mateo's cousins showed up a couple of weeks ago, demanding to see Buda's accounting records. They spent the day inquiring as to where the diesel was being bought, which hunter paid for the *joca* and who was an invited guest, how many crabs and sea bass had been sold and at what price . . . a litany of details repeated ad nauseam every year and whose repetition inevitably ends in exhaustion and shambles because some disgruntled cousin or brother has convinced themselves that something should have been done differently. Honestly, at this point, do they need to complicate their lives like this? Karen can clearly envision Mateo separating himself from Buda. He'd suffer a bit at first, crying over a lost love, as the song goes, but then he'd discover the blessings of freedom. As long as he remains entrenched in battle, though, his personality is starting to sour again. We're sliding backward, Karen sometimes thinks.

And while Natalia feels the same, Karen can't count on her. Maybe one day. For now, they don't have the right chemistry. Often she thinks the problem isn't with Natalia herself but with the way parents and children in Spain relate to each other, with children always being more attentive to what their parents can do for them than what they can offer their parents. The parents keep giving and giving and giving . . . until when? It's also true that the reality of life in the delta cannot be directly compared with Colombia, that such a comparison would be unduly unfair. Perhaps time itself will offer a solution. What's not in dispute here is that they're all adults, and that everyone is dealing with their own issues . . . which often include their families.

Fortunately, none of that keeps Karen up at night. Literally. She sleeps for eight hours, no matter what happens. Nothing upsets her. Ever. When the sun goes down, she can be ranting, raving, bawling, whatever you want, but when it's time to go to bed, she closes her eyes, and that's all. See you in the morning.

"Nobody can make me suffer. Absolutely not. I've got my ego to protect me," Karen says, though she bolsters her defenses by always carrying with her some lucky pebbles and the image of a virgin she found one day while out for a walk. She doesn't know which virgin it is—she believes it's well loved in Andalusia—and while she recently went on a pilgrimage there, the enigma of this particular virgin continues.

Another one of Karen's tricks to getting a perfect night's sleep is to go shopping in Tarragona. She's an expert in how to alleviate tension and reduce stress through shoes and bags. It's an infallible sedative, and, well, she also enjoys the privilege of now having two sisters, a nephew, and a niece in the delta, and with her South American family nearby, she can better weather the emotional swings at the Gallart household. All her needs are completely covered, though it's true that lately she's been feeling a bit more anxious than normal because she suffered a significant setback: a phone call from Colombia letting her know that her brother had been stricken with COVID-19 and was near death. She immediately flew back there and settled in the city to be near to him, even though she couldn't physically be at his side owing to quarantine restrictions.

Since her mother was in the jungle region, she couldn't see her either. People were dying at such a rate that, in the streets, cardboard coffins were being put together, something her brother would never be subjected to not only because she'd spend whatever was necessary to preserve his dignity but also because, against all odds, he slowly began to recover. It was then, though, and just as unexpectedly, that her mother fell ill.

When Karen went to the hospital, she was denied an oxygen tank: "We don't have enough to go around, and there's a young man who needs it now."

"Are you telling me they're choosing to save one person instead of another?"

"If you were the patient, you'd get the oxygen," the nurse replied. "Your mother is an elderly woman, she's lived a good life, and we have to prioritize those who still have a long path ahead of them."

Karen's mother died in June. She returned to the delta immersed in a cloud of sadness that still shadows her whenever she thinks about how odd it is when certain moments come together: her mother dying as Natalia was announcing that she would be a mother for the second time.

Night falls. Everything appears exactly as it is in the colors of both dawn and dusk. The virtues of balance are captured when the light is exactly right, illuminating the nuances, the wrinkles and smoothness, proffering a glint of the truth that brings peace with it. With a bit of luck, it can also remind us of the few things that matter as much as or more than food. One is to have shelter. The dung beetle's rolling ball, the flamingo's lagoons, the red crab's mole-like tunnels, and La Casa de la Pantena are all housing complexes of varying architectures into which unexpected tenants will sometimes appear. Like the one announcing its presence on my roof.

When I heard it for the first time, I was startled, not because its footsteps were any louder than those of the usual birds but because this animal was moving so quickly my first thought was of a hungry mammal on the hunt. Now it has stopped. Maybe, when it heard me come home, it grew wary before curling up in a ball of alertness. This presence is a strange one, because birds don't normally perch on rooftops at night. We both wait in silence.

The animal moves again, and—as if I wasn't already sufficiently startled—I now realize the animal isn't outside the house but inside. I notice a few droppings on the higher shelves and elevated baseboards. When the intruder moves again, from the way it scurries I conclude that it's a lizard that's set up shop in the irregularities of the chipboard insulation. I settle into a chair, hoping to locate its position overhead. It moves. Slower than before. Advances toward the large window that overlooks the reeds, until it pokes its head through a hole in the stucco. It is, indeed, a lizard. A big one, though not as large as its steps had suggested.

In the distance, sound cannons can be heard as we tie off pincers for the final time this year. It's August 18. The cat's claws are retracted and dry like the plants and shrubs along the edge of the porch.

"I'm going to be a father again," Artur announces.

I congratulate him with a thump on the back.

Dylan already knew. "I've seen country folks with more than a dozen kids," the Peruvian says. "Back in the day, there wasn't any money to earn, but there was plenty of food to go around."

He snatches a crab from the barrel, pinching the left claw so Artur can tie it with a rubber band.

"Back then, people weren't thinking about sales," Dylan continues. "You dropped off your leftovers at the neighbor's house, and your neighbor did the same for you. Now, people would rather watch their neighbor's fish rot than help them out. Now they're all scumbags who only pay attention to their neighbors so they can outdo them to the point where they end up with nothing. You've got an Audi or a Mercedes? I'll buy a private jet. That's how it goes."

He tosses the cinched crab into the basket for the males and grabs another.

"Here we've released as much as four hundred kilos of fish back into the water. When I asked why, they told me it's because if the market is loaded with fish, people pay less."

"Well, all that could change," I say with a grin. "You're the boss now."

Dylan takes his eyes off the claws and focuses them on me. "Yeah, I'm the boss," he says with a laugh. "Well, I'm not coming to work tomorrow since I've got a doctor's appointment and they won't be able to fish, so, yeah, I guess I'm sorta like a boss."

Quim pulls up in a pickup to haul the last shipment of crabs off to market. He lights up a cigarette while Dylan and Artur finish tying off the final few. "I love the summer," he says. "Girls in skimpy clothes are fine by me."

We all laugh.

"The Mestres are gonna have to harvest soon," Quim observes, looking out across the fields.

There are rows where the rice stalks are doubled over from the weight of the grains. Even a gentle breeze could knock down the mature plants, prime for picking.

When they finish tying off the last claw, they set the crabs in trays, weigh them on the scale next to the porch door, load them into the trailer hitched to the pickup, and drive off. They kick up a trail of dust that follows them down the road straight toward El

Mas, where, they've said, a group of yogis will be settling in this weekend.

The wind has risen, dimming the sunshine. There is scarcely a bird to be heard, their cries diminished even more by a distant purring which turns out to be the engine of a small plane. It flies low, in broad circles, generating a strange sound strong enough to drown out everything else. The engine imposes its overbearing cadence upon the earth below. When it's on the far side of its loop, the plane sounds soft, but its stridency quickly grows, the plane eventually roaring like a monster as it flies over La Pantena. It's spraying pesticides, but it only releases its chemical rain on the fields surrounding Buda, making absolutely sure not to drench anyone. We're in the midst of summer, and who knows how many tourists are scattered across the island.

The poisonous spray targets the mosquito larvae with the goal of reducing the overall population by a few million, providing a bit of relief to humans, but most of all preventing harmful bacteria from growing around the rice. This is a critical time in the growing season, where farmers are looking to stave off any sort of contagion, which is why, along the edges of the fields, they've also driven in some stakes permeated with pheromones that detect the presence of *Pyricularia*, a fast-moving fungus that spreads along the neck of the stalk, causing the infected plant to brown from the stem to the panicle.

Warning stakes, fungicides, pesticides, and various other compounds released from gas-powered vehicles are some of the solutions resulting from a Green Revolution that fed millions of people while simultaneously weakening seeds that were magnificent in their own right until they became a monoculture. Just like crossbreeding wild plants, crossing rice, corn, barley, potatoes, or what have you improves productivity and resistance to predators and diseases. Monocropping weakens them. This maxim is part of Agriculture 101, but since one of the key tenets of the Green Revolution was to ignore the basics and enthrone their own system, the paper on which the original textbooks were printed is now soaked with modern chemicals. From the 1960s through the 1980s, the United States set about revolutionizing world nutrition through free and unabated monocropping, exporting a model which, for example, managed to prevent the demographic explosions in China, India, or Indonesia from leading to widespread famine.

But, soon enough, the price to pay for having saturated the Agriculture 101 textbooks revealed itself in the form of mass infections. In 1970, genetic uniformity resulted in corn blight sweeping across farms at a rate of eighty kilometers a day. It killed off crops with the specific Texas trait, something Robert Barbault explains clearly in *Un éléphant dans un jeu de quilles: l'homme et la biodiversité*: "At that time, in Asia, the rice dwarf virus was devastating rice fields from India to Indonesia, where a high-yield strain had been used. The International Rice Institute was forced to test 6,273 types of rice before finding a variety resistant to this disease: an otherwise unremarkable Indian species, *Oryza nivara*, that had only been discovered by scientists a few years earlier. It was crossbred with the most widespread farmed type, and the resistant hybrid that resulted now covers more than 100,000 square kilometers of Asia's rice fields."

In Buda, there hasn't been any dwarfism nor blight, but *Pyricularia* has forced scientists to crossbreed seeds until they achieve mutations immune to both the fungus and the powerful fungicides. The fortitude of these unnatural freaks has a calming effect on Mateo, while unnerving Luzia Galioto and Joan Barberà, who know resistant strains open the path to insects with immunities of their own: superspecies capable of withstanding increasingly lethal poisons while their existence simultaneously serves as an excuse to continue spraying pesticides from light aircraft. It's as if

Rachel Carson had never existed, as if she hadn't already denounced these abuses committed by the Industry Against the Planet, reminiscent of Agriculture 101 and the warnings about destruction caused by chemistry under the cover of language and euphemisms like "Revolution." As American ecologist Paul Shepard once asked, "Who would want to live in a world that is just not quite fatal?"

Carson and Shepard felt no fondness for small planes like the one currently flying over La Pantena. When it comes to large machines used to spray pesticides, the least harmful to humans is the tractor. Next come the small planes, followed by the worst of all perpetrators, the helicopter, whose rotor wash spreads chemical rain in a scattershot manner. They say tests are being conducted on spraying fields using drones. The European Union bans fumigation by plane, though it allows for certain exceptions, and some must be granted here. Buda hasn't been sprayed from the skies for the past two years because tractors soak the leaves better while using less liquid and being more profitable.

The plane has stopped its circuitous passes.

The birds return to the sky.

Other than spiders and dragonflies, the mosquito's natural predators include the sparrow, a flock of which is currently sweeping a rice field some two hundred meters from La Pantena. Oblivious to the sun, thousands of insects buzz in the humidity while squadrons of sparrows swoop low across the crops, gulping down mosquitoes simply by opening their beaks. The birds cut back and forth in the air at such a dizzying speed that the field looks like a dance floor.

Along the edges of the rice fields and the lagoon, a black-tailed godwit pecks at the mud. A Eurasian reed warbler is making its own rounds while some fifty-odd glossy ibises pass overhead in perfect V-shaped formation. At any rate, whenever I catch myself thinking "wow, it's hot," it's usually because I'm seeing a hoopoe and a few magpies. Two dragonflies are copulating while attached to a sun-bleached reed, the male extending his hyperlong penis, shining in the noonday sun amidst the stench of a clump of algae clogging an irrigation ditch. The ferment is somewhere between tonic and toxic. I clear the algae with an oar. Simona recommends doing it at least twice a day.

When I bike down the road to Sant Jaume, I see Pakistani and Indian workers crouching in fields looking for weeds. They don't hire them in Buda because the Bomba variety of rice grows taller than the J. Sendra and the Argila, and weeding by hand can lead to plenty of drooping plants, so it's not worth the trouble. With the Bomba, you have to trust in its roots, in its autonomy, to keep an eye out for any encroaching fungus, and to make sure the stalks don't droop so much they drown themselves. All that's left is to hope for favorable weather until the fat, healthy grains of rice reach the ideal moisture content of 18 percent, and certainly no more than 21. Beyond that point, you're earning less per kilo. And you must harvest not too soon, not too late, so the product is at its peak.

All of this is on Mateo's mind, which is why he's seemed more tense than usual recently. The rice is already getting heavy, and the approaching harvest isn't looking like what they'd hoped for.

"It'll be more or less the same as last year. Everything was looking okay for a while, but then the nematodes showed up. Maybe there was a problem with the fertilization. If you overfertilize the Bomba, the fungus gets you, and if you underfertilize, the nematodes will. It's really that hard to measure it. You can't go based on predictions, because, well, this is what you get."

The vast fields of gold are occasionally interrupted by small stretches stained brown by the nematodes. The damage doesn't look overly alarming, but as Natalia says, profitability is king here. Survival depends on it, and the microscopic worms have cut into profits to such an extent that Mateo might have to give up on dry planting altogether, since that's what's endured most of the punishment. He'll also have to listen to Natalia again as she repeats her arguments against experimenting with fertilizers, plant proteins, and other products recommended by Simona and her uncle in the interests of who knows what: Dad, listen, if it's not a clear win, then play it safe, because we're the ones risking the euros here. Not them.

For Xènia, the harvest promises to be great. Just look at her, this unique individual from the delta who only got involved in the family's fledgling rice business to help her mother keep the books up to date: now she's earned the respect of a trade union which, until her arrival, seemed exclusive to men, Simona notwithstanding. Buda's supervisor is a unique case. She's almost an extension of Mateo, and when people look at her they see a member of the Gallart family. Simona brings tremendous value, especially when you consider that being a woman doesn't open any doors for you in this business. She alone knows the battles she had to win to earn this position . . . though, to put it bluntly, Mateo is the one who rice farmers fear, respect, and keep a watchful eye on. When Simona was brought on board, people accepted her out of a sense of obedience; sex might not have been the primary factor in her hiring, although it matters somewhat. Xènia, on the other hand, has been accepted despite the drawbacks, the disadvantages, the taboos of being a woman. Not even she knows how to express it. The rice farmers have seen her go and earn her stripes, whereas Simona had responsibility thrust upon her.

Simona's nature would cause problems later on, but right from the start she stepped seamlessly into her role there in the rice fields. In addition to sowing and harvesting, she fished, hunted, barked orders, and got pissed off. That unique attitude of hers, which dispelled the myth of traditional "femininity," allowed many to begin seeing Simona's sex as equivalent to that of their brusquer colleagues. "*Aquesta tia és un home*," they all agreed: that woman's a man. And that was that.

Regardless, Xènia sees Simona's case as so unique that it constitutes a statistical anomaly. This is why she feels that, by establishing herself in rice country as an agricultural entrepreneur, she's opened a more "realistic" path, a feasible option for women looking to prosper in the industry, and to take pride in doing so. And she didn't even intend to do this. Sometimes the winds of fate blow in your favor, and just when Xènia most needed a stable job, the family business had started to do well enough to add more staff.

Xènia was twenty-four, she'd been chipping in since she was sixteen, and after working in the fields picking broccoli, Brussels sprouts, and tomatoes, she ended up as a server at the discotheque where she met Pablo. When her father approached her with the offer, there was little reason to think she'd decline. She wasn't tied down to anything, so when her brother chose to pass on the rice business, Xènia started joining her father in the fields and at meetings.

One day, when they were out in the fields, Xènia walked up to a tractor, only to be rebuffed by a group of guys who told her to forget it, that only men did that kind of thing. So she took the tractor operating test. If Karen couldn't become a police officer, Xènia would redeem her, albeit unwittingly, by getting behind the wheel. On the day of the exam, she was the only woman in attendance. "You want to try this too?" the instructor asked her as she approached the piece of machinery.

"I came here to take the test. What else would I be doing?"

Oddly, when Xènia's father saw how driven she was becoming, he began treating her like a man, appointing her as a family representative to the Consell Rector de la Cambra Arrossera. Being the only woman among eighteen seasoned and strapping farmers is no piece of cake. She wasn't heading out among the rows every day, and she hadn't spent much time in the field, which added to the awkwardness and made it difficult if not impossible for her to engage in certain conversations. But she settled in, she learned, and the men assimilated her. The respect she's garnered has been reinforced, thanks in particular to her efforts to extol the virtues of rice in the delta: she crunches data and generates reports that allow her to confirm Mateo's pessimism whenever the Budero declares that the government's new food policy is going to deal a major blow to rice.

"It wasn't all that long ago they started this massive anti-rice campaign, arguing that it uses up too much water and emits all these greenhouse gases," Mateo states sometimes. "The objective is to take down rice farmers one by one until we're all gone. They want us dead and buried so they can have their precious water and take it up to Barcelona."

Xènia has no idea how accurate Mateo's intricate conspiracy theories are, but what's unquestionable is that the European Union's new Common Agricultural Policy is costing them a hundred euros per hectare, forcing them to cut back on the herbicides they've been using effectively until now while authorizing them to use some expensive pesticides that, as it turns out, are absolutely worthless. The consequences will be immediate: "We'll be producing less and less, and eventually we'll have to stop growing rice altogether because we won't be able to cover our expenses. People are already looking to quit. And then what?"

Better not to think about all of that. But Xènia's adamant that not even the potential bankruptcy of the family business will nudge her toward helping Pablo and the bulls. When it comes to her children, no, that's not going to happen. She's already had it up to here after getting up early on countless mornings to feed the cattle, sling bales of hay, and clean the damn corrals . . . and for what? So he can then give her the same amount of attention?

"By the way, if there's no rice, let's see how many ducks show up," Mateo says. "I'm not a hunter myself, but I make hunting possible for a lot of people. If there weren't any hunters, we wouldn't have a hundred and fifty thousand ducks in the delta. Ninety percent of game species feed here, and that's in addition to the protected ones. What would you rather have? This, or the animals rummaging through the local dump? When you see animals rooting through the garbage, it's because they don't have enough food. And do you know what happens to protected species when they can't eat? They either leave or they go extinct. Yes, human beings throw everything off balance, but within that imbalance there are ways of maintaining order . . . if you want to maintain it."

The hunting business helps sustain rice farming, creating a chain of economic dependencies that, according to some farmers, benefits the ecosystem. Environmentalists, on the other hand, claim that the landowners are mainly interested in making money, and that they compete against one another to attract more birds by dumping sorghum and corn into their fields.

"You have to distinguish between the ecologists and the environmentalists," Mateo says this afternoon, sitting on the porch in front of La Pantena. "Ecologists talk in terms of the way things are. There's no ideology. They understand that there has to be room for everyone here in the delta. For humans, too. The other ones have a radical objective, and they don't care what they have to destroy to achieve it. They live in this parallel world where people don't exist, or if they do, it's only the like-minded ones. Anyone contradicting them is dead wrong."

There's a common refrain in the delta, which a farmer summarized for me: "Let me tell you a story. The story of this ultra-environmentalist who decided to start growing her own rice. She was so radical she planted organic rice on her own environmental organization's property. One year, a large flock of flamingos showed up and settled in the rice field. They looked so pretty and tourists were so drawn to them that she let them stay and didn't plant rice of any kind. When the European Union satellites photographed the delta to identify the fields, they captured some wonderful images of flamingos on the environmentalist's property, but no stalks, so when it came to distributing annual rice subsidies, she didn't receive anything. She went ballistic. She wanted to get paid despite not having grown a grain. This is the situation we're in. If her family's livelihood depended on rice, you know what that environmentalist would have done with those amazing flamingos."

A cannon shot thunders across the island. The birds dispersed across the fields aren't even startled anymore. Meanwhile, four workers board the boat that has been anchored in the channel for months. Simona, the only one upright, punts toward the lagoon. They're on their way to prepare the *joques* and the tubs for hunting season, which begins in October. On this calm afternoon, the boat slips on glassy water between clutches of reeds. A kingfisher slices through the air three meters above the surface.

The boat makes its way across the lagoon toward the tubs, which are located on the stretch of sand and shrubs that divides the Gran Calaix. The four workers, all sporting knee-high waders, disembark and begin covering the hiding place with palm fronds. There was a time only reeds were used, but palms aren't as hard to manipulate and offer the same level of camouflage. The water can reach nearly a meter in depth, so the tubs are slightly deeper than that; they're made from either concrete or polyester that's designed to keep the feet dry, especially in winter. Simona and the three men brush the dust from the stools no one has used since last year, set the decoys on top of them, and seal the tub with a heavy lid to insulate the interior until autumn. They repeat the operation with each tub, watched from afar by birds either floating on the water or flying through the sky.

The tubs are a luxury offered by Buda, because Spain's Sociedad de Cazadores only provides *joques*. This means that hunters are exposed to the elements, including rising waters, and since they require thicker camouflage, they're draped with many more palm fronds. Buda also offers *joques*, which are available for rent at a more reasonable price. Most have enough space to accommodate two shooters.

Simona's team confirms that the wooden benches haven't rotted out and that the palm fronds extending above and around the corners of the structure are secure.

By the time they return to the channel, the sun is already low in the sky. There are still several tubs and *joques* to prepare, but tomorrow work begins on the La Pantena canal, and it's still more than a month until the first shot is fired.

As dusk is falling, I go inside the house to fix dinner, having forgotten I've left the door open. Hundreds of gnats, known here as *rendillas*, let themselves in. Hundreds or perhaps thousands more have attached themselves to the door itself; closing it would mean bringing even more insects into the house, so I resort for the first time to a cloth and the insecticide the workers keep stashed in the laundry room. Even after that, several are still hanging on, or perhaps others have taken their place. I close the door, accepting that a few more will sneak inside.

Dozens of gnats land revoltingly in the middle of the living-room table, mere centimeters from the plate of asparagus with scrambled eggs and unripe garlic. Some dare to raid the food, though the majority either remain still or move about slowly in clumsy little hops. They drown in the glass of water and rest on the napkin. I begin smashing them with paper towels: they make no attempt at escape, but as I'm gradually eliminating them, others appear out of nowhere, descending from all sides, indifferent to the carnage below. For some reason none of them deign to approach the asparagus; they like the table, perhaps due to the light reflecting off the artificial wood grain. But I'm still eating my dinner surrounded by too many gnats. Overhead, the lizard is scurrying around underneath the roofing, and I find myself wondering where it's left today's excrement, which I occasionally find stuck to shelves, ledges, and high up on the walls.

I wake early. The sun rises, tinting the delta saffron. From the porch, I see a tablecloth of spiderwebs spreading out across the fields. The dew hanging from the silk sparkles in the morning light, draping the rice in sequins and pearls. Some are so well outlined by the drops of moisture that they could be necklaces. Hundreds of dragonflies perch on the tips of the reeds silhouetted against the dawn, wings spread wide. As soon as the sun dries them, they'll begin to hunt.

Quim, Dylan, and Artur pull up in a truck filled with massive stakes. They have sobrasada, tuna, and fuet sandwiches for breakfast. When Pol rolls in with the tractor, Quim and Artur hop into the canal, where a flotilla of crabs still moves around.

"If you keep moving, they won't attack," Quim says.

The water is almost up to their armpits. They lash a rope to the top of the first of the stakes lining the canal in front of La Pantena. They tie the other end to the tractor's front-end bucket, which is then raised, pulling the stake from the mire; the bottom of the stake drips with greasy, toxic mud and attached vegetation. The extraction is repeated with the rest of the stakes along the causeway. Next, the men drag fresh stakes to the locations from which the old ones have been uprooted. Quim holds one in place while Pol skillfully maneuvers the bucket directly overhead before dropping it, delivering a sharp and precise blow that sinks the post a few centimeters into the muck.

He hits it again.

And again.

The bucket hammers the head of the stake with the right amount of force, as if it were a pile driver.

When the stake is securely embedded, they move on to the next one. Dylan is in charge of having the stakes ready and supplying tools and gear to the men working in the water. To help it sink better into the muddy bottom, sometimes he'll sharpen the tip of a stake that's been blunted. Looking to help, I drag a few of the posts nearer him, but he immediately furrows his brow and tells me it's best if I don't get involved in case something happens, leaving them with a problem. This is how the day goes.

On Monday, August 30, Buda reclaims its age-old silence. There is no background noise, no launches, no massive speedboats tearing up the water behind the wall of reeds. Swallows and starlings are scattered like confetti across the rice fields until a light rain begins to fall, catching me as I bike along the jetty. As it grows into a downpour, I see Dylan in the distance opening the outlet valves, allowing the excess water to flow more swiftly without flooding the fields. I wait underneath a black poplar for it to die down.

Back on the bike, the island smells of eucalyptus. Simona is coming the opposite way in the truck. She pulls up alongside me. "It's not a good day to be out riding around," she says.

I'm not sure what she's referring to. Apparently, she can see the confusion in my face.

"I saw you were riding your bike around the lagoon," she adds. "With the way it's raining, the tires will kick up the soil and ruin the roads. So don't be riding around there."

My passage has left the slightest of ruts. It certainly isn't damaging anything. "It's just a bike."

"Stay off the roads, okay?"

I continue on toward the sea while Simona fills the gas tank of the truck whose four mud terrain tires weigh twenty times that of my bike. She's on her way back from making her rounds of the lagoon near La Pirenaica, one of my new, off-limits areas.

The following morning, a world the color of steel appears ready to crush us. The men spend the first hour driving stakes into the mud. Simona takes a look at how everything is going before heading off to do something or other. Right on cue, the first peal of thunder unleashes a cloudburst. The copious rain falls reassuringly straight.

"Thunder's harmless," Quim says. "The wind is what causes damage, and there isn't any."

Here, people still think in terms of rice, even if everyone is focused these days on getting ready for hunting and fishing season. Artur is a hunter. The other day he showed us a video in which two enormous and efficient hounds cornered a wild boar. He said he's got the endurance to trail game for a long time, and that if his canteen runs out, he doesn't mind drinking from a puddle. Dylan is already on record as having said he's not much of a hunter. Quim tends to avoid the topic.

"You hunt?"

We're on the porch. Quim and Artur have emerged from the canal because it's hard to work when the rain is coming down in buckets, but also because of the lightning. They're soaked to the skin. Since it appears this storm will be lasting for a while, they change into dry clothes there on the porch. Quim lights a cigarette.

"I've never really liked hunting. Duck, roe deer, pork, *bou* . . . I'm all for that, but I want it on the plate. Already butchered and grilled. Especially with the duck. All I want's the thigh."

"With rice?"

"If I can avoid rice, I avoid it. When I have to eat it, I go for pearl rice. Around here, it's a tough thing to escape. As for me, I'll take pasta with vegetables."

An impressive flash of lightning illuminates the men on the porch.

They tell hunting stories. A few about fishing.

They end up deciding that eel fishing was prohibited here—they gesture toward the canal—because Simona had banned the Sociedad de Pescadores de La Cava from Buda's waters. She'd rather save the catch for people from her own town, although La Cava legally grants fishing permits. So the ban is actually a story of retribution.

"And, in the end, she'll lose the catch," the men agree.

Apparently, this year nobody wants to serve as secretary, which is what around here they call the hunter's assistant: the person who's on the ground solving problems. It pays around a hundred euros a day, but that might not compensate for getting up at four in the morning and going out into the cold only to be yelled at by a woman with an overwhelming sense of self-importance.

"It's getting harder and harder to find secretaries. People don't want to show up and get chewed out. And she'll always be duking it out with Mateo, because Simona wants to hunt and fish while Mateo's telling her to focus on working."

As the stories unfold, the rain picks up, obstreperously machine-gunning the roof. You have to raise your voice to be heard.

"Nothing's gonna get done here until the afternoon," Pol says. "I'm going home to eat."

Since he's leaving Buda by car, I ask if he can drop me off in town so I can do some shopping. The rain is coming down in sheets, blinding our vision to three meters at most. There isn't another car out there, but the road is carpeted in red crabs scuttling across as fast as they can. The storm seems to have summoned them, drawing them out of their burrows and directing them who knows where. They're crossing in both directions, from the canal to the rice field and from the rice field to the canal, flexing their claws to defend themselves from possible aerial attacks before potentially being crushed under the tires of Pol's car. They don't match the gnats in terms of sheer numbers, but they're much larger, and their impressive turnout, combined with their armor-plated clatter, is suggestive of an amphibious invasion. Pol speeds along as if under a clear sky at noon, joking about his relationships with women.

The deluge continues into the night.

The gnats on the door have magically vanished, as if in a puff of smoke, and I'm able to wipe out those remaining on the table from the previous day.

I have dinner by the fire, listening to news reports about flash flooding in the upper part of the delta. The waters have inundated a campsite, cut off two main roads, and swept away vehicles, people, and dogs. The Red Cross has designated the Alcanar civic center as a shelter for anyone who has been displaced. The coastline hasn't been damaged. The waiting continues.

"The moving waters at their priestlike task / Of pure ablution round earth's human shores," wrote Keats, who never knew of climate change, and whom I recall on my dune. I like to venture out at a time when nothing ever happens: that interval between the end of lunch and the beginning of the afternoon when everything comes to a halt. The sun doesn't hit as hard if the wind is blowing and your head is wrapped in a bandanna.

Hundreds of white seagulls undulate like foam atop a copper sea.

Foam.

I don't tend to ask many questions these days, because most of the answers arrived a long time ago. One of them is this: set your reflections aside for a while. Today I'm not thinking about what I see. I'm simply filling myself with images and intuitions until I sense that the waves are dying down, as they always do, while I've grown enough to know that what I'm writing is sea-foam, and that it's beautiful.

I've witnessed the delta dry, inundated, and sprouting.

A sea of seven colors.

The sky reflecting infinity every day.

And yet I still don't know if this island will accept me.

Barry Lopez, American nature writer, wondered about ways of letting a place know that you are present in a way where you're both in a mutual state of occupancy. "The key, I think, is to become vulnerable to a place. If you open yourself up, you can build intimacy," he wrote. Getting hurt by or getting lost in a place allows you to understand it much more deeply. The blood, the pain, and the sense of helplessness focus your thoughts on the forces of the space surrounding you, on the ways you can relate with it so it may offer up its treasures to you.

I don't know if my father ever thought such things, but when he was in the water he'd belly up and float like nobody's business, letting himself be rocked by the waves and tugged along by the current. It's where he found his solace. He swam precariously, head always erect, huffing and puffing along in a hopeless breaststroke reminiscent of a *bou* in distress. But he could spend an astonishing amount of time floating on his back. I haven't seen anyone do a dead man's float like my father. He's a robust, powerfully built man, having spent thousands of hours slinging brushes and scrapers, moving furniture and ladders, and hauling around gallons of paint. And, with age, he's added a belly that, when he reclined in the sea, stood out like a hypnotic islet that only increased my sense of wonder at how it was possible for him to remain supine for so long. Because when I tried to imitate him, I couldn't hold on for long despite my slight build and my best efforts at arching my back, relaxing my legs, and not taking on any water.

Now he no longer bathes in the sea and I've burned several ships, I understand that his secret was to be calm in the place where he wanted to be, letting superior enormous forces which he never questioned take care of him, as they care for the jellyfish and the seaweed. My father the drifter had managed to make himself recognizable by the sea, and if one day he's able to bathe in the Mediterranean again, the sea will welcome him as one of its own, because nature remembers the shapes, the smells, the tastes of the skin—even more if it sweats paint. And it will sway him in its immensity as if it hadn't been years since the last time.

I still have a hard time with that dead man's float. I suppose it has to do with my nature, with my inability to disconnect and fully surrender myself to other forces. But diving into the delta at least allows me to perceive what it feels like to be in limbo, hell's frontier space where there is neither glory nor torment: that neutral void which not even fire can reach.

My drifting dad would close his eyes to the sun while I open mine beneath the murky surface of the water. We are two very different Gabriels, with the common trait that we both like to lay ourselves open and enter into some sort of dialogue with death. He never suggested to me that it was something to fear; we never talked about it at all. For many years, I was terrified of it. Being a child of my vertiginous era, I became obsessed with time, inciting me to take advantage of it, to squeeze it, to profit from it. To achieve something I'm not quite sure of . . . experiences, perhaps. I suppose death stood as the one great obstacle to uncovering the world as the clock ticks down. If dying would prevent me from knowing, then why would I have been given life? I dove headfirst into the world in search of sensations to justify my existence and offer some sort of answer.

Now I have lived, I understand my father's calmness. I understand the primitive wisdom which allowed him to reach this point long before I did. He didn't forge ahead with artificial urgencies. He's known a sun that doesn't scorch, freezing winters that bring snow, and seas without plastic. It's true that, for many years, he ignored the extent to which people's sordidness and morals could reach, and now with the daily tsunamis of stomach-churning news, he's been consumed with a rage he often unleashes in the form of curses. I find myself wondering if he still knows how to float.

The river rejects floaters. It simply sends them toward the sea. As I lie on my back, the current carries me aloft, and I drift along with the logs, the boats, the seaweed, though in my case still alive. I return to a vertical position, facing the open waters, and breaststroke with astonishing ease. I move slowly yet calmly, as if the countercurrent doesn't matter. No matter how long I swim, I won't tire, because the rhythm of the strokes is my own. Periodically, I'll dip beneath the surface, and when I open my eyes in the turbidity it's as if I'm swimming through a dream, or in the fog of a dream that dissipates without leaving any memory in its wake. I separate from my own body, which I govern like never before, driven by a euphoric detachment, something closer to lucidity than joy.

When I emerge from the water, I feel so clean that my trunks bother me. I don't normally expose myself in public, but there's nobody around, and everything is too wild and natural to dissimulate with a bit of cloth.

I strip down.

I reenter the river to swim some more.

Up and down the stream.

Breaststroking keeps me parallel to the shore while the crawl stroke moves me into the midst of the current. I suppose when I put my face in the water, I lose my sense of orientation, and I drift a bit off course. For some, balance is style.

As I head back along the shore, now quite dry, a conclave of plovers scampers a few meters ahead of me, keeping their distance. A flock of seagulls retreats from my path, though they don't fly off. The confidence of these birds suggests that I'm getting close to something, that I'm starting to occupy a space in their world. This suspicion is confirmed when, as I enter the clutch of reeds, two dragonflies collide with me. As if I were a leaf. On an afternoon that arrived with thoughts of death, I ended up skinny-dipping, and the insects no longer recognize me as they did before. I cast a glance toward the sea. From this vantage point, escape routes either don't exist or are very far away, perhaps because there is no need to flee.

RICE

UNTIL RECENTLY, the delta wasn't considered a delta. Historians from Tortosa denied its existence, reducing it to the misleading name of La Ribera, as if an uninhabited immensity worthy of its own name extended little beyond the banks of the river. There were economic reasons for this too. Tortosa was the centerpiece of the delta, the large, regional city through which everything passed, and the increase in small towns and villages outside of this beating heart meant opening up new veins for commerce that undermined Tortosa's power. Naming the delta—even just naming it—meant giving that space a body, making the existence of an alternative more apparent. Hence their efforts to silence it.

But the delta still existed, as did the people who populated it. Given the impossibility of keeping it nameless, Tortosa attempted to taint it, saying "*el delta és fang*" ("the delta is mud"), reducing that space to little more than a terrarium for miserable bands of swamp people literally bogged down by life. As a result, lagoons and swamps, orchards and shacks became ghost towns unvisited by working-class people from Tortosa, giving rise to legends and rumors of voodoo.

It wasn't until the rice boom that they started calling it a delta. At that point, writers began telling stories that evidenced the existence of the people who toiled away in the fields, tending to fig trees and bathing in the river or the sea. They didn't necessarily dedicate many lines to the area. But Benito Pérez Galdós left a record, Ernest

Hemingway wrote a story, Josep Pla contributed a short chapter, Josep Maria Espinàs also got involved in a foray of sorts—riding a contraption that resembled an electric bicycle and which helped him verify the appearance of rice—and Josep Vallverdú was obviously mistaken when he predicted that rice's days were numbered. When it comes to travel books commenting on the delta from the perspective of the sea, Carlos Barral contributed one that included photographs by Xavier Miserachs. And yet all this is so anecdotal, peanuts next to the novels of Sebastià Juan Arbó, who reflected the pride of people who had nothing. This is a common profile when it comes to deltas, vast expanses generally inhabited by castoffs, pirates, criminals, or poor folks of any sort who create domestic microcosms until the minstrel on duty, in this case Arbó, shows up and articulates a transcendent tale. Either that or a luminous idea, like the one proposed by the autochthonous Jaume Vidal, who counted the number of water-covered fields in the delta (12,306 glistening mirrors reflecting the heavens above), proving that it's the world's largest art gallery.

For us outsiders, the delta has existed only since it started being narrated to us. This narration is so recent, the stories that sustain it are so few in number, that in our imagination it's a volatile space, its ground constantly shifting. Its histories haven't been repeated enough, and without repetition, nothing lasts long. When someone finally gets up to tell the story of a place, the danger is that the place will no longer be there, as has happened before. When a narrator needs to consult someone's neighbor regarding a particular incident, it can turn out that both they and their family are long gone. In Buda, many of those who could have kept their stories alive were expelled, the waters have been filled with American crabs, and the lighthouse has been moved so far away that, from certain points of view, the only traditional things left on the island are the indomitable wind, the tenuous land, and Mateo.

Mateo believes that if the lagoons could talk, they'd say the Gallarts are the ones looking after them, even though the land grant now belongs to a state that has abandoned them. An example? It wasn't long ago that the director of the Parc Natural visited the Gran Calaix with Mateo, who showed him a heap of fish killed by the encroaching sea. "Salt water supports the reproduction cycle of the Spanish toothcarp, which is like a Spanish guppy," the director explained.

"That's exactly what he said to me: destroying most of the lagoon's flora and fauna was a good idea if it supported a particular species. What about the rest of the animals? What about biodiversity? You're gonna destroy the entire wetlands to save a single species?"

Mateo affirms that, in and around the delta, there are multiple interests intent on expropriating it. They want the seventeenth-century form of the delta, he says, and they all follow the same, exact script.

"La Administración buys, expropriates, or exchanges lands that the park and the naturalist then manage. Scientists who can't see beyond sediment management dedicate themselves to conducting studies and designing incredibly expensive projects that end up as worthless stacks of paper on dusty shelves."

"So what does La Administración get out of all of this?"

"When the rice fields are gone, La Administración will keep the water rights. That's their big cut. La Administración wants what any other company wants—to do business."

La Administración is the godfather of a Mafia syndicate that involves people from many different strata of society, as described by Karen. Every time she attends a La Taula meeting with Mateo, she leaves feeling equal parts shocked and stunned.

"At first I thought it wasn't that big of a deal," Karen said to him after one of those meetings. "But, wow, are you kidding me?"

She didn't have a full grasp of the breadth and scope of it all, but Mateo has proof. Judges tend to dismiss much of it because, as he says, there are a number of "dons" and bosses who also want to see him overthrown. He's close to proving his case, but at the same time he wouldn't be surprised if they simply ignore his documents that lay bare the extent of the persecution he's been subjected to over the years. To illustrate this, he cites a story he must have told me at least three times since I moved in. It goes back to when he was in his early twenties and La Administración rescinded his family's right to hunt on Buda.

"While we were banned, we found people from the Ministry of the Environment trespassing on our private preserve. I figured there had to be some favors being exchanged, but the fact is, officials from the Parc Natural were serving as guides for invited hunters, shotguns in hand. Their goal was to bring home as many ducks as possible."

Mateo bought an entry-level video camera which he gave to Pedrito Vilaplana and his son so they could document the irregular hunting. He was confident that, being tenant farmers, the Vilaplanas wouldn't be worth a second glance as they slipped stealthily through the reeds.

A few weeks later, Mateo called Josep Vehí, a hunting buddy who hadn't fired a single shot in Buda in four years because of the ban, and suggested he invite the director general of the Departament de Medi Ambient, Magí Font, for some paella at El Mas. Font accepted. In addition to the director general, a number of his local subordinates came as well. When Roberto, Mateo's most vehemently pro-hunting uncle, saw one of the officials who had promoted the ban enter the house, he grabbed him by the lapels and spat a few insults under his breath. The official, flushed, took a seat at the table next to Mateo, at that time still a boy with whom he was on good terms and who must have inspired a certain sense of security in him. When it was time for dessert, Uncle Roberto dropped a bag filled with photographs, cassettes, and videotapes in the center of the table. "Here is documented proof," he said, "that people are hunting in Buda. And we're not the ones doing it."

In the reflected light, the images in the negatives taken by Pedrito and his son appeared in sharp relief.

"Can I keep this?" Font asked, pointing to the bag.

"It's for you."

"Are there copies?"

"No."

Font looked at the Parc Natural staffers. "Care to explain what you've been up to?"

The men lowered their heads in silence.

Shortly after, Buda regained its hunting rights.

That's how the world is. Evidence isn't always enough, though. In the case of the two-bit geologist who had designated the wetland a marsh, Mateo's family had gathered such a mountain of evidence to refute his arguments that the judge agreed with them. But then the machinations that take place so often in court came into play, and the Gallarts and company ended up conceding because, as Mateo says, the decision was ultimately not legal but political. There are too many judges aligned with political parties and businesspeople. That, or they're simply cowards. Mateo has grown so accustomed to losing that he's assumed his position as the lamb. When faced with an unjust ruling, he gets angry at first before capitulating, convinced that "if this same thing happens to anyone else, the story will end like it did in Puerto Hurraco": in a bloodbath.

Since that legendary paella in El Mas, the delta has been governed by different parties, each looking out for themselves and for Barcelona, which is in charge of everything. Because if Mateo is clear about one thing, it's that the people waving environmental flags in Catalonia, mobilizing to defend a few meters of coastline, are the same people who, here, seem to deny climate change and instead simply accept that the sea is flooding not meters but kilometers of land. The delta's fresh water is too succulent a bounty for the big city. This is why they avoid discussing things like coastal regression, arguing instead that the sea is only recouping a space that once belonged to it, that whatever happens is "natural." Natural. What's natural depends on how much you're receiving in grant money and other subsidies.

Of all the places involved in this battle of (natural) space, Buda is going to be the first to fall, but what's more unbearable for Mateo is that La Administración wants him to bend the knee and succumb in silence. There's no way of muzzling him in the delta. He knows too many people here who are also being treated detrimentally, and nobody can completely stifle him because his voice represents others. But beyond Arenal beach and La Ràpita, who will hear his calls for help, for solidarity?

When he realized nobody outside the delta was going to hand him a megaphone, he tried to think up some other way to get his message out. And when asked what he had to offer in return, the answer was simple: rice. In a move to shrug off the yoke of wholesale distributors, he decided to create his own brand: Arroz del Faro.

The competition around here can be intimidating, but Mateo and his childhood friend Paulino Mestres tracked down an Argentine professional who designed some eye-catching bundles made from a blend of paper and plastic. The packaging jumps out at you, the texture encourages you to touch it, and the hodgepodge of materials is so odd it's all but impossible to tell what it's been woven from. And thank goodness for that, because he knows he should be eliminating plastic, which has become increasingly unpopular.

The problem arises when he crunches the numbers; time will tell if he can establish the brand a bit and eventually be able to dispense with the damn plastic. What's good about the packaging is that it incorporates a good amount of information about the type of rice it contains, about the island of Buda. There's even a map situating it in the greater delta, and the lighthouse's illustrated structure forms part of the logo. Every bag is like a tiny cookbook where, in addition to extolling the wonders of rice grown in Buda and showcasing the Bomba variety—which is perfect for paellas, along with a round Marisma grain ideal for creamy rice dishes that cook in thirteen minutes and brothy ones that are done in fifteen—it also highlights the conservation work being done on the island by Garrobud Associats and summarizes the history of the iconic lighthouse, which, when it was built in 1864, was emblematic for being the tallest metallic lighthouse in the world at 51.5 meters and having a beacon that could be seen from twenty nautical miles away. It's about encouraging people to consume history, not just rice. About choosing a brand based on the story it tells. About convincing them that this island has value, that it deserves to last. Which is why, when they hear it will soon be flooded, they wonder why nobody is doing anything more than what's being done in the Amazon rainforest or the Ganges Delta. Seeking out allies among consumers appears to be generating some results.

For consumers to pay attention to the island's history, to listen to what Mateo is intent on telling them, the rice had better be good. Trust is earned through quality offerings. No matter what your ads say, if your product is worthless, nobody with standards will believe your tall promotional tales. And the quality, the audience, and the credit are all at stake here during the days of harvest.

At ten in the morning, the combine sits at the ready, waiting for the dew to fully evaporate and the atmosphere to become dry enough to harvest the rice at the appropriate level of humidity. At 12:12, the massive machine's engine stirs to life alongside the tractor pulling a large trailer known colloquially as a grain-o-vator. The vehicles begin to roll forward in sync.

The force of the combine's sickle blades stirs up waves of rice which are automatically swallowed up by the threshing cylinder, separating the grains from the stalks. After that, the rice is fed through a tube, the mouth of which hangs directly over the grain-o-vator being pulled by the tractor parallel to the combine. Thousands—no, millions—of grains of rice are ejaculated into the grain-o-vator's bin like a white waterfall flowing with an unstoppable vehemence. In the wake of these two machines, the freshly reaped land is soon rife with herons, egrets, and gulls milling about like a cortege of nibblers.

Simona collects a sample of rice, clambers into her truck, and speeds off to the nearest cooperative, where, within the hour, they'll confirm the humidity of the grains to be right at twenty degrees. Spot on. If the minimum amount hadn't yet been reached, the supervisor would have called in the order for the combine to stop. But the humidity level is exactly right. This season, Mateo decided not to introduce the antifungal spray, persuaded in part by the price, though the savings came at a cost when some of the plants became infected. Still, though, the harvest has been a decent one, with the healthy grains coming in full, dense, and tender. Something to be proud of. People will continue associating this rice with something worthwhile, and that's what counts the most, all monetary benefits aside.

He knows each successful harvest boils many people's blood, a fact he enjoys. Why deny it? Doing things well is a much more effective form of revenge than actions that are more spectacular yet anecdotal. Like the persecution of the damned Luzia Galioto, who snuck onto the island this summer without permission. If she had permission, she didn't communicate it as she should have. And after the geologist's scam study, the paella with the Parc Natural representatives at El Mas, the countless prohibitions, the oh-so-many boycotts and embargoes and instances of ostracism that take place whenever there's occasion to do so . . . he's certainly not about to grant some recalcitrant environmentalists even the slimmest benefit of the doubt. If it's a war they want, bring it on. After all, aren't they the ones saying Buda's days are numbered? Well then, let them begin the count.

IN DEFENSE OF SPACE

LUZIA HAS ALREADY STARTED COUNTING. She figures the island has twenty years of life left, though if it were up to her, it would disappear sooner. Because in this day and age, what sense does it make to maintain a rice farm on the seafront by wasting tremendous amounts of electricity on generators connected to dozens of pumps whose sole mission is to facilitate a crop that needs one hundred liters of irrigation water to produce one kilo of rice? Are we aware of the waste this signifies? No matter how much effort Mateo's *iaio* put into it, the rice field may well die. We have to change the dynamics, prioritize the common good. Then again, what does the common good matter to someone who claims to be a champion of diversity but is just another one of those people growing mostly dry, upland rice with the excuse of avoiding apple snails? What they're actually doing is driving away birds like the northern lapwing, which, when it doesn't find its preferred flooded areas, moves on. And then, in winter, the farmers dry the fields because it's more convenient for them. So what do we conclude? That it makes no difference to the birds. Not even the hunters agree with drying up the delta, because the ducks need their fresh water, and if the fields aren't flooded, they may well leave for good.

Since she's interested in birds, in June she went to Buda to conduct a census of the reed bunting, a passerine bird acutely threatened by the deterioration of wetlands and agricultural intensification. Luzia hates visiting Buda, but the island is one of the last paradises of the reed bunting, so after asking permission from the Parc Natural, she told one of her colleagues and two volunteers to prepare for an expedition on the island. A few days later, she was leading investigators into the realm of the unmentionable.

Having crossed the two fantastical kilometers, Luzia became excited again, both because of the beauty and because such an extension allowed her to divine what the entire island would soon be like. She went to the wharf equipped with a pair of binoculars, notebooks, a hat, and all the other equipment a professional ornithologist would carry.

Luzia hasn't had SEO BirdLife or Greenpeace bumper stickers on her car since her side mirrors were ripped off once she was outed as an environmentalist. She wasn't in Buda—the delta in general is a hotbed for radicals—but she was nevertheless left mirrorless for the same reasons one colleague's tires were slashed and a group of gun-wielding hunters forced another to leave a farm. The precautionary act of not labeling her vehicle at least allows her to move about with relative calm, and since she had permission to enter Buda, when the day came to count reed buntings she crossed the Migjorn barrier without warning a soul.

She parked in front of the wharf, entered the clutches of reeds, brandished the birdcall, and began to blow. Every hundred meters or so she'd pause, blow, wait a few minutes for a male to appear, record it in the log, and move on. Nothing makes her happier. This is why she became a scientist: to tread across soil, sand, and wetlands collecting the data that allows her to tell her stories. To conduct science, one must collect data, and to collect data one must be in the field. Which is right where she wants to be.

After some three or so hours of searching the kilometer and a half of the island where the reed bunting lives, they returned to the wharf. A weathered ATV, the sort of thing workers use to move around the island regardless of whether it gets encrusted with dust and salt, was parked on the opposite side of the road, blocking the biologist's vehicle from leaving. Luzia maneuvered a bit, encroaching into the thickets of brush, crushing a few plants while craning her neck out the window, eyes on the ground, focused on not rolling over or getting stuck in the rice field. She managed to avoid the ATV by a couple of millimeters, and departed.

As Luzia left Buda, she cursed whoever had the gall to block the road with their utility vehicle. What right did they think they had . . . Though it wasn't hard to figure who this genius might have been. She deduced that her invisible enemy's intent was to immobilize her for a time, perhaps even observing her from a distance, and that's why she also experienced a sense of euphoria, amplified by the adrenaline of rage, of having slipped away.

She drove back across the two fantastical kilometers, crossing the Migjorn once again, passed the beach, and entered the main roadway. Just before hitting the long straightaway toward Sant Jaume, she saw in her rearview mirror a truck coming at full throttle. Luzia sensed enough of a threat that she pressed down a bit on the accelerator. There was no doubt in her mind that the vehicle, on whose doors the Garrobud logo was clearly visible, was coming for her, because while the SEO BirdLife's car was packed with people, the person that driver was chasing was certainly her. She took her foot off the gas for a second, hesitating. Her pursuer did not. The truck roared up behind her, overtaking before swerving into her lane, forcing her to brake hard and stop as if it were a movie. Simona was behind the wheel.

"You! *Què fas!*" screamed the supervisor as she got out of her car. "What were you doing on the farm? Why didn't you get permission? Who the hell do you think you are?"

Luzia showed Simona the authorization forms. She explained that the census was being conducted throughout the Parc Natural, but that the tracking site could only be accessed via the private part of Buda. That there was nothing to worry about because they hadn't disturbed anything, certainly not any animals. Simona countered by saying that she was the only one who could grant permission, that if she wanted access to the island she had to talk to her, and that Luzia didn't have any respect for anything.

When the pursuer had blown off steam, the biologist returned to her car. I hope the sea floods the island soon enough, she thought as she turned the ignition key with a shudder.

Power, money, and violence help us understand who occupies what spaces, but spaces are also inhabited and defended by telling evocative stories. Venice is so assured of its beauty that it will build all the necessary walls to safeguard itself, and the world will approve. For centuries, the city has been able to narrate its charms to the point where we're convinced we can't allow it to sink. Regardless, one day, in the not-too-distant future, it will succumb, at which point its legendary status will continue as a sunken city, equaling Pompeii, Atlantis, ancient Alexandria, the Yonaguni Monument, Dwarka, or Port Royal. No one will say Venice was a dream because it will continue to exist in millions of memories of those who learned of its bridges, its palaces and pergolas, its cloaked strangers who turn down its alleys, and will remember it as if they had seen it themselves. Venice is a floating story with the endurance of Adam and Eve, and that's why it has always been able to recruit volunteers to fight for its salvation, thus increasing its own legend.

There aren't many places like Venice, but now, with advertising, you can come to believe Venice is anything. It's important to determine the authenticity of a pearl, though it's also true that thinking you have a Venice close by gives you an incentive to investigate further and, even if you discover that maybe it's not such a big deal after all, appreciate its value and talk about it until it eventually becomes a symbol. Nafplion, Suzhou, Recife, Vylkove, Tavira, Ganvié, Udaipur . . . we depend upon storytellers to fill the world with little Venices, and in Barcelona some fantastic ones have appeared, enthroning what Mateo calls a puddle of frogs and what the locals know as La Ricarda, in the Llobregat Delta.

La Ricarda isn't Venice. Of that there's no doubt. Instead it's a 135-hectare estate with a large lagoon surrounded by marshes replete with spiked reeds and pine forests on dunes where spartina grows and where you can find herons, egrets, bitterns, and Kentish plovers, just some of the protected species common to this river mouth at Barcelona's gates. La Ricarda is the penultimate little green corner of a delta that, since the 1950s, has been increasingly encroached upon by factories, apartment complexes, and even some farms, slipping like an islet between the hulking logistical masses of the seaport and the airport. The greeny delta has been losing ground for more than half a century without anyone raising their voice in protest. La Administración, ever a supporter of inertia, recently noted that the opening of a third runway at the airport would involve cutting back another good stretch of wetlands. But La Administración was taken by surprise. Since La Ricarda is next to Barcelona, and since it had become fashionable during the pandemic to talk about climate change, local storytellers (whose population density per square kilometer is impressive) mobilized to oppose the plan. They wrote, filmed, painted, and produced a substantial, coordinated environmental story that turned La Ricarda into a collective icon, despite the private property being owned by the Gomis Bertrand family and including seven historic homes, among them mansions and architectural structures regarded as national cultural assets.

Yes, La Ricarda isn't Venice, but it's mobilizing thousands of people to stop a multimillion-dollar investment. Meanwhile, those clamoring for a much more unobtrusive amount to help them protect a few miles of coastline in the Ebro Delta wonder where that money might be allocated if officials end up not spending it on a third runway. Mateo is convinced it won't go to the island because, even though its bags of rice emblazoned with their lighthouse image can be found on many grocery store and supermarket shelves, Buda is far enough away from any large urban center that most people think of it as little more than a poignant eccentricity.

Mateo also doesn't think the Ebro Delta will receive much support. Most of Spain's wetlands are far from large cities, which, perhaps, is why they're being lost. The majority of storytellers see them as remote: they do not speak of them, nor have they been told about them, and therefore they lack concern for the wetlands and are indifferent to their future. Unless the wetland is in La Ricarda. Which isn't Venice, but nowadays it may as well be. Funny to see the influences of perspective and storytelling. To see how a wetland of 135 hectares can mobilize many more people than a delta of 7,736.

The Gallarts aren't the Gomis Bertrand family, Buda doesn't have seven historic homes, nor is it near an international airport or one of the densest cities in Europe, but Mateo believes that if he could round up a few accomplices to help spread Buda's story beyond L'Ampolla and Camarles, the island could become another Venice. But how, though? Having someone write about Buda after having spent a considerable amount of time there . . . Well, that might work.

Ask Pablo Archer, who has studied the French and knows how the story of a delta is constructed beyond a bag of rice and a lighthouse. Camargue is Pablo's main point of reference because the space in the Rhône Delta is rife with lagoons inhabited by the largest population of flamingos in Europe, by countless Louisiana crabs, and, among other similarities with the Ebrenc environment, it's notable for raising horses and—here's the crux—bulls.

An important nuance: in France, bulls don't carry the same political burdens as in Spain, something which has made it possible for the animal to be valued regardless of ideologies. In Camargue, there are seasonal cattle drives, livestock festivals with music, the old pasture trails are maintained, and bullfights are legal, fostering heated debates that are markedly different from those in Spain, in part because of intellectuals like Matthieu Duperrex, who, while qualifying bullfighting as "a ridiculous yet nevertheless painful pantomime," is also capable of accepting in public the ritual value of that iconoclastic spectacle: "In a world where industrial slaughter is a denial of death, ritual execution has the advantage of lifting the modest veil draped over the objectification of animals. The bull doesn't have a shadow of a chance, but he has a name, a personality. He is *someone*, he is *himself*." Killing *another* is intolerable for Duperrex, though he does believe that the same sacrifice helps remind us of the value of a dignified death in a world bent on denying finality.

Pablo has learned that the Camargue bulls carry stories that spread by word of mouth as legends or fables, that not only are they worth preserving but that they also define the region's character. One of these myths is that of Prouvènço, the male selected as the father of the breed after ranchers crossed their most powerful animals in search of the One Great Stud. They called him Prouvènço because he embodied the resilience of the Provençal language in his strength. It's been said the country revered him as much as the recortadores (Spain's famous acrobats, who perform leaps over bulls in the arena) feared him. In 1909, when the champion among all the Camargue breeds was enjoying the height of his celebrity, his sons gored him in what Duperrex has described as "a Shakespearian patricide, his guts strewn across a mound of clay as if an altar before the nascent dawn."

Pablo envies the discourse they've created in Camargue in defense of the animal that defines his life, which is why, during the hit the Bernabés took upon losing the Russian tourists, and his subsequent depression and separation from Xènia, he spent a troubling amount of time thinking of ways he could explain the bull here. The cattle drives stopped when too many animals were hit and killed while crossing newly built roads. They had been expelled from Buda, their fields had been curtailed, and since legislation has been almost unanimously aligned against them, against their extensive way of life, the fighting bulls of the delta had all but become another farm animal.

Pablo weighed the option of reclaiming the *lligallos*, the Ebrencs' word for the paths historically used by the *bous*, the bullfighting equivalent of sheep-droving roads. To many, the initiative would ring as stale as the words: for plenty of today's city kids, using words like bull and *lligallo* in the same sentence is like talking about Martians. Even worse, perhaps, because it sounds so old-fashioned. And of course it wasn't going to start any revolutions, because reclaiming livestock pathways was already being done in places where herding and grazing were taken seriously, but at least it would introduce the story of the bull from a familiar, friendlier place, one linked to history and the shepherds. Besides, you have to start somewhere, right?

He was beginning to outline the plan for the *lligallos* when the possibility arose of working on an island with an exceptional herd, one that distinguished the space as unique on the planet. Pablo's one for hyperbole, but that's the reality of the situation.

Vinallop is an island in the Ebro River located forty-five minutes from Tortosa. Here, a herd of wild bulls and cows lived without the presence of even a single human. For decades, herders had brought the *bous* to the island to graze. The animals would ford the river and enjoy twenty hectares of absolute freedom among willows, ash trees, and, above all, white poplars: fire trees. After animals were prohibited on Vinallop in 1994, the bulls continued to swim there, but institutional pressure ended up regulating these visits until they were shut down completely. Groups of youngsters took over the island as a place for bonfires and getting drunk, and it was rumored among locals that it had become a virtual whorehouse where the kids would go to get high and hook up.

One day, a rancher brought two wild cows to the island so they could die in peace. Only they weren't dying. They were pregnant.

Their calves were born on Vinallop.

They survived.

And eventually their offspring mated with and impregnated them again.

History is replete with sordid tales of incest, but it's still true that when the authorities contacted Pablo, the island was inhabited by twenty-two animals, and while some scandalized and religiously inclined Ebrencs criticized the "Dantesque spectacle" offered by the island, La Administración, animal activists, bullfighting aficionados, and a majority of informed neighbors believed this was a singular event that needed to be preserved, and that it was important to mobilize.

When a public call for tenders to manage Vinallop went out, several of Pablo's acquaintances encouraged him to apply. One of their arguments was that, despite Pablo being a cattle rancher who had gotten into his fair share of scrapes over the years—after all, when you're working with bulls in the delta, how could one not get into some sort of trouble?—he was good at negotiating. He had a broad outlook on things and a manner of speaking that went beyond simple personal interest, and he could mediate between the animal activists and the bullfighting aficionados who were constantly locking horns because both parties saw the Illa dels Bous as a flag symbolizing their respective causes, and both were taking advantage of the international attention the island was receiving. At the time, both groups were coming to Vinallop with food for the *bous*, showing that both had the same intention: helping the animals. But whenever they encountered one another on the island, fights would ensue.

Pablo was emerging from a gruesome period in his life and didn't want to get involved with another experience that might end up the way the one in Montsià had, with La Administración ordering his herd to be shot from helicopters, leaving the countryside to reek of rotting carcasses all summer long. People who don't know this world can't begin to imagine how traumatizing it is to have your animals killed, bulls and cows you'd named as if they were your children. He didn't want to go through another experience that might end up like that ever again. But it's true that the opportunity to mediate between two radically opposing sides drew him in some way to a noble cause. One not unlike the one his *iaio* had led when he was asked to preside over the local farmers' and ranchers' cooperative at a time when 80 percent of the land was owned by people from outside the delta, several of whom held baron-like status in La Llanada, La Comandanta, and La Isla de Riu. After forty years, Pablo's *iaio*, or rather he and the other members of the cooperative, gleefully managed to get that same percentage of land into the hands of local families. In addition, Illa dels Bous was a high-profile symbol, and if that bet turned out to be a winning one, it could go a long way toward promoting the *lligallo* project.

On Christmas Day 2017, Pablo paid a visit to assess the situation. He found twenty-two *bous*. Regulations required there to be 1.2 animals per hectare, so that number would have to be reduced. The herbage spread out with the anarchy appropriate for a deserted island. The clear birdsong, the quiet approach to the shore, the freedom of the *bous*, and the possibility of taking on a project like this in relative tranquility despite the commotion which was undoubtedly going to be raised on the outside led him to accept this challenge and toss his hat into the ring.

Six candidates were considered. Four presented plans formulated by animal rights entities. Another proposed a business model that combined tourism with local gastronomy. Pablo represented the sixth option, based on his experience with livestock. Assuming these bulls were wild fauna that should be allowed to coexist with people instead of being managed by them, he suggested keeping them as free-range animals while building a holding pen on the island so he and the veterinarian would have a facility to periodically review the animals' well-being. It was all about not altering anything while still offering professional supervision.

In October 2018, while the jury was deliberating, representatives from Medi Ambient called Pablo, asking him to remove a dead cow from the island. The cattle rancher took it as a wink and a nod indicating possibilities. A few weeks later, his proposal was chosen as the winner. In February, he started his work at Vinallop.

And that's why, this morning, shortly after dawn, we're loading fifty kilos of feed into the little outboard boat, which takes on a little bit of water as we cross the Ebro with Chip, Pablo's dog. The river gleams with the day's first light between the greenery of the island and the continental shore. The whirring of the little motor is the only thing ripping through the sylvan silence.

"They can hear the engine, so they know I'm with someone," Pablo says.

Somewhere in that wilderness lived twelve animals. When Pablo first arrived, there were eighteen left, and six had to be eliminated to meet the legal requirements for density. The veterinarian detected high levels of inbreeding among the herd, with a coefficient of between 87 and 92 percent, meaning that the genes of those incestuous *bous* were already deteriorating rapidly. Each animal was examined to determine who would be sacrificed: the one with a lump on the eye, the one with the injured leg, the one with the hernia. And then the three oldest. Six in all. Then, even though the males weren't fit for reproduction, they were sterilized. The twelve survivors were chipped and marked with ear tags. They're the ones we'll attempt to locate amidst the fallen trees and undergrowth.

To bring them all together, Pablo uses a couple of tactics. One consists of spreading the contents of a feed bag behind him as he walks. The smell of food will immediately attract even the most ill-tempered of beasts. The other goes by the name of Chip, and is the option he's using today.

First, we take a walk around the island. There are stretches of hermetic forest. The treetops screen out sunlight while the humidity soaks through, darkening the wooden boards of the holding pen. Sometimes Pablo lets out a few cries and shouts: his way of communicating with the *bous*, alerting them of our presence so they'll keep their distance. They probably wouldn't bother to inquire, but one never knows, and it's always polite to say hello.

We traverse the island, our boots sinking into a multiplicity of fresh, decaying leaves. Pablo shoots a glance at the shore where the herd usually likes to stay. They're not there.

"Go get 'em, Chip!"

Chip takes off in the opposite direction. We follow him across the island to a particularly entangled area where the density of moss and foliage has been thickened by fallen branches. We force our way through thickets and brambles, vault over toppled tree trunks. In the distance, two black shadows pass fleetingly before us.

"They're here."

We hear and feel the trotting of several beasts, enough to make the island tremble. They're less than a hundred meters away, crossing a small lake. Their legs splash as they run, creating a veil of water that only adds to the vegetative curtain separating us from them. The bulls situate themselves on the opposite side of the lake.

We are so cloistered we can't see the herd as a whole, segmented as it is by the undergrowth. Pablo holds Chip's collar while he coos at the *bous* as we make our way deeper into the island's interior. They continue to surround the edges of the lake until they finally appear before us, some forty meters away. Two massive, downed logs are all that separate us from them.

We all look at each other while Pablo continues his calls.

The logs don't seem like they could be easily jumped, but they're still only logs, and we've all seen images of bulls leaping over a burladero in the ring, pursuing the poor matador hiding behind it.

When the bulls have departed, Pablo and Chip accompany me to the last tree standing before a large, open field. "Wait here," Pablo says. "Don't move. There's nothing to worry about. If you don't move, they'll just pass right on by."

Pablo and Chip go out again in search of the herd. I can sense where he is from the calls he lets out. Maybe five minutes later, the rancher appears on the other edge of the clearing while, a little farther out, not far from the shore, the bulls gallop past with little Chip following close behind. Pablo brings up the rear. They all disappear back into the forest. Several minutes go by, during which time I hear voices ringing out behind the brush. Then Pablo reemerges at the clearing at the same instant that twelve massive animals materialize before me. No more than fifty meters away. With nothing but clear terrain between us. Not a single tree or scrub or rock. I evaluate whether I could climb the tree I'm standing under; I look for anything stout enough to serve as harborage. Across the way, Pablo raises his hand, suggesting (I can only assume) I stay where I am. The twelve bulls have aligned themselves in perfect formation, occupying a good part of the plain before them. Pablo grabs Chip, almost parallel with the animals but several meters away, near the edge of the wooded area.

For some reason, one of the bulls moves forward, trotting directly toward me. He then angles his torso slightly and cuts diagonally across the clearing. The other eleven follow, legs churning en masse.

Most are moving in single file, though one or two run parallel to another.

The tremors from that race are now reaching my feet. The animals churn forward like a short, black train, coming within thirty meters of me before thundering down a knoll into another small clearing. From there they continue running, unimpeded, toward the forest, eventually becoming shadows first and then a memory.

Pablo and Chip approach, both as radiant as could be.

"Hey, pretty impressive, right?"

Back on the mainland, Chip lays his muzzle on the bow of the boat and closes his eyes, the wind blowing back his ears. Pablo's hand grips the tiller. How could he want to change anything, now he's enjoying this new life among aquatic bulls? The island has been a gift, perhaps compensation for all he's suffered. And the evidence of his quality work is that the debate surrounding how the *bous* should be cared for, and by whom, has evaporated. That no news is good news. Pablo is demonstrating that it is possible to reach agreements, to look after the bulls as a rancher would, and perhaps even restore the animal's public perception. Who knows if the Illa could be a first step toward promoting the *bou* as an icon of future transformations. Pablo can occasionally get a bit grandiloquent, but he has reason to believe in making significant changes, even with the knowledge that a new day and age may force him to give up certain wishes, like maintaining what some call "La Fiesta." The bullfight.

If it were up to him, he'd legalize another brand of *bou* that would allow him to participate in bullfighting. He has plenty of personal and philosophical arguments with which to defend the existence of this ritual, but he also knows it's neither practical nor socially accepted, not in Catalonia nor in much of Spain. And if he genuinely wants to move the business forward with a certain amount of peace and tranquility—while keeping the waters calm on the home front as well—then the future must involve accepting the new rules of the game. And it's not that big of a sacrifice. Pablo not only loves his animals, he admires them. And in some ways maybe he's starting to come to terms with the logic of those who oppose their unnecessary killing, sensing that he might be able to let go of the passion for bullfighting his *iaio* instilled in him, however distraught he might be by this apparent betrayal. The guardians of the bullfighting tradition are accusing him of buckling under the pressure of the easily manipulated mob, because once you've acknowledged the fighting bull's imminent mortality, it's as if you've drunk the animal rights movement's tincture and started treating the bulls as if they were sheep. The guardians might be right to some degree, but his *iaio* lived in a different era and hardcore bullfighting fans will have to acknowledge that times have changed. If the fighting bull is to live on and be honored by as many people as possible, certain conditions will have to be met.

As much as the bullfighting aficionados blame him for all but putting an end to La Fiesta, Pablo is taking advantage of every legal loophole there is, and while he abides by the ban on bullfighting, he's not given up on the *correbous*, the *embolats*, and especially not the recortadores. And then you have people on the other side of the issue, who have no idea what they're talking about yet are nevertheless berating him and accusing him of profiting off the animals, torturing them, and all that typical sort of . . . well, bullshit. There are many fronts on which he's not ceded ground. On the contrary, his herd is made up of fighting bulls from Navarre and the Ebro valley which he continues to select based on their combativeness, on how hot they run, on how they convey the sense of real danger, which is what counts in terms of the spectacle, of the excitement. Because that's what people want, whether it's here or in China. To be excited. He lives off that stuff. It's why he's devoted himself to cattle ranching: that thread which connects him with the thrill of his ancestors.

During this trip, we debated as we've debated before about the lengths to which animals should be used as a spectacle for humans. After getting a bit heated, he declares, assuredly, "I've written articles and gone on television to defend La Fiesta, but I'm more comfortable defending the *bou* in the fields. In shows where there's no blood. That said, the bull has to earn his keep by working."

He parks in front of the vela where he grazes his herd. He's added a gangplank connected to several elevated walkways to make it easier to pass above the animals and work in less danger. From above, Pablo observes the behavior of each, looking for bravery while still confident that his bulls don't feel the need to attack the muleta, the matador's famous red cape. That they don't have to lower their heads. "A bull that won't bow down is no good with the cape," he says, alluding to bullfights preferring animals who charge with their horns low, almost parallel with the sand, because it looks more spectacular that way. "With a male from the Domecq ranch, a bullfighter can perform somewhere between seventy and ninety passes with the muleta. With the ones from Miura, Victorino, or Fraile, you can expect less."

With the Bernabés' bulls, passes with the cape would be as minimal as they are risky, because these animals attack with their heads high, never losing sight of the target they intend to gore. We're talking about milliseconds, a spark, but still enough to multiply the risk that a sudden turn of the neck could catch even the most skillful matador by surprise and either flip him or, worse, impale him. The first black bull to enter a house is the one that fled the plaza.

The Bernabés seek out wild bulls that won't humble themselves before anything, which is why they provoke increasingly mixed reactions among both the town councils that hire them and the young recortadores who intend to leap over them in the runnings and spectacles. Bravery is a word on everyone's lips, especially those sorts of men who brag of pushing limits and staring down challenges, puffing out their chests and putting their bravura on display for all to see, but when they find themselves face to face with something truly valiant, well . . .

Since 2006, the Bernabés have refreshed their herd by purchasing animals from the breeders Rebomba and José Luis Cuartero, the two official lineages with which they've won several competitions during which the animals' drive and virility were thoroughly tested. And while that seems to somewhat favor signing contracts and garnering prestige at local festivals, lately there have been people suggesting that it might not be entirely necessary to continue with such bullish bulls. Which is understandable, because you attend one of these afternoon shows with your crew or your family, often with children in tow, and the intent is to show off in front of the crowd, run a few times, take a few jumps, and then get in the car to go grab a bite to eat. There aren't many people out there looking for *bous* that are going to present a serious challenge, nor are town councils looking for the afternoon to end in drama. Understandable. But don't then try and make up all these tall tales about balls and bravery when what we're really talking about is a pastime, a circus, or whatever might better suit their bourgeois purposes. Because respecting the animal means conceding to its nature, and, if you're a rancher, establishing conditions where it can develop and grow. This is what Pablo has always tried to do. Respect the animal. Respect its nature. Nature itself. Respect the tradition and legacy that runs five generations deep of not seeing the bull as entertainment to be enjoyed with a spritzer and an olive but rather as an equal, one that presents an honest challenge even today, when such acts are spoiled by chatter from thousands of presumptuous blowhards who brag about things only they have done. Pablo has accepted the end of bullfighting in Catalonia and the growing societal opposition to any sort of festival including bulls, but he's drawn a line in the delta sand beyond which he will not compromise, and that line is marked by the essence of the animal itself. He's not going to domesticate an animal that's wild at heart. He's not going to present an increasingly tamed public "un toro pasado por agua": a soft-boiled bull. He finds this expression amusing, especially considering that delta bulls literally live in wetlands, and that twelve of them inhabit an island.

In thinking of those who prefer to take in their entertainment from the couch, as well as anyone who might be curious enough to peer into this world without the use of adjectives or other intermediaries, he plans to request permission to put up cameras that will broadcast the daily life of the Vinallop bulls on a YouTube channel. He also wants surveillance cameras, because there are a lot of crazy folks out there. And for those venturesome enough to want to enjoy a picnic on the island or leave food for the bulls, he's proposed sectioning off areas where they can disembark safely. It's all about people finally learning a bull's true value, about creating stories where people and animals are able to understand one another. Maybe then someone will also learn that he used to apply St. John's wort oil to the animals' skin before branding them so the wound would heal more quickly, but now he's chipping them all since he doesn't see a reason to sear and scar them. That in November and December they cleanse the cattle with deworming supplements and run blood work to prevent brucellosis, leukosis, and tuberculosis so the cattle can live full, healthy lives and die peacefully of old age. With enough respect, anything is possible. He's even heard talk of a vegan bull ranch in Jaén. He's clearly taken charge of the family business, and he wants to continue adapting it in accordance with his ideas. Anything and everything with respect. And respect means putting them to work. Critics and others unfamiliar with his way of approaching it tend to mock him when he says "work." They say it's a euphemism for the extreme stress the *bous* are made to endure. Pablo, however, is convinced that a bull, like a cow or a dog, feels greater stress living under confinement, going to the vet, or participating in a running, than engaging in an *embolat*. To this day, he has yet to encounter a single bull that has suffered consequences from a performance that lasts no more than fifteen minutes. American, Uruguayan, and Argentinian cowboys ride American rodeo bulls for eight seconds—eight seconds!—and the animalistic discourse is the same. But when he presents such arguments they are ignored, while complaints from animal ethics groups like Prou Correbous spread faster than the commandments of a new religion.

Rebutting the anti-bullfighting propaganda machine has only been possible in recent years by demonstrating that the animal itself rises above all the nattering blather and can take its place by our side, festivals included. In Camargue, there are twenty-nine thousand head of cattle and nine thousand annual festivals. French lawmakers are monitoring bullfighting, which includes the animal's ultimate sacrifice. From Brussels, the European Union seconds this approach, and the Comunitat Valenciana both permits and supports bullfighting while promoting certain Rutas del Bou. Both regions share a desire to establish a *bou* route that would link the two Mediterranean countries.

Pablo knows that today, in Catalonia, this is a utopian dream, but he also knows that, to prevent the fighting bull from disappearing from the face of the earth, it has to be put to work. It must take advantage of phenomena like Vinallop, where insults have fallen silent in some cases and transformed into congratulations in others, establishing the place as a symbol of how things can be done the right way. He's already traversed what's perhaps the most difficult part of the path, he's stepped back from the edge of a precipice or two, and with the Illa he's found something iconic that both supports and illustrates the viability of his strategy, but it will require the kind of time and patience Xènia doesn't seem willing to grant him. He has faith that now she has begun to see and perhaps even appreciate that much of what he has been predicting has come to fruition, though the look in his wife's eyes reflects a weariness that doesn't bode well. She's tired, she'd like to have a few weekends here and there to enjoy like normal people. Those are her words. By normal she means taking the kids on a trip, doing something special once in a while, and by special she means something not involving bulls or rice. Which is fine. But when he suggests they go on a trip together, the two of them, to commemorate their ten years of marriage, she balks. She's not going anywhere without the children.

Sometimes it's too hard for him to understand her. When Xènia gets like this, Pablo considers it unfair, because she seems to have forgotten all the good times they've had together. In any case, they're both used to these blowups, and the island's success has impressed her enough to acknowledge that he's done a decent job. Which means that, for the first time in a while, Xènia is seeing the hard work paying off without the need for Pablo to point it out. The numbers show that at least he's achieving something instead of getting bogged down in administrative entanglements like Mateo, who, no matter how right he may be, seems unable to alter his fate in Buda. Because, among other things, he lacks discretion. A deft touch. Diplomacy, Mateo, diplomacy. Pablo attends the Parc Natural meetings with a voice but not a vote, because they won't allow anyone to seriously represent the *bou* ranchers of the delta. Though at least he stays informed on local issues and sees the stances being taken by those able to vote. And when he hears Mateo in public, often it's painful. Because Pablo supports him when he says that if, as environmentalists claim, nature must run its course, there wouldn't be anyone left in Holland living near the sea, considering that a good part of its coast is full of dikes and polders; with nature running its due course, we should simply blow it all up and let water flood the entire delta. Pablo supports him on this and many other things, but when Mateo speaks his mind, he does it in such a vehement way that eventually people stop listening to him. It doesn't matter what he has to add to the conversation, because they've either tuned him out or come to detest him. It's certainly true that several members of La Taula don't share some of the Budero's arguments, but mostly what they don't share is his tone, and if he were to refine his sense of diplomacy he'd surely be able to achieve something more.

It's not that Pablo once acted the way Mateo does now; he simply recognizes that he expresses himself much more convincingly. At the end of the day, he's his *iaio*'s grandson, a *bou* man from the delta, with everything that entails as a revolutionary, a pariah, a benchmark, and a homeless person with a fighting spirit. Furthermore, Pablo has known both sides of the political spectrum, because while his father's family sympathized with right-wing ideologies, his mother is a left-wing nationalist. While his father was a senior manager at Spanish telecom company Telefónica, his mother was being promoted at the nonprofit Institut d'Estudis Comarcals del Montsià. What the two sides have in common is a visceral rejection of injustice and inequality. So there are times when Pablo feels he's reaped the benefits of having witnessed firsthand how interests are negotiated: the spectacle of the balance of forces required to move nothing less than an entire family forward. Add to that a spirited upbringing that resulted in some memorable disappointments and the teachable moments he accumulated during his many years of poorly calculated outbursts; these more than anything left him with a sense of confusion if not an outright lack of understanding, from which he's molded this moderate nature which allows him to expend the least amount of diplomacy required by decisive circles. Pablo is version 10.0 of his *iaio*. He's not lost an ounce of his Bernabé character. The problem with the restraint that's called for in these modern times, with its damn political correctness, is that sometimes, by the time he gets home, he's tired of restraining himself. He gets more angry than necessary, and the little ones get into spats that, truth be told, could have been avoided. With Xènia he is, shall we say, blunt.

Yesterday Bernat told him that sometimes he turns into an ogre. While Pablo was embarrassed that Bernat said it in front of a stranger (me), he's grateful his son trusts him enough to express his discontent, because that means that things, however imperfect they may be, aren't all that bad. He knows the children's love is unconditional, that they're devoted despite his ogre-like episodes. With Xènia it's something else entirely. Which is why it seems so important to him that his dear figure skater, rice cook, and lover enjoys his success with Vinallop in her own discreet way. That should mean a little more time, a truce that allows him to continue dedicating himself to the *bous* for a few more months without being on the receiving end of too much extra pressure from his wife. Occasionally, he'll try to imagine his life without her. It's hard for him. He wonders if it's the same for her.

Dylan has agreed to let me help him, and our hands still smell of the silt from the stakes we dragged and hammered into La Pantena, while Artur is warming two servings of the roe deer he bagged back on March 27. Almost half a year ago. After field-dressing and butchering it, he stored it in the deep freezer to be consumed at designated times. Today we're celebrating the return of calmness following the tourist season. He shot the deer with a .30-06 rifle he also uses for wild boar, goats, and red deer. Roe deer and horsemeat are atop his list of favorites. Wild boar isn't bad, though it seems to have a particularly strong flavor.

"I'm a big carnivore, but I never buy meat at the supermarket," Artur says as he stands in front of the microwave in which the venison is rotating. "I always go to a butcher shop that sells horsemeat from their own herds that graze in the mountain passes. My father buys grass-fed lamb and goat meat. We eat animals that eat grass. And we eat what we hunt."

Occasionally, a wild boar will find its way into Buda, though large wild mammals are rare on the island. Their rarity is partly because they tend to be hunted if they show up. If you wish to hear stories of large, aquatic vertebrates coexisting with humans, you must pay heed to other rivers, other waters. In Thailand, swimming elephant races are held. There, as well as in several other Asian countries, are pachyderms that roam great distances because, according to extraordinary (if uncredentialed) evolutionary anthropologist Elaine Morgan, the elephant evolved, like the whale, as an aquatic animal. In the water, weight is no obstacle, and size is an advantage when it comes to conserving body heat. Elephants still instinctively use their trunks as breathing tubes when fording deeply channeled rivers. Morgan cited the case of an elephant that traveled some 320 kilometers from island to island in the Bay of Bengal, which at times meant swimming more than one and a half kilometers from land in the open ocean. It took this fresh- and saltwater elephant twelve years to complete its journey around the archipelago.

The Ma'dan buffalo and the Indian elephants let slip stories that sound as fantastic as that of George Orwell's assistant on Jura, Bill Dunn, who's said to have swum across the Gulf of Corryvreckan with a wooden leg. What he did was remove the false leg, slather himself with sheep's fat to reduce the drag on his body, and swim the crawl stroke for the 1,340 meters that separate Jura from Scarba, all the while escorted by a flotilla of small watercraft ready, if necessary, to help him.

Jura, the island where there were so many red deer that its name is derived from *hjörtr*, the Norse word for deer.

Jura, the cervine island where Orwell would write *1984*, the novel, they say, that he at one point considered titling *The Last Man in Europe*.

Orwell had passed as a vagabond in hop fields in Kent, lived penniless in London and Paris, fought against fascists in Catalonia, run a small business in Wallington, herded goats in Marrakech, and—aghast by the incorrigible morality of the world he'd seen—settled on Jura, where he tended to his garden and wrote a classic. His talents had already been on display in his previous books, but by the time he arrived on the island, he was clearly disappointed with the human species. It would also be worthwhile to consider how the whirlpool that once trapped him in that same Gulf of Corryvreckan had affected him, making him fear for his life as he realized he hadn't accurately calculated the influence of the tides. The whirlpools, insular wilderness, and disappointment in his fellow humans stirred in him a freedom of thought and transgressive actions which, in Orwell's case, took the form of science fiction.

Jura.

Buda.

The Last Man in Europe.

1984.

The Last Man in the Delta.

2027?

The blending and instability encourage us to picture cocktails of islands, titles, dates, and words that won't be blown away by the wind because I'm writing them down and because this afternoon is a gentle one.

I've come to the beach to bring closure to the day. Out at sea, the spume seems to rise much higher than normal. It's the birds. Standing on the dune, I see more movement than there actually is, which is due to my lack of vision: I seem to have removed my glasses. Myopia suggests nonexistent realities. Perfect for both imagining and making mistakes.

Back along the shore, the world appears asleep, though some beings seem to be on the move. The tiny sounds are all part of the dream. Today I pass through the clutch of reeds with the sun closer to the horizon than it has been the last few days, and, as with the light, there's a lack of dragonflies. A mosquito bites me on the neck. Two more get me on the leg. I can see them building their strength in numbers. I take off, waving my towel, swiping it through the air as if it were a broadsword, swearing that, for as long as this summer lasts, I'll never again cross this corridor at this time of day without the dragonflies.

LIGHT

BLACKOUT

NATURE DOESN'T ACCEPT absent-mindedness, excessive confidence, or delays of any sort.

Pablo came by yesterday to chat for a bit. He also wanted to show Buda to Xènia and to the children, who had yet to set foot on the island. Then the family headed off to the vela where his *bous* are corralled. Xènia stayed on one side of the fence chatting with Ángel while the kids played in the field. When Pablo entered the vela, a bull was challenging the leader of the herd. Pintoret, the ringleader being challenged, found an ally in Estrellito, and both bulls began goring Navarro, the upstart candidate. The field had been watered a few hours before and their hooves kicked up curtains of misty spray. The violence troubled little Bernat, who had never seen such savagery in all the years of accompanying his father to the fields.

"Mom, I'm going back to the car."

The bulls fought their way across the field, crashing into the holding pen hard enough to bend the bars before ending up in a corner not visible to Xènia, Ángel, and little Biel, who could only hear Pablo's calls as he tried to calm or separate the beasts, the thundering sound of the earth being trampled, the dry, heavy thudding of the hulking masses.

Pablo had seen his *iaio* and other veteran cowhands deal with similar situations. He knew he shouldn't intervene despite the fear that one of them could end up badly hurt or worse, so he waited. The pair hit and gored Navarro repeatedly until he was left still on the ground. Pablo thought they'd killed him, that he was gasping for his final breaths, and he ran forward, shouting to scare off the attackers. Estrellito and Pintoret backed away slowly, though without ever taking their eyes off Navarro. When they had retreated to a safe distance, Pablo sensed something moving behind him.

Look, the old folks had told him. He knew better. He always has. Never put yourself between two animals. And yet there he was, in the middle of the pasture, far from the fence and right in front of a mad bull that had caught a beating and was looking to let off some steam. There he was, like a dumbass or, worse, a smart-ass, wondering how this could have happened to someone with so many years of experience.

There was no time for more thinking, as Navarro's half ton of bulk and horns was now galloping directly at him, neck held high like a good Bernabé.

"What's going on, Ángel?" Xènia asked when she no longer heard Pablo's calls.

"Nothing. They must have stopped fighting."

Pablo had taken off running. He didn't look back, not wanting to lose focus and trip, pouring all his strength into the race in hope of reaching the hillock that rises to the fence. On the incline, Navarro would undoubtedly catch him, the muscular haunches of the bull allowing him to power uphill at a much greater speed, but the animal would also be feeling less steady and wouldn't be able to thrust his horns with the same precision as on the plain.

As his foot hit the first stone at the base of the mound, Pablo felt the impact in his back. The bull's head pitched upwards, tossing his body into the air.

"Did it get him?" Xènia asked. She still couldn't see anything from where she stood.

But Bernat had. It all happened right in front of the car. He saw his father flying through the air.

"Ángel, it got him!"

"No, ma'am, no it didn't."

"It did!" Xènia shouted as she started to run along the outside of the fence toward where her husband was.

As if through someone else's eyes, Pablo saw himself floating through the air.

He was in the air for what seemed like forever.

When the rancher finally came splashing down in a gravelly puddle, he curled up, covering his head with his arms. At least the bull had launched him forward, allowing him to land uphill. He thought about his son Bernat and how he'd made a rookie mistake, how his normally reliable self-preservation alert system had suffered a catastrophic failure. His *iaio* had told him a thousand times not to get too sure of himself, not to get involved in a fight like this one. And he never had before, goddamn it! But it sure as hell looked like his time was up.

Just play dead, Pablo thought. He was no more than a meter or two from the bull's hooves, which were all he could see of the animal from his position. From Navarro's movements, the rancher knew the animal had reared up on his hind legs. The bull thrust and twisted his horns in the air as if still hunting the body which, seconds before, had flown overhead. Navarro crashed to the ground, front hooves landing centimeters from Pablo and spewing gravel and pebbles like an explosion of shrapnel, plenty of which hit the rancher. He was on the verge of being trampled. Navarro had located Pablo yet again: the man was lying directly before him. The animal was turning his neck in preparation for the coup de grâce when Pablo noticed another violent scattering of stones; simultaneously, he felt the dry thud of a brutal collision. As his eyes struggled to focus, Pablo realized Pintoret had struck Navarro, lifting the attacker off the ground. This had garnered the rancher a few precious seconds. Pablo rolled across the stones, which jabbed him like ice picks as they dug into his already beleaguered back. The pain was bordering on unbearable, but the adrenaline rush erased any doubt: he wasn't going to stop now, his self-preservation instincts had kicked in, alerting him that his life was in imminent danger of being extinguished. He stopped his roll and began to crawl, army-style, up the muddy slope while Pintoret thrashed and battered what it thought must have been the dying man.

Inside the car, Bernat was bawling.

Xènia was still en route, running blindly.

With difficulty, Navarro separated himself from Pintoret and once again set his sights on Pablo, who had managed to get to his feet and was limping, hunched over, toward the corral. This time, the cattle rancher risked glancing back. The bull was rushing up the slope, ready to impale him against the post. Pablo reached the fence, set one foot on the lowest board, grabbed hold of the highest one, and in the split second before his executioner arrived, he was able to vault himself over the barrier, collapsing safely to the ground on the other side. He could hear the bull huffing and panting through the gaps in the corral. He could see the finely tipped shafts of the horns aimed directly at him. The animal butted the boards a few times more, before returning to the grazing lands.

Xènia and Ángel ran up. Pablo picked himself up slowly, checking to see whether, despite the pain, everything was more or less in working order. He was drenched in sweat. His back was cramping, as if his body weight was greater than it was, and the contusions that dotted his entire body forced him to move gingerly.

"Are you okay? How are you?"

"Leave me alone!" Pablo grunted.

How could this have happened to him? Especially in front of Ángel and his family. How?

Pablo limped to the car, where Bernat was still crying. Xènia followed in silence; she knows full well when to step in and when not to, especially when it's not worth it. Seeing his older brother's tears and overwhelmed by the stress of it all, Biel also began to cry.

Pablo decided not to have Xènia drive. He wanted to handle that task himself, to confirm that all his parts were still in working order, or at least good enough to bring the family home. He tried to calm himself, to assess the damage, but his fury at his greenhorn carelessness and what could have happened ignited something within him. He couldn't hold it together anymore. Idiot, idiot, idiot. Gripping the steering wheel while unleashing the tremendous amount of tension that had accumulated, along with the fear, the rage, the shame, the certainty of death that had possessed him when he hit the ground, he let it all go, vomiting up a cascade of curses that lasted the entire drive from the field to the Amposta while the children cried silently and Xènia fixed her eyes on the asphalt.

The threat of death is ever present. The secret lies in our awareness of it. If you can accept the next stretch of inevitably disappearing coastline, imagine the fragility of life. A speeding car, an unexpected storm, a malignant bacterium, a deceptively dying bull . . . and it's goodbye. It's a beautiful challenge to come out ahead in life while remaining vulnerable. To enjoy this experience, you must simply accept that one day you will die. That one day pain, weakness, and helplessness will overtake what was once your radiant vigor. That one day the threat of death which for years has been expressed in terms of distance will appear there yet again.

After the bull charges Pablo, my mother breaks the news to me that the doctors have detected a pulmonary tumor in my father. Somehow, the excrescence which had been affecting his prostate and was somewhat under control was now reflected in his lung. Tests must be run. I return to Barcelona. Opening day of hunting season in Buda is October 10, but I'm in the city with my family. Just when it seems that my father is starting to recover, he develops pneumonia and is admitted to intensive care. We visit him every day. Although he breathes through a mask that provides him with oxygen and often grunts from the pain of being forced to lie down for many hours, he jokes with the nurses and criticizes politicians with his usual intensity.

A few days later they replace the mask with a more unobtrusive oxygen inhaler, move my father back to a standard room, and the doctor signs the transfer orders to a French hospital conducting a clinical trial that, apparently, is producing impressive results. Two nights later, we get a call at three in the morning warning us that my father has gotten worse, that we should come quickly.

I arrive with my mother, my brother, and my sister accompanied by her partner and my niece from Seville, who works in the city. They set us up in a waiting room at the front end of the hallway. Only one of us at a time is allowed into my father's room. I find him there, breathing artificial air, as he has been the last few days. He doesn't look any worse, though it seems as though his lung is already saturated with that substitute for the pure, natural air which is keeping him alive. We talk about whatever, he keeps smiling, until he falls silent. He turns to me, and without losing that grin of his, says, "Whatever happens, I'm at peace."

His voice, his expression, the distention of his body all say the same thing. There is a sense of peace that my father has managed to achieve and now transmits to me from this boundary he now inhabits. I admire him more than ever.

My father makes it through the day. The following morning, he struggles to breathe, pounding his chest in search of the air he can only access through a mask. The brutal overexertion coupled with the tranquilizers plunges him into unconsciousness. My son arrives around three in the afternoon. With his entire family surrounding him, we decide to take him off artificial respiration. The nurse warns us that the end may come quickly. We all gather around the bed, me on one side holding his left hand.

Dad.

Your fingers are so big.

You've brought so much color into our lives.

So many castles, bridges, and moats that we've built with you there at the edge of the sea.

My father is able to breathe on his own for another three minutes or so. He dies, his left hand in mine. Everyone who needs to be here is present.

The wake is attended by many people who go on about my father's greatness. About the greatness of my parents. For the memorial cards, we've selected a verse from a song that always moved him.

> If on one unfortunate day
> The reaper comes for me,
> Shove off my boat into the sea
> With an autumn easterly
> And damn the studding sails
> To the scrapping of the winds.
>
> Bury me without mourning,
> Where the beach meets the sky,
> On the slope of a mountain
> That juts above the horizon,
> I want a view of the dawn.
>
> My body will be the way
> Of lending green to the pines
> And yellow to the flowering Scotch brooms.

Near the sea, for I,
I am a man
Born on the Mediterranean.

It is autumn. We cremate him on Montjuïc, the hill in Barcelona overlooking the sea. Then we bring his remains to my grandparents' burial niche. My maternal grandparents. The way he wanted. This is the part of the family we associate with love, and if eternity exists, it will be the best place for him.

It's hard to shrug off the grief. The memories continue to pile up. But, even with the feeling of profound loss inside of me, I shed not a single tear. I'm as calm as him. I don't mourn death the way I was told I was supposed to. At least not for now. Time will tell.

LIGHTHOUSES

AFTER TWO WEEKS, I RETURN TO LA PANTENA. The boom gate that marks the entrance to Buda swings shut with a bang due to the weight of the rain-soaked wood. A powerful easterly storm knocked down nearly twenty trees the day before yesterday, and trunks are strewn across the swamped road. The men have painted the house. On the wall behind the sink they've installed a board on which to hang pans. La Pantena is ready to open for fishing season, but we'll have to wait for Dylan to return from Peru, since he's the only one authorized to fish.

"Get ready. You're gonna have to deal with us every night," Quim warns, eyeing the large net used primarily to catch eels but also other fish.

"Pantena" derives from the ancient Greek word *pantherion*. *Pan* signifies "everything" while *therion* means "beast." The art of "la pantena" fishing consists of laying a net several meters wide in part of the canal and folding it around a point, creating a one-way funnel through which the "beasts" can enter but not exit. Our thick mesh net is still lying in a heap by the canal. The workers stretch it out by draping it across a line of stakes, though they don't actually unfurl it, displaying its length but not its width. Since the water level has risen, the planks of the smallish dock are soaked. In two days, Dylan will arrive, and northerly winds even stronger than today's gales are expected: a good omen for fishers.

I start a fire in the fireplace. A thread of black smoke sneaks into the living room. The wood is damp and the wind fierce, but the flue draws well and quickly redirects the smoke up the chimney.

Next morning, I step out onto a porch surrounded by expanses of greens and browns. The leaves of the cat's claw have curled up and the bushes are tangled. The rows in some of the fields are gone, having been turned into a miry paste. Herons and seagulls alternate between dizzying downwind flights and static suspensions where they remain twitching and trembling in the air like marionettes held by an invisible thread.

The path toward the sea has turned to mud. I make my way, trying to step from one clod of hardened excrement to another, lending me some semblance of assuredness. The mud spreads well beyond the confines of this fecal corridor. The hall of dragonflies no longer exists: the reeds have disappeared along with the summer's last predatory insects. The men have cut back the reedbed along with the intervening vegetation, clearing the way so the sea can now be seen from more than a hundred meters away. Without the reeds, there's nothing to shelter the path from the wind. It has lost its mystery.

There is less litter on the beach but many more cormorants than two months ago. Autumn and the storm have transformed Buda. A long, flat cloud like a Mexican sombrero crowns Montsià, which is silhouetted in high definition, as are the windmills in Camarles and the Cardó Massif on this morning so crystalline that even the lighthouse, with its perfectly delineated profile, seems to have made its way a bit closer to the shore.

Lighthouses stand against death, and the Ebro Delta had three. Someone once said that for a time they actually contributed to the number of shipwrecks by misleading captains who weren't aware if they were navigating in the vicinity of the Buda, La Banya, or Fangar lighthouses and made the mistake of piloting their boats directly into the mire. But this is nothing more than a fable intended to insinuate that too much light can be confusing and even fatal.

Whatever the case, the coastline was named the Costa de la Muerte by local sailors. Like coral reefs, icebergs, or sea spires, the delta's sandbars have been a graveyard for ships. The sheer number of disasters led to the construction of an impressive lighthouse built with Birmingham iron on the backs of English workers about whom almost nothing is known, save that many of them succumbed to malaria. On September 15, 1860, the octagonal lantern with its white, spherical dome was lit, and it became the tallest iron lighthouse in the world and a point of reference for engineers of the time. The lighthouse keepers settled in a cabin with a thatched reed roof alongside the great tower constructed on what was then dry land.

The retreating coastline has been calculated based on the lighthouse's position. As writer Sebastià Juan Arbó recalled decades later, during the first forty years of the twentieth century, "the lighthouse was so far inland that the sea couldn't be seen from where it stood. We ate in the shadow of the lighthouse and then went up to the top, contemplating with awe the immense panorama of the riverside fields, enclosed by fences and dotted with huts, the winding Ebro at the center of it all, which came to die at the foot of the lighthouse."

The boom in dams and reservoirs in the late 1940s and the resulting lack of sediment flowing downstream caused the coastline to begin receding at a rate of thirty-nine meters per year. By the time Pepo Cabezas was appointed lighthouse keeper, it was already reachable only by boat. Every morning, he'd teach classes to his children, Manolita and Antonio, before going out to fish or hunt. They had a plot of cultivated land that supported watermelons, goats, and chickens, and staples of their diet included fish, elvers, frog legs, and duck.

Since the fall of that lighthouse, a few more have been erected, though those familiar with the original prefer to use other words to define them. Watchtower. Platform. Beacon. All substitutes for the virtuoso work of engineering that, for decades, had been identified as a lighthouse. Back in the 1990s, the port authority considered removing the platform still flashing there in front of Buda, believing the construction of the Cap de Tortosa lighthouse would render the older one unnecessary, but the fishers asked to keep it there because it helped them quickly locate the entrance to the river's mouth. Which is why, in 1995, the old and corroded tower was replaced by a new, stainless steel version that has continued to move steadily away from the coast. This is the tower I can now barely make out, reduced to a matchstick in the offing, its increasingly remote flashes providing nightly reports on how its separation from this dying shore continues to grow.

But nobody here is thinking of that now.

The house is freshly painted, Dylan has arrived, and it's time to fish.

"What are those logs doing there?" Simona says, pointing to the firewood I've gathered in a sheltered corner near the hearth, where I've lit a fire. She puts a flat-screen larger than my own TV down on La Pantena's living-room table.

"There's nowhere else to put them," I reply. "And I need them to dry out. They got soaked in the storm."

Simona shutters the large window at one end of the table, connects the flat-screen and a PlayStation console to a wall socket, and presses play on the remote control. It's a quarter past six in the evening. The supervisor let herself in earlier with a salutatory wave and is now installing her equipment without having consulted me. She knows I'd never refuse access to whatever they might need, but there are such things as manners and this is my home now.

Obviously she sees it differently, but this is my home. She rubs her hands together.

Dylan, Quim, and Artur enter carrying two fisher's baskets and a bag filled with drinks, canned food, a loaf of bread, and a couple of baguettes. Simona's daughter follows, brandishing two PlayStation games. She puts one in the console.

"Use one of those baskets for the logs he's left on the ground here," Simona orders. "The wind should be strong from ten to one. Let's hope so, because if it's just a breeze it's not worth staying out for a handful of bream or sea bass. That's barely enough for dinner."

She claps her hands as if to say *Come on, let's go see how the pantena is looking*. The supervisor and the men set out into an evening still shaken by the recent gale. There is a new moon, and the darkness is already so opaque it's hard for me to see Quim walking barely a meter in front of me. The men's headlamps are off, though they move swiftly as their retinas are acclimated to the blackening shadows. Since I can't see, and one wrong step will drop me into the canal, I switch on the flashlight on my cell phone.

"What the hell are you doing?" Simona screams. "Turn that off, goddammit!"

It's off as fast as I'd turned it on. Fortunately, Artur now has his headlamp lit; he's standing at one end of the pantena, serving as a reference point for me. The men take down the net, unfurl it, attach the ends to the stakes, and stretch it across the water. It reaches almost as far as the bend where the straightaway to El Mas begins. That's the point where the net begins to fold over itself, creating the cylindrical passageway through which the fish will pass. The water level has surpassed that of the dock, but everyone is wearing chest-high bootfoot waders. They move swiftly and sure-footedly along the muddy slope leading to the dock. We make our way back inside the house.

From one of the baskets they produce some chorizo, blood sausage, a jar of homestyle olives, and bags of peanuts, while the girl starts playing *Farming Simulator* on the PlayStation. The challenge is to manage a virtual farm, basically driving tractors of any sort in all imaginable situations. We chat for maybe forty minutes while the kid plays with the volume on full blast. I toss a massive hunk of wood onto the fire. The men head back out to check the pantena.

"We'll eat when we get back," Simona says. Turning to me, she adds: "You can stay and set the table, right?"

I get the plates, silverware, and glasses ready. It doesn't take long for the fishers to return with bream and sea bass. Simona's father also makes a brief appearance. I see him wave and then drop something squirming into a garbage bag before leaving.

"We're gonna have ourselves a heck of a meal tonight!" Simona exclaims while her daughter drives a tractor through electronic fields.

Quim tosses six live fish into the grill basket. A bream makes a break for it, only to end up writhing on the coals, coated in ash. Quim relocates it to the grill, crushing the gasping fish's final hopes, stokes the glowing firewood until he has an even bed of embers, and leaves dinner to slowly smolder.

We dine with the kid at the head of the table. She scarfs down her food in a flash and returns to *Farming Simulator*, which she's still playing at full volume. The rest of us have to raise our voices to hear one another. Simona remarks that there are people out there with plenty of money who'll never enjoy a dinner like the one we're having. Fresh fish, a solid campfire, homemade wine, seltzer, and, for dessert, Terry, the brandy that's said to be "the water of the delta." She pours herself a glass along with two tablespoons of sugar while Artur opens a plastic container of chocolate-covered pastries: a 100 percent corporate product.

"Fuck the rich!" Simona shouts.

"Hola, bona nit!"

Two bundled-up men wearing headlamps enter the scene. They introduce themselves with a wave of their hands, though they mostly engage with Simona, who invites them to help themselves to anything they'd like. They're fishing for elvers, which is legal in Buda for anyone with the appropriate license. Dylan doesn't. His license only allows him to go after other fish. The law is the law. Here, though, they've learned how to take advantage of every loophole, which is why those charged with managing Buda allow licensed outsiders to fish for baby eels on the island in exchange for 50 percent of the profits. And tonight the fishers will be going out to set traps near the old dragonfly corridor: the reason why they cut back all the reeds.

Simona is in good spirits. She's joking and laughing endlessly. Everyone else is smiling to a certain degree, glancing at each other out of the corners of their eyes. They look uncomfortable. Quim and Artur dig into the peanuts. The girl has stopped her virtual tractor while rain falls on the TV. She waits for the fictional storm to clear while, in one corner of the plasma screen, a digital clock continues spiraling forward at a vertiginous rate: we watch as the afternoon, the night, and then the dawn all occur in the space of three minutes. The field fans out from the operator's perspective, as if she were sitting in the cab herself.

At the table, Simona and the men talk about elvers. They say that, in a few days, the Migjorn's gullet will open wide and Buda will once again be an island. We'll only be able to access it by boat. Simona goes on a rant: apparently the floodgates haven't been unlatched in roughly a decade, and reviving that tradition means workers won't be able to access Buda with the same facility as before, will always be forced to keep one eye on the ferry. Their movements can then be more closely controlled.

On the flat-screen TV a light drizzle is falling, through which a bright sun sparkles. The girl stirs her tractor to life. The sound of the motor mixes with the voices of the men. I stare into the fire, losing myself in my thoughts, whatever they may have been.

When the eel anglers leave, the men don their waders once again to go check the pantena. "You stay here and wash the dishes," Simona tells me.

The girl sets the controller on the table; the tractor is parked in a machine shed, the *Farming Simulator* screen still pulsating away. She zips up her waterproof overalls and heads out with her elders. While I organize the cupboards, I see Quim and Simona carrying two black bags across the porch in the direction of the rice field. A couple minutes later, they return without them. The wind whips up the shrubs outside and whistles through the half-open, porthole-sized windows, clearing the smoke. The group returns to the room with a flathead gray mullet, three striped mullet, three bream, two sea bass, and a few other fish the size of a pinkie. All are together in one of the baskets.

"Nothing. Not even worth it," Simona sighs. She looks at her daughter. "Come on, let's go." She looks at the men. "Stay a little longer, and if there's still nothing, head home."

As soon as the pickup's headlights are aiming down the straightaway to El Mas, Quim, Artur, and Dylan shut off the TV and tear open another bag of peanuts. Artur rubs his head and leans back against the mantelpiece, shaking his head, while Quim tells me to get ready for the real island, because once the floodgates open, we will be truly isolated.

"They're not gonna show you how to cross the river, because they don't want anyone touching that boat. So you've gotta ask permission every time you want to go out," Dylan says.

"What if I need to leave on a Sunday?" Most Sundays, Buda is deserted, unless there are tourists staying at El Mas. At that time, though, it was usually empty.

"Then you'll just have to call and have someone come pick you up."

"And if there's one of those big storms?"

Quim looks at Artur, who seems as expectant as I am.

"Run."

With his fingers he cracks open the shell of a peanut.

"And while you're running, get on the horn. Sometimes things get hectic, but you should have coverage. If you don't, look for a place that does. Anyway, I suppose someone will remember you're here."

The three of us laugh.

"This thing gets hot," Artur says, moving away from the fireplace.

Glasses of wine are served. In late summer, Mateo had offered Artur an open-ended contract, and while he liked the job and found the island an amazing place to work, he was hesitant to accept. Putting up with the supervisor day in and day out is a high price to pay, and he wasn't sure whether it would be worth the effort. And beyond that, working for your father-in-law not only complicates everything a little bit more, because you're left with divided loyalties, but it's also a means of garnering preferential treatment when your coworkers—who, by now, are also your friends—are involved in some sort of high jinks. Like that day Simona started laying into Dylan and Quim before turning to Artur, saying how lucky he was that she couldn't curse him out the same way. Which is when Artur blurted out, "And why not? Why not me?"

Artur would rather put up with that nasty woman's rantings than come across as a spoiled brat in front of his colleagues. But somehow he can't. He's lived a pampered life, yes, growing olive trees and feeding rabbits until he was eighteen, though for the past eleven years he's been working nonstop, accepting what he's paid instead of what someone who dedicates eleven hours a day to their travails should receive. Artur knows what his coworkers think of Simona, but at the end of the day, Quim and Dylan also know that the boss is Artur's father-in-law, which means he'll never be measured by the same standards as they are. For this reason, he refuses to accept any favors, but at the same time, he won't do anything Dylan and Quim wouldn't do themselves. He's not looking to benefit in any way, and he certainly doesn't expect to be cut any extra slack. The best way to achieve this harmony would be to keep quiet, fit in, and only speak out in protest when it's in unison with his colleagues. To demonstrate that the three of them experience both suffering and enjoyment as a team, as he would in any other job. But the thing is that Natalia is his wife, and when he comes home after work, he can't help telling her about how his day went on the island. And then there's the fact that Natalia owns the farm. Not legally, not yet, but if Buda manages to hold on, one day she'll inherit a percentage. Beyond that, she feels as though the island is an extension of herself, and since she can't stand anyone abusing either the space or the people taking care of it, every time Artur tells her something about the supervisor's misdeeds and transgressions, Natalia feels angry. Even with herself, wondering how she could have been so wrong about this woman whom, at first, she liked very much. She even considered her a model of new femininity: a truly empowered woman who had burst onto the scene in an ultra-macho universe, breaking all the molds, even the physical ones, with her short hair and impressive musculature. Everything about her was impressive, yes, even the bad temper that raised its head on occasion, especially when someone attacking Buda needed a good tongue-lashing. She liked having someone like that close to her father. She wanted him protected. Armored, even. But now she thinks about it, how strange, right? A recently separated woman attached at the hip to her father all day every day, and yet she never imagined any kind of history between them. No matter how much Mateo appreciated Simona, no matter how much he sang her praises, she'd always considered their relationship to be a connection clean and clear of any desires. Any interests, too, though when you work closely with someone it's easy for feelings to mix. Simona seemed so unsensual to Natalia, so far outside the contours of her father's profile, that she'd never even considered this possibility. On the other hand, Simona made her think a lot about gender roles, and I'd even venture to say that she came to feel something akin to admiration for that rarity of a woman.

During those years when Natalia was heading up to Pas's shack, sometimes to spend the weekend, other times for longer periods, Simona had always been attentive to what she might need, joking in that crude and boisterous manner Natalia sympathized with because it seemed genuine. Sometimes Natalia would ask Simona to take out her garbage because the nearest container was several kilometers away, and Simona never had any problems with that. She seemed like a kind soul who was concerned with Natalia's safety and that of the island, as well as Mateo's, of course. The ideal supervisor, regardless of how many people in the town, her Uncle Gonzalo included, claimed she was some sort of despot and told objectionable stories about her. Gonzalo had gotten himself into a lot of trouble throughout his life; he had a tendency to lie a lot, and Natalia's father, who knows Simona best and has firsthand knowledge of the kinds of things people at the helm of companies have to put up with, defended the supervisor to any- and everyone, meaning there wasn't anything more to discuss.

Natalia used to catch the train to L'Aldea. She'd usually arrive on a Friday afternoon or evening, and, since she traveled by bike, she'd pedal from the station to Sant Jaume, where she could party for a few hours before heading to the island, sometimes with others in tow. It was on one of those days that she invited several friends from L'Ametlla for a barbecue. They entered Buda. The afternoon dragged on, night fell, and since there wasn't any food to be found, they went into town to buy pizzas. The anglers had already opened the Migjorn's maw, inaugurating their fishing season, so the young folks headed for El Sifó to catch the barge across the river. They returned, loaded up with Italian food: they feasted with beer, wine, and song, and around three in the morning they crossed back onto the mainland, where Natalia bid them farewell.

Since she had to use both hands to turn the ferry's enormous crank so she could return to the island, she left her phone on the ground. When the wheel began to turn, the docking ramp rose, and her phone slipped into the river through the gap. Spending the night on the island incommunicado would be inadvisable. She hopped on her bike, wondering whether or not to tell Gonzalo and Teresa about the situation. Normally she'd have illuminated her path with her phone's flashlight, but instead she set out pedaling through the darkness. As she was invisible, she figured she'd be able to tell if a vehicle was coming down the opposite road along the river with its headlights off. There's no explanation for why she did this. Perhaps it was the recklessness of youth combined with a certain feeling of invincibility that comes from being in a familiar space that prompted her to turn back and go looking for a car . . . which, when it saw her dead ahead, did indeed switch on its lights. In it were Simona and Felipet, the man who had moved into La Pantena after the deaths of Ramoneta and Pep. Natalia couldn't say who was more surprised.

"What are you doing here?" Simona asked. Natalia could tell the supervisor was nervous, which was disconcertingly strange, considering her usual confidence.

"I came to spend the weekend with friends. What about you?"

"Just here with Felipet, who wanted to show me a few things. He was out late fishing and I'm going to drop him off at the house."

A few things.

In the wee hours of the morning.

Natalia returned to Pas's shack, still not thinking about sex. Yes, Simona was married, but Felipet was a bit of a head case. The two had known each other since forever, and their sexual chemistry was less than zero. Whenever they were seen together, they looked like a couple of buddies. The faces they'd made when they almost literally ran into her suggested something more complex than an affair. At the end of the day, Felipet wouldn't care if he'd added one more romantic tryst to the dozens, perhaps hundreds, that he'd accumulated. The look on his face had been the grimace of a guilty man. Of someone who could be expelled from the paradise he'd been enjoying for the past two years in La Pantena. There, face to face with those two, Natalia realized that, even if she didn't buy into all Gonzalo had to say, this situation fit with the stories he'd been telling her over the years. These were no longer hypotheses or narratives potentially shored up by resentment; she herself had seen something worthy of heightened suspicion. Now she had two things to tell her uncle about that night. But she wasn't going to wake him before daybreak. Besides, why sow more division? Tomorrow would be another day. Things would look different in the light, and she was tired of the often-gratuitous tensions which never served any purpose. She went to sleep.

As the relationship between Natalia and Simona continued to remain cordial, Natalia quashed any suspicions raised by that encounter. Until Artur started working in Buda. When her husband started talking about the supervisor's behavior, it seemed as if he were telling her about someone else. Insulting the workers, belittling them, shouting at them, and worst of all, murky accounting.

Natalia knows her husband well. He doesn't invent stories, nor does he cause any harm, especially when it comes to family matters, which he regards as sacred. As a result, he was returning home increasingly upset about what he was witnessing in Buda. Even if he hadn't told her anything, she'd have sensed something was wrong, because ever since Artur started shooing birds from the island, Simona had stopped talking to Natalia. Now, the supervisor doesn't even say hello to her. Natalia isn't greeting Simona either, but she's not about to tolerate such an illogical situation. And while Artur sometimes asks Natalia to casually slip a detail or two to her father, or even suggests it might be better for her to wait and let him be the one to wait for him to slip some details to Mateo himself, Natalia sees no reason for patience. If anything, she feels a need to tell her father. An immediate need to tell him what she's feeling, which is why, when things started going wrong, she didn't hesitate before calling Mateo.

"For the first time in my life," she said, "I'm really angry with you."

Her parents' separation had hurt, and for a time she'd blamed a good part of that breakup on her father, though she couldn't call that anger. It was somewhere between dejection and rage. A separation is a disagreement, an incompatibility. It's often hard to assign blame, and when it came to her parents, she couldn't and shouldn't point the finger at either of them. But, yes, her father bore direct responsibility for the supervisor's abuse.

Natalia spilled everything she'd heard from Artur, resuscitating old criticisms levied by Gonzalo and many others and adding her own concerns about the company's progress. She also asked him why he pays so much attention to Simona when she proposes changes to the farming techniques used in the fields or suggests adding new, likely ineffective substances to the cultivation process. Mateo answered in the same way he always answers those who question his right-hand woman: that, on these fields, Simona is Messi, that she loves Buda as if it were her own. Dylan, on the other hand, is a reliable worker who lacks global perspective and the ability to operate a tractor. Quim is extraordinarily strong and a very fine person, but that's about it. Artur has a bright future before him, but he still needs to learn more. If Mateo were to go off on someone, he'd do it to the Generalitat, the state, or La Administración, the latter of which is truly responsible for everything.

And that's what gets Natalia heated at times. Messi and La Administración? That woman treats her own people like garbage, and her bad manners, well known throughout the region, paint a terrible picture of Buda, Mateo, and the entire family. Natalia told Mateo to give Simona an ultimatum. This time she wasn't talking about another one of those reconciliation meetings where Simona, Dylan, and Quim would supposedly come to some sort of understanding, because those theatrics never result in anything other than the supervisor softening her tone for a couple of days before returning to her old ways.

Natalia understood that her father wasn't going to put pressure on the Messi of the Delta in such a way. Yes, you heard that correctly. The Messi of the Delta. He could have compared her to Alèxia Putellas, who's Catalan and all, but okay, sure, Messi's more than that. Much more. The most. Mateo has a publicist's imagination, and many of his comparisons strain credibility, so his other daughter, Andrea, also started pointing out the need for a change in direction, suggesting that so many people with the same concerns might not be wrong, and that the years he's spent working with Simona and the close relationship they've fostered might be distorting his objectivity.

All for naught. Mateo isn't about to give in. The one thing Natalia's clear about is that her father aspires to be running the island by 2027, after which he might send it all to hell. On those rare occasions when he considers the possibility of her taking the reins, he immediately goes back to the technical and financial hassles that come with managing many hectares, and banishes the idea from his head. If Artur was willing, and had learned what was needed, he could handle the island's affairs on the ground, giving Natalia an incentive to look more favorably on an administrative role. They'd represent a formidable tandem. But her husband isn't happy, and the situation seems ready to drag on forever. Which is why, when the possibility of an open-ended contract presented itself, it was she who urged Artur not to sign it, to use the opportunity to get out of Buda. Think about that: in the beginning, it was Natalia who had encouraged him to work on the island. But now he's become aware of how true the adage is about mixing business and family. Natalia understands Artur better than anyone, and she's seen firsthand how, in a matter of months—well, in a matter of weeks or even days—things can change, because as soon as he started working on the island, disagreements began cropping up. She realized immediately that her husband had entered one of those loops in which he's unable to talk about anything, where he's reduced to complaint after complaint. Since the couple share almost everything, it was all about seeing him walk through that door, accepting his anxiety, and teasing out the problems he'd rather have ignored, because there are enough problems in life without having to taint yourself with those of your nearest and dearest. She's already had enough of the family fights that break out every time there's a shareholders' meeting.

If Artur's agreed to sign the indefinite contract, it's because Gonzalo and Ramon have convinced him that he represents Buda's last chance to be well managed by someone in the family when Mateo retires. They see him as the only one professionally qualified to both understand this space and act in it. But beyond even that, and essential to everything, they see him emerging as the only one Mateo can ever trust, giving him the necessary clout to one day take over. But, most of all, if Artur does one day take the reins, Simona will have to dial it down in terms of how she's behaved over the years. Ramón and Gonzalo have both told him he must consider Dylan and Quim. He can't leave them alone with . . . with . . . with her. If Artur's in it for the long run, the supervisor will have to continue restraining herself the way she's been doing the past few months. Everybody's noticed it. Artur's surprised to hear that Simona's become more restrained as of late, because everything he's experienced under her command until now has seemed excessive to him.

And, yes, it does indeed seem as if the supervisor is dialing it down. Artur likes to live peacefully, to hunt, to season his own olives like the ones he brought to La Pantena tonight, and that's why working in Buda causes him such unhealthy levels of confusion and turmoil. Nothing here is calming for him.

In any case, things calmed down a bit in September, and for better or for worse he's part of the family. He has enormous respect for Mateo, Natalia is the love of his life, and through her he's part of a lineage that's entrusted him with governing an important portion of its assets. Artur never wanted to govern anything—as a goal, it wasn't even on his radar—but sometimes sacrifices must be made to restore order, and perhaps the time had come to make them.

Given the circumstances, he gets along quite well with Dylan and Quim, Buda is a paradise, and Simona isn't spending as much time with them as she used to because now she's ducking out whenever she can. After correcting them, berating them, browbeating them, sure, but then she takes advantage of any opportunity to disappear. And besides, the calendar seemed favorable. After the harvest, hunting season would begin, which is Artur's favorite. Then he'd pull out the same pantena fishing net he'd helped restore, and he certainly didn't want to miss either the premiere or the experience of fishing in a place like that. And maybe later that fall they'd open up the Migjorn, leaving Buda romantically isolated and allowing him the time to discover a secretive side of the island, accessible to only a select few. In other words, he was looking at six months of no rice, during which time his obligations would be perfectly tailored to his tastes, while simultaneously learning from great colleagues and the support of Mateo's brothers. Besides, after all was said and done, he'd come to know and understand Simona, at least somewhat. If the supervisor could control herself, he'd thoroughly enjoy his time there, and if she couldn't, he'd have to postpone his departure from Eden for a few months. He knew that if he did decide to leave,

Natalia would side with him, and Mateo would have to understand that Artur's a free and independent individual who's at his own service and won't allow himself to be sacrificed like a pawn to alleviate other people's disputes at the expense of his own mental health. No. Life can be simpler than that. Hunt roe deer, fish for sea bream, and gather olives. If you're happy with that, everything else can line up nicely for you. But if you want to grow more and more rice, load up on herbicides, and buy state-of-the-art tractors and 4x4 pickups, all the while suspecting that everyone around you is out there to screw you over . . . Well, life isn't so easy anymore.

Back at La Pantena, Artur takes a swig of wine and shakes his head again. "I heard her tell you to stay and clear the table," he says to me. "She thinks you're stupid."

"Or that you're Ramoneta," Quim adds.

We laugh. The fire pops and crackles.

"This is a great night for poachers and the Guardia Civil," Quim observes, a peanut between his fingers. "No moon. Running up and down all night. Crazy."

Shortly after midnight, after another fruitless trip to check the pantena, they decide to go home.

As they drive off, the solitary flashing lighthouse beacon bids them farewell.

In the morning, I discover that the men have left an empty brown-paper bag on the porch like a doormat. Since Simona wants me to keep the firewood orderly, I grab some logs from the pile next to the river and stack them on top of the bag so they can be covered while they dry. Then I walk to my dune, which has been transformed. One side of the slope has sunk, creating a hollow, as if the water had pierced its contours, opening up a deep furrow.

A rickety-looking shrub is completely festooned with gull feathers and reminiscent of the trembling leaves of a blooming bonsai being shaken by a westerly Ponente wind. A boat is all but buried in the sand, only a tiny bit of stern visible. The sea moves against the wind. The waves rise one after another like links in a chain, and the Mediterranean itself seems to have swelled. It seems higher, as if growing.

At the mouth of the river, the sand spit where seagulls usually flock by the hundreds has all but disappeared. The division of the waters is extreme today, with the river and the sea being perfectly distinguishable in terms of both color and waves. The churning salt water is capped with foam that leaps and falls, exploding against the mass of the fast-flowing river driven even harder by a southerly wind. The two colossi collide, scattering spume. It's a natural battlefield so savage that the effect is something dreamlike: reality and fiction merging into a grandiose spectacle. Two fishers cast their rods, balancing on boats that sway like swings.

Back along the beach, I notice the absence of footprints. Impermanence is an unbelievable relaxant. There is almost no debris in the sand, just heavier objects like a large tire or a refrigerator door. Everything that could be dragged away is gone. In the old dragonfly corridor, two ducks, startled by my appearance, fly out of the canal. Male and female: a couple that reminds me of my parents. When I cry, the wind spreads tears across my face, releasing some, which fly.

To my father, my mother was everything. During his final weeks in the hospital, the visit he most looked forward to was from her, and when he was allowed to spend a few days at home, he was always looking for her even when the entire family was there. Their children are, truly, the fruits of their love. I think my father loved us more than anything because we came from his love for her. Because we are a part of my mother, who was the world to him.

A cormorant in the canal senses me, but between the wind and the brushwood it can't take flight, and after a desperate whirring of its wings, it chooses to dive instead. I enjoy seeing animals hunkered and hiding; what's clandestine is borne of poetry. I don't need binoculars to appreciate the harmony of this orchestra which even the most ignorant among us finds moving. Few know how to interpret Pau Casals or Manuel de Falla, but we can all feel them.

I lie down on a bed of reeds, letting the wind blow overhead. The radio announces that today's high is thirty knots, and tomorrow it will accelerate to thirty-six. Such precision for this volatile world. For days now I've been jumping from one thought to the next without recalling the previous one, stopping only at strange realities. Fortunately, oddities still appear during any walk, so I'm able to make frequent stops and feel the connection continuing. The connection with the water, with the sand, with the delta. It's different now, because something as significant as death has happened. But the connection lives on. The wind sweeps across the fields and segments of grass drop like the automated keys on a player piano, interpreting the music of time on this colossal instrument. A magpie zigzags past the purple backdrop of clouds haloed by the sun, which has decided to show itself, if only for a few seconds. When I inhale, I think of my father's lungs stained by paint, tobacco, and the city. But I think even more about the things he taught us and the friendships he broke off because he considered many of his colleagues to be hypocrites, about how he digested their deceptions, their fraudulence, their betrayals, and about his efforts to maintain consistency. I think about how, after investing all his savings in the video rental shop that was supposed to stabilize the family economy, his two business partners started stealing movies to set up a parallel shop in Ibiza and brought us to the brink of ruin. To help him reclaim his financial footing, a friend offered him a job in a factory. He tried it for a month before literally becoming sick. My father's life has been defined by three pillars: doing his own thing, being sincere, and Eloísa, his wife.

I continue along the straightaway to El Mas, passing La Pantena on my way to Gonzalo's house. In the large coop off to the side the ducks huddle together, forming a mattress of feathers that sway like spikes of wheat. I cross the fields until I reach Gran Calaix. Fifteen newly built hunting stands are lined up along the shore of the lagoon. Each consists of four walls fashioned from vertical pallets camouflaged with palm fronds or reeds. A few spent cartridges are scattered about the water and grasses.

Back at La Pantena, I grab a coat hanger from the workshop and hack at the branches of the fir tree, breaking off plenty of pine cones for the fire. The Ponente winds blow with a silent ripple, as if everything is preparing for the night.

NIGHTTIME

LIKE YESTERDAY, the men, the supervisor, and the little pup arrive as soon as the sun is going down. The girl isn't with them this time. Simona asks what the logs are doing stacked on top of the brown-paper bag. "It's not for firewood?" I ask.

"It's the dog's spot. Come on, get that out of there."

They set the pantena. They bring two bottles of wine from the car, along with peanuts and a massive bag of sunflower seeds. They chat for a while about this and that, and when they're about to go take their first look at the net, Simona tells me I can start setting the table.

After the incursion, Quim and Artur leave a basket of fish at the entrance and strip off the top half of their slickers, complaining that they're too itchy and hot. They tie the rubber sleeves around their waists, leaving the men in short sleeves. Quim fires up the grill and begins lining up the fish. We dine on freshly caught sea bream and sea bass, along with some fresh lamb courtesy of Artur.

"Come on, man! Eat with your hands! Nobody's gonna call you out for that here," Quim says to me.

Yesterday I used silverware even though everyone else was pulling the meat apart with their fingers, but today I'm not about to turn up my nose at their table manners. The men grab fish directly off the hot coals with their bare hands. They'll drop the fish instantly if scalded, but more often than not, they hold on long enough to bite in. After the fish are denuded, they exhale wafts of steam. We eat with relish.

Before sitting down at the table, I watched as Simona dropped a basket of fish in the foyer. Then her father came, said hello to everyone, and left with another garbage bag inside which something was moving. The men tell hunting stories throughout the dinner. I mention a hunter from Extremadura who illegally imported Iberian ibexes and turned the screws on the neighboring landowners until he forced them all out and kept their land. I talk about poaching, abuse, and justice.

Simona may have either taken the hint or made a series of revealing associations. Whatever the case may be, though, she seems to have understood that I'm living in this house, that I've got a set of eyes, and that I'm not going to get volatile, so she chooses to be direct. As we're finishing dinner, with the television on in the background and our fingers still slicked with fish oil, she grabs the bottle of Terry and pours a splash into her glass. She adds two teaspoons of sugar. "So let's see," she says, looking at me. "Are you trustworthy or not?"

We all know what the question is about.

"I could tell you yes," I reply, "but how am I supposed to prove it to you?"

"Well. Alright then." Simona nods without taking her eyes off me. "There are spoken rules and then there are unspoken ones, but it shouldn't have to be that way. And we're not going to stop fishing for what we want just because of a few unjust laws."

And with that, it's her turn to launch into a monologue on justice until Rambo appears on the TV screen. We have, or rather she has, tuned into a classic film channel that, tonight, has already aired two movies, *Rambo* included, about war.

"Look at him," Simona says, following Rambo's every transition, every maneuver. "That's how it's done."

While the Vietnam veteran squares off with some corrupt small-town police officers and National Guard soldiers, Simona pulls out her phone and shows us a video from the day her daughter won the Spanish national championship for her age group in the hundred-meter butterfly. The girl is an elite swimmer. A true athlete. Eleven years of pure, stylized power that she consolidated during her days spent in the rice fields.

A few minutes later, the supervisor gets a call. "My husband," she says as she hangs up. "He busted the iron. I've gotta go and fix it."

It's ten thirty at night. Quim looks at me, his face showing nothing. Simona gets up, orders them to let her know about the next catch, and leaves.

"The iron?" I ask when the truck's headlights have receded down the road. "Really?"

The men shrug.

"Time for the drunk to visit the hunk," Quim says. "Come on, let's go check the pantena."

They head out into a night lashed by a colder and more violent wind than yesterday. When they return, there are five fish in the basket, two of which are undersized.

"Yeah, the wind has an effect, but so do the currents," Quim says.

Artur shakes his head, rubbing it with his hand. "It can't be like this," he says. "You know the situation I'm in . . . If someone finds out, what am I supposed to tell them? I don't want to get on their bad side, but at the same time . . . I mean, I'm working here, I can't say I'm not showing up. I'm just another worker here, so what am I supposed to do? Just say I wasn't there?"

"Come on, man, don't get yourself all bent out of shape," Quim says while he sorts through the night's catch.

Before setting the basket on the scale, Artur asks Quim how much he thinks it weighs. He's always amazed at how his companion is able to eyeball the loads of crab pots, fishing baskets, and bags of rice.

"Twenty-eight kilos."

When Quim drops the basket on the scale, the digital readout says . . . twenty-seven.

"What a guy," Artur mutters.

Dylan, Quim, and Artur start their rotations. Every night, two of them stay with me. They arrive as the sun is going down. Simona shows up around six, spits out a couple of orders, and disappears until the next day. She doesn't stay for dinner anymore. The men bring bread and other snacks and restock the refrigerator. I offer to share with them whatever I've got, but we have different diets and they'd rather not mix foods. They prepare "salads" of tomatoes, mussels, and fuet. According to their norms, I can eat their food—they even encourage me to do so—but they don't have any plans of their own to venture into my pantry. They leave wine, beer, meat in the fridge, and fish in the freezer.

"Do you like vegetables?" Quim asks as I down my scrambled eggs with spinach. After the fourth night, I quit trying to keep up with their carnivorous pace.

Simona calls in sometimes, asking what they've caught and whether they're still in the house. The wind has been impetuous all week, but the catch hasn't corresponded to what would be expected from such powerful gusts. The duration of these stewardships depends on the wind. One night, the men arrived at 5:48 p.m. and left at 3:52 a.m. Other times, they were out by 12 a.m. On average, they stay until about 1 a.m.

One night, Simona herself shows up and stays until one. Fifteen minutes before leaving, she takes the biggest log from the rack and hucks it into the fireplace. "That'll keep you warm through the rest of the night," she says as she puts on her jacket. The log immediately begins to sizzle and pop.

"That's putting out a lot of sparks," Quim observes.

"*Xeik*, I don't think anything's gonna catch fire here," Simona answers. "There's nothing to ignite. Come on now, let's go."

Once they're gone, I throw several glasses of water over the embers until they're completely extinguished.

At first I thought it would be hard for me to accept the possibility of these daily invasions of my space, which include nights of indefinite endings. They could become eternal, but we've enjoyed pleasant conversations during which we reveal ourselves a little bit at a time, we appreciate the company, and when silence does eventually fall, it's a natural silence. If I want privacy, I shut myself in the bedroom to read or doze off until the men come to say goodbye. If they leave at dawn, they'll most likely return to Buda the next day after eating.

I was recently told they're well compensated for working at night, among other things. Artur continues to be racked with doubt about how he should respond, knowing what he now knows, and how he should decide which family member he's going to betray. Dylan thoroughly enjoyed his trip back to Peru. Quim isn't about to forget what Simona has done to him over the years, because, he says, "It went too far. It's unforgivable what happened." Many environmentalists don't want to set foot on Buda no matter how wondrous it is. Simona intends to *xafar* the land over the next few days so it'll be flat enough to prevent the workers from tripping and stumbling during the harvest, and the men grumble and mutter to themselves, fully convinced this should have been done before they started fishing. I've also come to realize that Simona always starts our conversations with a warning, a piece of advice, or a reprimand. And I've been told that, on the day Artur brought over the fresh meat, Simona had said: "Now he's there, if we take the meat over to La Pantena he'll eat it."

I'd like for Simona to tell me about her life, about Buda, and about her companions. I've tried to get her to open up on a number of occasions, even going so far as to intentionally bump into her with the intent of starting a conversation. And yet she's always in avoidance mode, countering by saying that she'll come over one afternoon and we'll talk then. I've been waiting eight months for that afternoon.

The wind and cold have subsided enough by now to allow me to pick up my pen and go outside to write.

A day later, spring appears. Within a matter of hours, the spiderwebs are once again suspended in the nothingness and the wind smells of salt and the minerals churned up by the rotary tiller, the machine with steel teeth that evens out furrows by mixing soil with stubble, and which is followed by a black-and-white court of herons and ibises.

I walk along the beach toward the Migjorn. Security hasn't been around in some time. The birds are no longer nesting, and I want to explore that stretch of land which some consider forbidden. The Gran Calaix unfolds right before the sea. I make my way directly between the two massive bodies of water. The wind has raised up a small sandbar with two perfectly aligned steps, making it ideal for contemplating the lagoon, which on this particular afternoon is a mirrored plain where the water melts gently into the shore, no crashing, no foaming, making it difficult to think of words like *wave* or *death*. I can sometimes hear a slight lacustrine wave, contrasting with the roar of the sea behind me. It smells like earth tinged with seaweed and grass. The sun will be setting in two hours' time and yet the afternoon is still warm, as it is at the foot of the Serra del Montsià, where the sea exhales clouds that creep up the slopes, dressing the mountains in veils.

The star begins its plummet toward the peaks while seagulls screech, set off by the dun browns of the deserted paradises.

Everything is cream, ocher, and nothing at all. The lagoon conjures thoughts of the most fragile bastion standing at attention. Waiting. A place of both fortitude and finality.

Something to keep an eye on during the last hours.

Throughout the years, I haven't borne witness to many people during their dying moments, but what I remember most from those I've seen is their eyes, fixed on some specific horizon. During that final transition, when you understand that everything will soon be ending but there's still time to think clearly—whether it be days, weeks, or even a month—your sight searches for what's essential, and if my father's eyes always rested on my mother, those of my friend Daniel spent countless hours studying the sky through the bay windows of his home. And those of my beloved Pilar were shared among the many friends who, for weeks, made their pilgrimages to bid her farewell. My grandmother María tended to either close her eyes entirely or focus them on her tightly clenched hands resting on her skirt, and my grandmother Isabel woke from a coma to speak with my deceased grandfather, her husband, whom she saw. Yes, she saw him sitting on the edge of her bed, before telling him, "My dear, we'll be together soon." Two hours later, she would pass away.

Maybe, in the end, our eyes are seeking out what's distilled in our hearts. What we loved most, or those who loved us.

Back at the seashore, the sand and water are at the same level, elements of the same plane. Here, today, the wilds converse horizontally, as if recognizing each other. The action continues: a gull has just gobbled up a sonso, obviously relishing the taste of the sand eel; the plovers patrol the shoreline with their heads angled down in search of a snack; and a churning of bubbles indicates that something aggressive is happening ten meters out to sea, though the appearance of calm reigns supreme.

It's been said that waves are, in general, white noise, soothing in their own consistent, delicate way. Our body recognizes their cadence, regards it as reminiscent of the beating of our own heart. It has also been said that terrestrial beings, humans among them, have come from water, which is why it's entirely plausible that the sound of water was the first sound with which the first sensitive organisms interacted.

Ancestral cultures affirm that their music comes from nature. The rustling of branches and leaves, the wind on the plains, the roars, shrieks, murmurs, splashes, chirps, wailings, calls to the flocks, the herds, the shoals . . . all have inspired the musicians of history, though Debussy is often cited as the first composer who sought to align a work more closely with the sensations evoked by the sea. That particular composition is titled *La mer* and premiered in 1905. Roughly a century later, musician and soundscape-seeker Bernie Krause let a group of students listen to Debussy's theme without offering them any point of reference. When he asked them what the music made them think of, none of them mentioned the sea. Not even water. When people from coastal tribes who had never had access to that work, or other similarly sophisticated compositions, heard it, they spoke about the sea.

If it's true that we hear what we see, it seems that millions of people around the world have stopped looking toward the sea. They've ceased to recognize the sound of the element which occupies 71 percent of our planet. Perhaps all it would take to hear it again would be to stop . . . and listen.

VOICE

DRY

WHAT DOES THE SEA SOUND LIKE? It all depends on the slope of the beach, the distance from the shore, the depth the waters reach, the currents, the mix of floating and sunken materials, the salinity, the temperature, the seasonal weather, the prevailing environment of the land surrounding it . . . But, if the water continues advancing and the earth's entire surface is flooded, what will the sea sound like when there is no land, no rocks, no sand on which the waves can break?

Having reached the Migjorn, I turn for the shore, walking along Buda's marine contours to the river mouth where I swam peacefully back in the summer. Today, the fresh and salty currents collide, forming a long crest of foam. At this summit of confluences that is the mouth of the delta, while the earth and the sea proffer warnings about what humans are doing to them, it's easy to think heroes and hermits alike aren't welcome anymore. That the extreme, careless, and isolated personality of the asocial eremites who, for centuries, were dressed up as epic figures, has lost a certain appeal. That romanticism isn't what it once was, and that it's now time to give voice to the choir.

Giving voice to the beetle, the flamingo, *la bova*, or the beech marten—some nights I occasionally seen them near the Migjorn—to Ramoneta, Fabrizio Salina, Rachel Carson, or Simona, turning history into a symphony, and it's worth believing that their music will stand the test of time regardless of how strange it may sound to our uneducated ear. Things mix better without fear. For those who seek the purity in something, whether they call it *nature* or *humanity*, will never be able to fully enjoy what both cooks and rots in the delta: the gifts of the fruitful mud.

Demanding the isolation of our species from all the others is proving to be lethal to human interests, and those who have noticed this problem have proposed an "ecology of reconciliation" as the primary objective of this century. A physical interchange between plants, humans, minerals, and animals that gives rise to a new fertility.

To understand the benefits of combining species, it will be useful to have mixed people. The Ebro Delta is a cocktail of North Africans, Pakistanis, and Ebrencs with Valencian, Aragonese, Catalan, and Romani roots, among others who in turn coexist with stories of *marfantes*: the ghosts haunting the lagoons, lending nuance to the delta's hyperrealistic native spirit, because the soul is also stitched together with stories that are often unclear. That might be the reason why Henry Beston, after living in *The Outermost House*, went on to write two volumes of fairy tales.

Mystery and beauty are what sustain us. They both allow us to sense that there is something better, something infinitely greater, than this little puddle of numbers, neon lights, and suffocating palaver. For this reason, reality is occasionally filtered as if it were fiction and you're unsure which waters you're swimming in as you alternate between big and small, between Catalan and Spanish, between wealth and scarcity. We must be able to see how we're being governed by inexactness.

For all of these reasons and many more, there are now people out there trying to grant the Ebro personhood status. Now the Whanganui River in New Zealand has been granted its own legal identity, Ebrencs want to emulate the Maori and say, "I am the river and the river is me." Following the Whanganui example, the Ganges and Yamuna rivers in India and the Atrato in Colombia have also achieved personhood, and this new status helps both in terms of defending their interests and establishing a dialogue with them.

"Hello, Whanganui."

"Hello, Don Gabriel."

I've become friends with people who, shall we say, aren't exactly from this world, people like Fabrizio Salina or El Boga, like Rachel Carson and Josep Pla. So it shouldn't be too difficult to strengthen relationships with people who, objectively speaking, exist on the planet today, whether they're known as Whanganui, Yamuna, or Ebro. Henry David Thoreau, another such friend, once said, "I desire to speak somewhere without bounds." And, he added, "There are continents and seas in the moral world to which every man is an isthmus or an inlet, yet unexplored by him."

As a geographical feature, the human species might be more akin to a delta than an isthmus: a compacted chaos that can, in a short period of time, appear anywhere, expanding or waning, slippery and fertile, and in any case creatively so, for better or worse. To be a delta is inherent to existence.

We're like old poplar trees from the realm that coexist with eucalyptus trees from afar as well as the neighboring figs, kissed by floating seaweed and cattails. We're on the verge of becoming an Illawarra flame tree, famous for the bright-red flowers which can cover the entire tree even when it's leafless. We're an insecure, fragile organism prone to dissolution: the flesh of constant change.

Which is fortunate.

Because change implies expansion.

When you change, you seem to be more, you seem to recognize the plurality of yourself and are therefore capable of adopting outside perspectives, including those of the enemy. Change is the first step toward deciphering the sinuous, the serpentine. But not many changes occur over the course of a lifetime.

When taking stock of those moments in which something transformed me in an essential way, I note three peaks marked by disappointment, love, and death, always keeping betrayal in mind. For betrayal to exist, faith and truth are required. The good thing about a delta is that, right from the start, you know you can't trust it. That at any second its serpentine nature will put you in a compromising situation. The physical nature of a space determines the spirit of the beings that inhabit it, and here the ground moves, sinks, reappears. Some people do as well.

In any case, in the delta I can't be fooled by anyone because I don't know what expectations I have of the place other than the Big One. I'm just here to write and survive by witnessing how the Ebrencs make key decisions which affect their ancestors: will I be dry-planting or sowing in flooded fields? Do I offer a shitty job to a Santjaumero or an Indian? Will I be herding bulls or fattened ducks? Do I dance jotas or sardanas? To fish for eels or not to fish for eels? Am I against coastal recession, dikes, sediment, or nothing at all?

The identity of the delta and its people emerges from the answers to these questions, which will determine this territory's fate. And I'd observe all of them with a more or less notarial inquisitiveness if this reality hadn't asked me the same question that's eating away at Artur: are you going to betray?

"Are you trustworthy or not?"

That's what they asked me at the La Pantena dinner table, half a lifetime after that moment of disappointment in which I began to accept the serpentine nature of morality.

And now, almost three decades after my first visit, I find myself in this delta, immersed in my third great transformation after the death of my father. It's a mutation that takes place so calmly and quietly that it doesn't seem as if anything is changing at all, perhaps because my father died an elderly man and it's easier to come to terms with what's natural. Or perhaps because I've taken the blow as the culmination of a process that has, for years, been leading me to thoughts of life and its endings, enriching me without any sort of fanfare. Unlike what happened with heartbreak and love, the shock of death allows me to contemplate the landscape and notice my place in it.

"Are you trustworthy or not?"

Phrases hit differently depending on their positioning in time and space. Occasionally they can feel so swampy that you've no idea how you'll move forward, while at other moments you'll accept them like a dune you can ascend and look out from in peace. From my dune, I can see the clouds of hesitation being blown away by the gale that is my history.

I came here to write about a delta, and I found unexpected turbidity, murkier and more oleaginous than normal. When, back in summer, having swum through its brown waters, I stepped onto the river's sandy banks, there was no silt, no trace of dirt on my skin. But I know full well that the shit stains of complicity are sticky at first, only to later become embedded.

Are you complicit?

Perhaps. What I am is Gabriel's son, and there can be no doubt whatsoever about that.

The radio is broadcasting the conclusions of yet another World Climate Summit, and, as always, the news isn't good. What some people see as a tragedy, and what has brought me here, is considered by some analysts to be the result of a favorable climatological period. The planet follows cycles that alternate between ice ages and warm periods, and we're currently experiencing one of the latter phases dominated by high temperatures. The problem is that the globe's natural warming has been enhanced by unchecked human activity, imposing a veritable infinite summer upon the earth, scalding the seascape to the point where mass extinctions will begin: countless coral reefs are expected to succumb first, followed by certain species of turtles, dolphins, manatees, tuna, and cockles. Conscious that one disappearance will trigger others, resulting in a domino effect that could potentially knock down the human species, philosophers like Jorge Riechmann advise us that "we must prepare to die. Not individually, but collectively, with our civilization." And what sort of ending will we be facing? "This has not been a good civilization, and it will not die a good death," the philosopher adds.

Riechmann's fateful prediction coincides with the rampant pessimism of well-informed individuals who are amazed by how the massive operational entities powerful enough to transform the globe aren't immediately implementing countermeasures in the face of the planet's dizzying state of deterioration.

"Time has been broken," Miguel Cabello, a rancher friend of mine, once told me years ago. And I think the exact same word, broken, could be used to define today.

We want to dream of ourselves as being able to live beyond our natural lives. As gods like Cronus, owners of the clock. And in that dream we spurn the laws of time's profundity, the laws that govern our tides, our genes, our instincts, striving to forget the fables and legends that emphasize that time is not a game to be played.

But here's the thing: we know our dominance is a lie.

By lying to ourselves, we betray our ancestors who devoted so much time and effort to deciphering the pillars of life on earth and transmitting that elemental information so the species could survive. Self-deception is the greatest modern epidemic, the result of two centuries of unparalleled vanity. So here we are, spending so much time admiring ourselves in the mirror that we won't even realize what the rising water implies until we're nose-deep in it.

The heat has begun to drag on forever. *Time has been broken.* These days, I'm thinking about that even more. Last night, I dreamed of an endless summer during which heat arrived, undulating, like the sea. The climate in the dream was identical to what was going on in reality: the temperature rose from dawn to noon, welling up like a wave whose incandescent crest lasted for hours. The world roasted until late in the afternoon, when the heat broke and the unbearable exhaustion morphed into a feeling of prolonged suffocation that stretched into the night. As soon as dawn broke, traces of a new wave began to appear. It didn't take long to begin growing, and as it grew, it withered, it evaporated, it dried up. The following day, another wave charred the ashes of what had already burned. The day after that, the burning continued. One wave after another, and the sea, the earth, and the sky boiled. Heat, heat, and more heat. Like never before. Heat outside the days and months when it was to be expected, repeating itself, as unstoppable and indifferent to our desires as the waves. Heat, heat, and more heat.

I dreamed of myself there, ensconced in that summer in the center of an extensive beach. I saw lonely, emaciated, and sweaty people leaning against salt cedar trees whose branches still provided shade. I walked toward these people lugging a jug of water over my shoulders like a massive backpack. When I approached one of them, the individual would open his mouth without moving or looking at me; most had their eyes closed. I twisted the handle on the spigot, which was connected to a cannula: only the thinnest of trickles began to flow, but it was enough for the thirsty people to open their eyes or simply look at me as they drank. At points, someone would say "water" or "more," though most remained silent, scrutinizing me as if wondering where I'd gotten the water or as if they'd understood something I hadn't.

I wove my way through the salt cedars, distributing trickles of water and exchanging glances while I listened to the dying of the waves. Soon enough, water stopped flowing from the tap. When I looked up, I saw an endless beach where thousands of people were seeking refuge in the shadows of the dunes and the precarious salt cedars stretching to the horizon. I had to refill the jug, and I had to do so quickly, because all those people were waiting, and somehow I knew they couldn't go in search of water on their own. I crossed the beach toward the river; I climbed the highest dune. As I crested the ridge, I saw that the river was gone. How could it not be there?

Then the totalitarian impact of the sea and the summer hit me.

A blow delivered by the water and the heat.

And that's how the dream ended.

During the last two centuries, monoculture, monotheism, and monogamy have been imposed upon a significant part of the world, displacing ways of acting and thinking that integrated diversity, and it seems as though the impact of this new uniformity has had an effect on the climate because, in many places, we've gone from four seasons to practically two. Soon enough, scientists say, they could all be reduced to one. And we might just inaugurate the era of the monoseason.

The Pleistocene included the last ice age. Now, however, we're talking about the Summercene.

It wasn't all that long ago that it was common in many latitudes to hear fantasies about the wonders of living in an infinite summer. Now, though, with the real possibility of such a thing knocking at our door, the consequences are intimidating. If a summer that dries up rivers and crops, expands the deserts, stifles the air, or melts glaciers has no end, then what? Billions of beings require dissimilitude to survive. The Earth and the Sea need their cold . . . at least as we've come to know them to this point. The question is how to get it back. How to return the heat to its three-month arrangement. Who or what can curtail these summers?

Buda didn't appear on the list of dying islands released by the World Climate Summit. Today, a tractor opened up the Migjorn, turning Buda into a literal island. The tractor drove its front-end loader into the layer of wet sand separating the river from the sea, creating a small declivity through which the Migjorn's waters drained. On the continental shore, the tractor bulldozed land to form a large dune running parallel to the new channel, through which a tiny thread of fresh water could dribble toward the Mediterranean. An hour later, the thread became a string. After that, the string will become a rope, a cable, and, finally, a tiny delta of its own whose amplitude will depend on the winds.

This inconspicuous bit of engineering is designed to favor eel fishing. The mini delta will allow the hatchlings, eager to change their environs, to enter the waterway, where the submerged cages await them. There are currently four cages on the mainland shore and three more on mine, all lashed to an anchor on dry land. The fishers have parked a massive shipping container-like dwelling behind the artificial dune. They'll be spending the next few months there, living nocturnally, checking the cages every hour in shifts, as we're doing at La Pantena.

At my feet lies one of those cages, which here are called *buzones*. Mailboxes. A rectangular iron lattice with a small entrance is coupled with a narrow and impeccably woven green net, because the eight-centimeter elvers weigh less than a gram. The eel fry will circulate through the funnel, turning in a gyre until inside the buzón, where the net opens up and the eels, pantena-style, can no longer find their way out.

The wind kicks up clouds of sand, projecting it like shrapnel toward the sea, diluting the figures of the three men supervising the tractor, hands in their pockets, still as statues. The riverbed is still shallow, and I cross over to the continental side, walking along the seashore. A man with a limp approaches me. He's the president of the Association of Professional Eel Fishers of Sant Jaume, founded by his father and his uncle. Whenever someone starts talking about elvers, the figures start flowing unremittingly. Each buzón can accept twenty-five kilos. For one kilo, you need around three and a half thousand animals, although, since they're somewhat larger in northern Spain, three thousand will suffice. Though when it comes to the miniature eels of Santo Domingo, you'll need ten thousand to generate the same weight. In the delta, a kilo is worth around five hundred euros.

"Four years ago, we earned seventeen thousand euros in a single week," recalls Vicent Tena, who's been fishing for elvers since he was six and credits these fry as having saved many people, his own family included, from going hungry. His sister's wedding was paid for with the money from the eels.

Vicent grew up in a shanty house in El Serrallo, not far up the coast. I've seen it in passing while biking. It's a structure embedded in the middle of a sea of rice. When the fields are flooded, it stands like a sheer outcropping over the immensity. It's accessible via a spit of land which, for years now, has been protected by a fig tree. Vicent is allergic to that tree—if he touches it, he develops blisters—but his father always tried to have one nearby: "Son, you just don't understand how those figs took the edge off my hunger."

Hunger has been the measuring stick for this fertile vastness which, for centuries, was so paradoxically miserable for the many people who sustained themselves on figs, tench, and eels. These single-gram animals were so abundant that they were cast before swine while simultaneously saving people's lives. Today they've become so scarce that it's barely worth catching them at all. There are fewer and fewer eel fishers with every passing year, and many have given up on the overnight shifts because the catch doesn't compensate for their time. Or so they say: there are still around four hundred buzones in the delta.

In any case, Vicent is convinced that, within the next couple of years, the European Union is going to ban eel trapping.

"What if you stop fishing, let the population recover, and then start up again?" I ask.

He shrugs. After beating around the bush a bit, he ends up saying that no matter how much they defer fishing, Europe is intent on banning trapping. The eel enters the Mediterranean through the Strait of Gibraltar, but it does so with hesitation because it prefers colder waters. And while the number of eels that reach these waters was never high, the population has declined even more due to the chemicals used to combat the apple snail and the proliferation of the blue crab. Europe, being aware of the potentially devastating environmental effects, has tightened regulations, opting to protect it.

Fishers aren't too terribly worried, because what they earn from elvers only supplements their regular income. Vicent, for example, is a cook. He's expert at preparing eel *en suc* with crab, garlic, guindilla peppers, parsley, tomato, and a splash of cognac, although his restaurant also serves thirty-two types of rice. Vicent grew up in a shanty house and now, in addition to running a successful restaurant, he presides over the Associations of Professional Eel Fishers, of Angling, Teranyina, Sport Fishing, and Trolling, having emerged as a new self-made *siñor* from the delta who defines himself by saying, "When you get down to it, I'm a pretty simple man. I don't like going to restaurants—a ham sandwich is fine by me. I'd rather sell a kilo of elvers for two hundred euros and buy a free-range lamb than go to the grocery store every few days. That's just how I was raised, saving money and eating healthy, and I don't have any real complaints. I was better off than plenty of others because my family had two shacks, one to live in and the other for sleeping."

The tractor continues to widen the breach, while the wind seems intent on covering it back up. The channel will broaden when the wind blows from the northwest. Talking about the air feels inevitable, and Vicent brings up something that happened recently. "This time it was my turn to fall," he says. It was a rainy night, with temperatures right at freezing point, and he was trying to haul in a mailbox. Each cage costs around three hundred euros, which is why he wasn't about to let it go, so he went to the water's edge, trying to maintain his balance while wiggling the hook, attempting to bring the mailbox closer to the shore without having to get into the water himself. He should have lashed a safety rope around his waist for his companion on the shore to anchor, sure, but he'd been doing this for years now, the trap was almost within reach, and he'd recovered plenty of times without ever needing a safety harness of any sort.

The downpour was starting to grow into a storm.

Vicent's mind wavered. He didn't want to get wet. He didn't even want to risk it. But as he hesitated, the softened clods of riverbank soil shifted under his feet, unbalancing him.

There weren't any branches or shrubs to grab onto.

He went in the dark.

Vicent managed to cling to some vegetation along the shoreline, but the current was pushing hard against him. He'd have to clamber up half a meter of muddy riverbank to reach dry land, an objective that was more of a feat, considering that Vicent once weighed over two hundred kilos, and while he was a bit lighter on his feet since having a gastric bypass, his movements were still slow.

The wind was blowing at well over fifty knots, the frigid temperature of the water could soon enough result in death by hypothermia, and the weight of the fisher's layered winter gear was dragging him down: a short-sleeved undershirt, a long-sleeved thermal shirt, a hoodie, and a parka, along with two pairs of pants, one thermal and one waterproof, the kind you use in snow, plus his heavy-duty boots, all of which were preventing him from floating. His partner threw him a rope, which Vicent was able to grab. He tied it around his waist, and the two of them worked together to hoist him ashore as quickly as possible.

"When you're going for eels, you always have to go in pairs."

As soon as he reached the shore, he got into his van, cranked up the heater, took off all his soaking-wet clothes, and raced back home, where he managed to avoid hypothermia.

Incidents like this reinforce you. Surviving on figs does too. Which is why Vicent can't understand why his paisanos from the delta seem to have such a low sense of self-esteem, completely the opposite of the northern Spanish eel anglers he met when he moved there with his father to work a rice farm in Tudela. He'd go on to live there for almost twenty years.

"The Basques believe in themselves. Here, the Trabucador spit has two winters left, maybe three. With Buda, it's ten at the most. If they were facing the same situation up north, they'd have already put up jetties and breakwaters. If they hadn't, they'd be demonstrating by the thousands."

The tractor's front-end loader excavates more sand at the point where the small channel splices with the river, widening the watercourse by a few more centimeters. When the grade increases, the flow gains strength. Vicent says elver fishing in Buda still isn't profitable, which isn't unusual: eel anglers have only just started trapping near the old dragonfly corridor, and sometimes it can take a fishery five or six years to get going. If that's the case, and if this type of fishing is going to be banned in the delta, then what's the point of anchoring mailboxes here?

I make my way back, biking against the wind, alternating periods of furious pedaling with long stretches of walking. On the El Mas straightaway, I hop back on the bike. The wind is at my back, and what was once a great difficulty becomes an impetus that shoots me along like a kingfisher. When I reach Gonzalo's house, I stop in front of the fig tree. It's rooted so close to the irrigation ditch that the tree itself leans toward the water, which is why, earlier in the summer, I had to jump up on the outermost branches and climb the thick trunk in a dangerously acrobatic position to pick even a tiny handful of figs. The rest, unreachable by humans, were left for the starlings and company. Now there are no fruits left, but Vicent's story invites us to admire the fig tree that much more.

It's been said that the fig tree was one of the first plants cultivated by humans, and that they did so in the Jordan Valley delta around 9400 BC. It may have been the first domesticated plant to have fed us, well before wheat, barley, legumes and rice. In Ancient Egypt, monkeys were trained to collect the fruit. It features in the foundational mythology of Rome, because Romulus and Remus were nursed by the wolf Luperca under a fig tree. This is separate from Adam and Eve covering their nakedness with the same lobed leaves which, today, wave in the wind like ancient Japanese folding fans. The fig tree symbolizes fertility, sexual initiation, and good luck.

Both the fig tree and the elver are part of the delta's mythology, now as silenced as the eel that saved those who traveled on the *Mayflower*. This little-publicized triad invites us to wonder why we often agree to remember the stories others want us to while forgetting those that might reveal to us a much more real world. For example, little has been said about how a fig tree revealed Christ's capricious sense of cruelty, though the Gospels lay it clearly before us. Mark tells us that, when Jesus went to the fig tree looking for fruit only to find nothing but leaves, he became angry. "For the time of figs was not yet," the apostle points out. But Jesus cursed him: "No man eat fruit of thee hereafter for ever." And with that, by the next morning the fig tree had withered and dried down to its roots.

In this chapter, Jesus demonstrates not only his lack of knowledge about the tree's periods of sexual reproduction but also a childish impulsivity that's contemporary, and which leads him to punish a being he undoubtedly considers inferior because it doesn't give him what he wants when he wants it. Jesus's rage at disobedient nature, and his repressive reaction, has parallels with the utilitarian attitude held by millions of people—not just urbanites—in the twenty-first century against all the natural things that surround them. Of all Jesus's miracles, this appears to be the only destructive one recorded in the Bible. Also the only one he carried out in Jerusalem, the only one that took twenty-four hours to take effect, and the only one priests don't read during Sunday Mass.

Vicent and the fishers are wringing elvers out of the Ebro just as Jesus strangled the fig tree. Both are doing away with living beings that sustained their ancestors. And it's difficult to understand why, years ago, no one decided to lift the ban on elvers that would have prevented us from reaching this point.

I get back on the bike with a tailwind. The horses grazing in the La Pantena fields watch me fly by on wheels. Ahead, the cohetera and the sea.

ON AUTHORITY

IN WELCOMING ME TO THE ISLAND, Mateo was putting his trust in me: a trust he's been underpinning during these recent months based on private stories which for whatever reason he's decided to tell. His invitation to settle me in La Pantena didn't imply silencing anything I might witness during my stay, but after more than a year of coexisting and having shared delicate situations where secrets were revealed to me, I sensed a certain pressure to keep quiet about anything that might upset my hosts and colleagues. Don't bite the hand that feeds you, as the saying goes.

It would be dishonest to tell of certain problematic events while simultaneously ignoring other elements of the story. Nobody has committed any serious infractions, merely slight deviations from the norm, which would only be worthy of fines or lose them a permit, but none of that is my concern. I could choose not to write these lines and stave off future disagreements, I could avoid being called an ingrate or a snitch, or whatever other reprisals I might suffer, but literature isn't a matter of fear versus friendship. And, even more importantly, I don't want to offend my father. He raised me to be able to write exactly what I have in this paragraph. To do the best work I can. So, cutting to the core of the situation, the question that remains is the same one Artur asked himself, the question we're both facing: who should I betray?

The rice fields, now *xafat*, have become massive puddles of mud and clods of earth. Feces and feathers garnish the dismantled surfaces that spread out in shades of straw and ocher. On the beach, a scourge from the northwest kicks up the half-warm sand, sending millions of these tiny particles in a breakneck charge against the sea. It's a spectral avalanche in which the gusts are chained together, reworking the ground, shaving down some of the dunes while forming new ones, higher and more convex, near the water. As far as the eye can see, mineral life is all that exists. Time is being expressed in its most mechanical dimension. The rawness of the planet. I press forward, peppered with grains I can only feel through my clothes because my hands are jammed into my pockets and my face is covered with a scarf. When I pull one hand out, gripping my binoculars, the crystalline flecks stick to me like microscopic pins. A marsh harrier hovers hungrily over the mire of the *xafat* fields. The wind increases its savagery.

A kingfisher darts across the reedbed. Alone, as usual. Most birds appear in flocks, but not this one. It's too quick for even its own kind. From the remnants of the dragonfly corridor I see a vehicle at the intersection of the road to La Pantena. Simona's pickup. Artur is next to the river, refueling the generator and accompanied by a truck driver.

As I'm arriving, Simona calls out to me from her vehicle. We approach one another, me at a quicker pace than her. When we meet, she puts her hands on my shoulders. She's taller and stouter than I am. "Hey," she says. "Don't take this the wrong way, but stay away from the beach. Don't even walk along the lagoon. The hunters will be coming soon, and if the ducks see you walking around here, they'll learn that people come through here and won't be back."

"Duck season doesn't start for another ten days."

"Well, it's still better if you're not out and about," she says, removing her hands from my shoulders.

"I can stay away from the lagoon for a few days," I reply. "But not the sea. That's what I'm here for. I'm more interested in that island there," I say, extending a finger in the direction of the beach, "than I am in the rice."

"Has anyone authorized that? Who authorized you?"

"Mateo is letting me live in La Pantena. I'm here because of the sea."

"And we're here because we have to work."

"Well," I say, digging into my pockets, "I'm here to work too." One hand emerges with a small notebook, the other with a pen. "Why else would I be here?"

Simona stares at me in silence, lips pursed, body tense. "Are you authorized? Hey! Do you have any authorization?"

"Not in so many words, but maybe now's the time to clarify that."

Simona pulls out her phone and calls Mateo. It's on speakerphone. She tells him that I'm wandering along the edge of the lagoon, that I've also been going to the sea, and that I'm going to disrupt duck hunting. Mateo suggests I stay away from those areas for a few days. My response is that I don't make any noise and I don't startle the fauna; many of the birds have incorporated me as part of the landscape itself and don't even fly off when I pass by. And, well, the whole point of me being here is to go to the sea and the mouth of the river. Mateo hesitates. Maybe, he says, if I'm extra careful . . . At this point, Simona turns off the speakerphone and exchanges a few words with Mateo, only to hang up on her boss while he's still responding. I can hear it all.

"Alright then," Simona says, looking me in the eyes. "I'm authorizing ten days for you to go to the sea."

The supervisor makes a half turn and heads toward La Pantena. I follow her, a few meters behind. We cross the tiny gangway to where Artur is with the generator and the truck driver. I enter the house. A few minutes later, the truck departs. Artur and Simona are on the porch; I can see them through the small window in the living room.

"I don't want anybody dropping off any food or water here," Simona says, quite loudly. "Nothing! I don't want to hear about anyone bringing anything to this guy!"

This guy is me. I listen to the sound of her vehicle vanishing into the distance. And to the tapping at the window shades. It's Artur.

"You heard what she said, right?"

"Yeah."

"Forget about it. If you need anything, just ask."

"Thank you so much."

"It's just how she is."

"Yeah."

It's getting dark.

A short while later Dylan arrives. We fill him in on what's happened. I tell them I can't trust her, I have no idea what such a person is capable of, that she's seriously pissed off.

"Calm down," Dylan says. "She won't do anything to you. She knows you're here because of Mateo."

The men fish until midnight.

When they leave, I don't feel particularly tense, but the awareness of being alone in Buda has taken on a new dimension. I think about all the latent threats. The drug traffickers, the poachers, the storm, but most of all the stories that point to Simona as having been responsible for poisoning water, cutting off electricity, slashing tires, putting sound cannons right next to Gonzalo's house, intimidating her workers . . . In a few short days, the island will be filled with weapons. They say dogs can sniff out fear and geese can sense whether a person intends to do them harm or not. Today would be a good day to be a goose. Lying in bed, I pay closer attention to the standard creaks and groans of the house. Though not for long because, after taking a long look at the two ducks in the painting at the head of the bedroom, I switch off the light and go to sleep.

Simona hasn't shown up at La Pantena for the past three nights. She supervises the catch by calling the men, who usually leave at dawn even though the tides aren't bringing in much. Simona's animosity toward me makes it easier for the men to disclose some new stories about the supervisor. Dylan in particular has squared off with her on a couple of occasions with an all but uncontrollable rage.

"She's done it all to me. In the beginning, when it was just me and her, the only thing she didn't do was break out her whip and give me twenty lashes."

Apart from the shouting, the gratuitous and unjustified corrections that slow everything down, never accepting suggestions from the men even if she ends up doing what they proposed while stressing that it had been her idea all along, the one thing that Dylan won't stand for is robbery. Being robbed, to be specific. Like that day when a boat with a cargo of drugs ran aground on the Buda beach. The traffickers had stolen the boat from a German resident, and when the man came to retrieve it, there was no way to drag it back to the water. The German man agreed to pay Simona to help him get the boat back out to sea, but the supervisor couldn't do it alone, so she enlisted help from Dylan, who got it unstuck. Since the entire operation took a significant amount of time, the supervisor was no longer on the beach when the boat was afloat again, so the German man gave Dylan two hundred euros, with one specification: "A hundred for Simona and a hundred for you."

When Dylan informed Simona about the German's tip, the supervisor told him to give her all the money, which she'd then distribute. Distribute? Dylan was right there in front of her; she could have given him his half straightaway. Regardless, he forked over the bills. A few days went by and he hadn't received anything, so he went to claim his share. Simona handed him twenty euros.

"What's this? The man gave me a hundred."

"Who handles the money around here? Me. I'm the one in charge of this."

Dylan returned the twenty euros. "Either you give me what's mine or you keep it all."

Simona took the bill. "Whoa!" she said.

Dylan informed Mateo of the situation. And while the boss understood his claim, he decided to pay the missing eighty from his own pocket. Dylan refused the gesture. It wasn't about that. It was about being fair, about ensuring Simona wouldn't continue doing whatever she wanted with impunity. The formula Mateo chose for solving the problem made it clear that, somehow, Simona had him in her clutches. Dylan had already noted that power imbalance on other occasions he'd reported the supervisor. Mateo always mitigated the violations, he mediated in situations that didn't merit arbitration because there were clear and present culprits. But the way he chose to solve the problem of the German man's tip, the fact that he was willing to put up his own money so the minisiñora wouldn't be put out or otherwise offended, demonstrated the power she had managed to consolidate on the farm. And if the men aspired to even a minimum amount of justice, hoped to draw a line in the sand regarding basic respect, they'd have to go about it their own way . . . Because Simona isn't open to suggestions. She's the type of person who only learns things the hard way. The damn law about the survival of the fittest.

One particular day, after Simona had thrown a piece of pipework at him and was shouting about how much she despised everyone, Dylan decided to hop in the truck parked on the esplanade between Paquito's shack and the toolsheds.

Through the dust-stained windshield, Dylan watched as the supervisor continued to shout at him.

He fired up the engine.

He popped the clutch, hit the accelerator, and floored it.

The truck roared straight toward the lone dark spot in that deserted place.

The supervisor was aghast.

Twenty meters away, and the vehicle was still gaining speed.

Simona stood swaying, not fully understanding what was happening.

The truck was just ten meters away when Dylan hit the brakes, skidding into a turn before leaving the esplanade.

Simona had turned white. And not just from the dust that had been kicked up.

The skid marks remained in the dirt for days, as if a sign of what might happen if things remained the same.

It hasn't helped much, because nothing seems to have changed. Now, Dylan is basically banking on how Artur's presence might have some sort of influence.

In the morning, I gather some logs from the pile next to the river and, as I'm walking back up to La Pantena, Simona's car pulls over at the junction where the road and straightaway meet. As I'm unloading the firewood into the basket by the fireplace, I hear the entrance door curtains rustling. It's her. "You're using up all the firewood," she says. "I assume you'll be compensating the workers for not leaving any logs for them."

I shrug, unsure of what to say. "Sure."

The sound of an approaching engine can be heard outside. It's the men. We step out onto the porch.

"The Parc Natural officials have prohibited us from using the barge," Simona tells her team. "But we'll be using it anyway, since how else are we supposed to work? Just don't cross with anyone not from the island." She looks in my direction.

"I count as being from the island, right?"

"No."

"But I need to go shopping in town, because if you're not bringing me food or water . . ."

"You'd better figure something else out, then."

"I guess I'll have to build a canoe."

The men grin.

"Well go right ahead then."

She leaves. I ask the others what options I have for getting off the island. The floodgates aren't fully open, so if I roll up my pant legs I can still wade across from shore to shore. Employees can still access Buda by car. Their vehicles have powerful traction that allows them to surmount the flooded areas and the sandy strip. In any case, within the next few days, the floodgates will yawn wider and there will be no choice but to cross via the barge.

"If you need a lift, give us a call," the men tell me. "You'll just have to wait till Simona leaves, and since she spends half the day outside . . ."

"What if she sees me in town or on the road?"

"Tell her you paddled your canoe over."

We all laugh.

"Is there really no way for me to get out on my own?"

The answer would seem to be no.

If I don't want to put my companions in a compromising situation, I should stay on the island and ride it out as best I can. Maybe I'll end up doing a little duck hunting. I have wild chard, crabs, and the fish from La Pantena, because now no one controls whether I catch anything, and besides, people are often prone to leaving the occasional sole or bream in the freezer. I evaluate my dry goods: two packages of rice, one of macaroni, and three cans of food. That's enough to guarantee dinner. I'll just have to make it through the rest of the day.

Regardless, La Administración and the supervisor have effectively locked me in, and the men don't want to teach me how to operate the barge because we're prohibited from using it, and if any sort of mishap were to occur, they'd be held responsible. It's a prime example of how tensions between public institutions, owners, and the occasional fool can end up impacting anyone. Why wouldn't the Parc Natural let them use the only means of transportation connecting the mainland to the island?

Many deltas are islands in and of themselves. Their inhabitants are governed by different codes than other, more sedentary societies. In Alexandria, *fellahin* along the Nile erected spiritual walls, creating a protected and accommodating space for folk and cabaret dancers. In Macau, the mouth of the Pearl River, the appetite for gambling, combined with unique legislation, has resulted in millions of tons of sand being dumped into the South China Sea, creating new spaces for casinos and hotels to be built. And in New York, as the population of the metropolitan area expanded across the mouth of the Hudson River, 90 percent of the city's wetlands were filled in and firmed up. Chinatown was once a wetland. The same with Coney Island and East Harlem. Eventually, on top of that mud and silt, one of the largest agglomerations of skyscrapers on the planet was constructed.

"So what are you gonna write about this?" Quim asks me one night, our fingers blackened from the freshly grilled eels he's prepared. "That these three are for private consumption?" he says as he grabs three more from the basket. One of the animals has slithered through the grates and fallen onto the bed of red-hot coals, writhing almost electrically and smearing itself with ash until Quim is able to grab it with the tongs and secure it once again on the grill. A few fish, generally bass or bream, always jump from the veritable frying pan into the fire, only to get coated in ash before Quim returns them to their fated grill, but the whipping, lashing eel, with its desperate, almost reptilian sashaying, is much more affecting.

As a cook, Quim is both patient and delicate. Despite the eels' spectacular convulsions and the jolting jumps of the other fish trying to scurry away, he's quickly able to seize the animals and gently return them to the grill.

"I won't be missing that book. I already told you I'll read it from cover to cover."

As he's grilling, he rolls up his sleeves, revealing a tattoo I'd seen on other occasions.

"You got your name tattooed on your arm," I say.

"You caught that. Yeah, I got it done when I was twelve. I was smoking a joint with my brother, and he thought it would be a good idea for each of us to get tattoos of our names. So we both went. Kid shit. If I could, I'd get it removed, but I'm not sure how the rest of the skin would turn out."

Dylan offers up his own forearm, on which a number has been tattooed.

"It's my ID number from Peru. Me and my brother did that too. When we were fourteen. We were obsessed with the whole identification thing, and then one day my brother says, 'What if they stop us and ask for our numbers and we don't remember them?' So here it is. Forever and ever."

Quim takes the seltzer bottle, angles the spout toward his mouth, and releases a stream directly down his throat.

"What the hell are you doing?" Dylan exclaims. "The carbonation will blow a hole in your stomach!"

"Whatever."

"Why don't they let you use the barge?" I ask.

"Who knows what the higher-ups are thinking," Quim says. "All I want to do is work, get paid, and for them to stop coming down on us with all this bullshit. But here, when you ask for an explanation for anything, they always shift the blame to La Administración. Maybe this whole thing about the barge does have something to do with them, but there's always a lot going on with these stories. Here, you can solve anything by blaming it on La Administración.

If a problem comes up, it's their problem to solve. But I don't know much about them. I know a few specific people who do a few specific things. And if we fix things with those people, then who knows, maybe La Administración will do better." At the conclusion of this speech, he looks at Dylan and says, "Shall we go?"

The men ready themselves for work, dragging the plastic chairs behind them. Quim adjusts the straps on his waterproof suit. We all put on our coats, and I follow them outside.

The wind seems stronger at night.

It forces you to lean into it as you walk.

We're guided by a crescent moon that shimmers on the surface of the canal. The fishers shake the pantena, pleating it as they go, forcing the fish to pile up in the last rectangular piece of netting. Perhaps a dozen eels, bream, sea bass, and gray mullet are flapping around, along with three crabs. The wind still hasn't brought what it was expected to bring.

The men haul the fish out along with the brackish water, struggling to maintain their balance on the wooden dock while being buffeted by the gusts of a howling wind. The red glow of the lighthouse flickers in the distance.

Quim grabs the basket and carries it inside the house. They add this catch to what they've already brought in and weigh it all together on the scale. "Not much," Dylan says.

Dylan's phone rings. It's Simona, asking how everything is going. She also announces that Mateo wants to set up a dinner at La Pantena, and that we'll have to get the house ready. After hanging up, the men head out.

CHORUS

ARTUR ANNOUNCES that the dinner at La Pantena will feature a wild boar stew prepared by his father. He asks me if I'll be there around four, because his father wants to let it simmer for several hours and will need my stove. That afternoon I'll be meeting with Vicent in town, so I'll leave the keys in a place agreed upon by Artur. Early on in my stay, I'd always lock the door if I was going to leave the house for a few hours, but as the months have passed, I've relaxed the habit, often simply closing it or leaving the keys somewhere Dylan suggests. However, the skirmishes with Simona have led me to start locking the door again. She's playing her own game, and if she wants to enter the house she will. But if something were to happen inside the house, at least I know I'll be able to ask some specific questions. If I were to leave it unlocked, it would be easy to attribute any sort of theft or damage to a random intruder. Of course, meeting a stranger here is practically impossible. During my solitary time on the island, I've seen one lone fisher on the beach and a couple of surfers who dragged their boards into the little pond that connected with the dragonfly corridor. I've also seen, especially on weekends, an unidentified vehicle pushing deep into La Pirenaica toward the dike facing the sea, although these incursions are rare enough that I'm comfortable attributing them to tourists from El Mas or temporary workers. In any case, nobody's come anywhere near La Pantena, unless they are accompanying Mateo on one of his sweeps through Buda. Now his dream of a shuttle train has been thwarted, he's volunteered to act as a guide to raise awareness among his visitors about the reality of life on the island.

After having impressed them with those two fantastic kilometers and the stately structure of El Mas, Mateo could show off Dieguito, the snake he keeps in the room adjacent to the El Pas shack. But he doesn't often include the snake as part of the tour, because Dieguito lives alone in a used wooden shipping crate in that dilapidated house, and such isolation is painful when compared with the images of the burros and horses in the open air, the tigerish blue crabs, the cohetera, or the sea.

Dieguito's confinement also stands in stark contrast with my freedom, so Mateo now tends to ignore the snake and instead ends the tour with La Pantena and myself. Before, he would conclude by grabbing a blue crab from the canal and letting it scuttle across the ground. He'd then crush the crustacean under his boot, pick up the carapace, and fling it back into the water while commenting on the disastrous effects of this species's unchecked reproduction in these waters. Since I'm now part of the tour, I might step out onto the porch after the crab show and say hello, at which point Mateo will report that I've been living in La Pantena for the past year to write a book about Buda and coastal recession. And so I've happened to chat a bit with one of Mateo's old friends, some, shall we say, high-flying businesspeople, several priests and bishops, as well as the owners of large neighboring properties.

These visits don't last long, ten or fifteen minutes at most. There might have been five or six during this year. Yes, that few. Still, though, I've been able to observe Mateo acting as a delightful host, his oratory abilities on full display. As a public speaker, he combines erudition with jokes while illustrating his words with perfectly gauged gestures that serve not only to captivate the audience but also to frame this fabled landscape. He's seductive to the point where it seems almost strange that this man can get as angry as they say during official meetings. In any case, he's a passionate man who believes that if he must jump through the hoops of becoming a tour guide, then he'll jump, because if he's to have any chance of saving Buda, then the show must go on, and for that to happen the island must be the main attraction. "Would you ever go to a circus without a clown?" he asked me one day at the end of one of his performances. "Well, here in Buda, that clown is me."

"What got Mateo thinking about arranging this dinner?" I ask Artur.

"I don't know, but Karen will be here too."

"And your father."

"You'll see how wild boar is cooked."

On Sunday afternoon I walk along the edge of the Gran Calaix. The wind stirs the reedbeds glazed with the oranges and siennas of autumn. The ruffled surface of the lagoon sends out flashes of languid light. In the distance, I mistake the felted tops of the reeds for a flock of birds. The din of thousands of plants clashing in the wind calms down to a near silence as I make my way around a bend in the path. The wall of shrubs to the south and the reeds along the shore of the Gran Calaix create a vast refuge where the wind itself is seen, rather than heard, on the lagoon.

This calmness reminds me of my father's words: "Whatever happens, I'm at peace." The certainty of his life well lived allows me to imagine that he'd have appreciated this haven, tells me that I'm enjoying it as he would have. I start to cry again, this time to the murmuring reeds. I let the cold tears roll down my cheeks until they either fall or are absorbed by my skin, recreating myself in the joyful sorrow of this beautiful reminder as it initiates me into another way of being, intoxicated with this feeling, making the most of it, of the cold on my face, of the warmth of memory, the air, the land, and the water in synchronous vibration, of the certainty that this—precisely this—is living.

The air dries my tears. The wharf's lookout tower appears. I enter and make my way up. The turret groans and sways like the timbers of a ship at the mercy of a storm. As soon as I break out the binoculars, a marsh harrier appears, gliding high before descending a few meters. It hangs there right in front of me, remaining impossibly still. Fixed like a star. The wooden tower creaks as it rocks, though it remains as firmly in place as the harrier. It's almost as if we're flying together.

I dispense with the binoculars to continue with the view. Something has startled a flock of coots, which are hurrying across the lagoon's surface and leaving little white trails like tracks in the water. A constellation of paillettes halos the cormorant perched on the protruding branch of a flooded tree, lending it a regal air, while behind it fast-moving plovers fly in groups level with the Gran Calaix. I rejoice in these scenes not simply because of their beauty but because I can explain it. Because I have both the vista and the words. And because, after many months, I now know that the smallish spot in the lagoon is an islet and not a moored boat, that the Gregale wind is blowing, and that the gleam from the southwest comes from the corner of a field through which the eddying waters sometimes flow. I know that the blots in the distance are goats, that the gap in the eucalyptus corridor is where the path to El Sifó begins, that what's flying farther away are lapwings, and that I can distinguish a human presence from several kilometers. I have sediment in my eye. Where once I didn't see, now I understand. From the flapping wings of the female marsh harrier to the screeching of the tern to myriad other ways the birds warn one another. The way they take in the colors, the air itself, and their ability to pretend, when necessary, that they're either dead or not there at all. Those who know how to do it best are often referred to by us, humans, as traitors. Even though their only desire is to survive.

You can choose. To act or not to act. A librarian in Alexandria, at the western edge of the Nile Delta, once told me: "A person looks at the world and asks, 'Why?' Here, our answer is 'Why not?'"

This posture, maintained throughout the centuries, has allowed for the construction of a modern library which aspires to reclaim the spirit of the ancient one, which had been one of the greatest in the world. The legendary Great Library of Alexandria was established in the third century BC and, though it would later find itself in decline, having suffered from the purging of intellectuals during the reign of Ptolemy VIII, and then again from Alexandria's resistance to Roman domination that drove Emperor Caracalla to cut off funding to the institution, what ended up physically destroying it was the Cretan earthquake in the year 365 AD and the tsunami which, hours later, would devastate the coasts of Libya and Alexandria.

The current library is also located a few meters from the sea. It was designed by Swedish architects and, while there isn't much in the way of physical books on its shelves, millions of texts can be consulted virtually. A few of these contain stories about the deltas of the world. Stories which insist that water always seeks the shortest path. Like the ones Elizabeth Rush told in her 2018 book *Rising*. Rush writes about eight American coastal communities which either have been or are being flooded due to climate change and property development failures and yet aren't candidates for receiving funding with which to confront the emergency.

Rush points out that many Native Americans whose families have, for centuries, existed in these sorts of hinterlands are now being excluded from certain government aid programs because, after generations of miscegenation, they're no longer pure enough to be considered Indigenous and therefore aren't entitled to compensation. Now, lacking both money and a place to call home, they've been condemned to wandering around as vagabonds.

Sea levels along North America's Atlantic coast are rising at a greater rate than the global average. And with that comes a wide range of critical situations being resolved in different ways, all of which depend on the race, population, and socioeconomic status of the people who inhabit these spaces. A resident of New York isn't treated the same as someone from Shorecrest, Florida. Rush expresses concern about the 90 percent of New York built on wetlands that were filled in and hardened with earth, and wonders what will happen not only to that city but also—and perhaps even more urgently—to Miami, whose sinking is now presumed to be inexorable. In this day and age it's striking to see how Miami Beach residents are benefiting from a large government investment to pay for the adaptation of structures vulnerable to rising sea levels, "but in Shorecrest, Hialeah, and Sweetwater—low- to middle-income neighborhoods where the majority of residents are people of color and municipal services have long been difficult to maintain, thanks to the discriminatory banking practice known as redlining and the resulting decline in property taxes—residents are expected to remove their shoes and wade through the water."

Rush pays attention to communities under pressure. She speaks with people who have left or are planning to leave, as well with those who will endure as long as they can, alone in their homes, for as long as the ground holds.

In Staten Island's Oakwood Beach neighborhood, Rush found a community that defended its interests against the various lobbies and, despite being obliged to migrate elsewhere, managed to remain united, staying in homes close to the landscape that had defined their lives. Which is why, today, old friends play cards, drink beer or tea, and relax and chat on their porches for as long as they like. The organized community of Oakwood Beach seems to have avoided the diasporic effect inescapable in other parts of the globe, allowing Rush to emphasize the camaraderie, the partnership, the feelings of being part of a group that Robin Wall Kimmerer, the Potawatomi botanist and author, also contends are still a possibility. You just have to learn when to retreat. Because, at some point, you will have to. "It is not a question of if but when," Ben Strauss, a sea-level rise expert and vice president of nonprofit news organization Climate Central, tells Rush. One day you will die. It is not a question of if but when.

Oakwood Beach's residents didn't want to endure until the end. They looked for an alternative that might preserve the way of life they loved. And they took the initiative. Some will see it as an escape, as having given in to pressure. Rush suggests that, over the years, she's come to understand the value of escape, even more so when it's timely and well planned. An escape which, in the Staten Island case, involves so many nuances and intricacies that it doesn't truly deserve the name, because it's more of a subtle displacement. A relocation of a group strong enough to have avoided disintegration. Of individuals who have come to learn how and when to retreat. They've discovered that if you move only a little but remain synchronized, things don't have to change so much. Which thus leads to the question: why don't we prepare for this withdrawal together?

This is what Rush is most interested in: "The radically egalitarian nature of retreat." In the affected areas, everyone must go, from the roseate spoonbill to the multibillionaire. Birds, fish, humans . . . Why can't we coordinate? A tactical withdrawal implies both humility and the recognition of the severity of the threat.

How might one go about it? Why trust that others will be willing to work with you? Gardener philosopher Santiago Beruete often recalls a favorite phrase from one of the teachers he most admired as a student: "Listen carefully to what I'm about to tell you . . . you are not alone."

Schools of fish, flocks of birds, herds of cattle: all are defensive formations to protect the group from predators and obtain food. Millions of animals believe they'll survive better together. This is why there are species that sing or bellow in chorus to scare off would-be attackers. Some birds, like the thrush, upon detecting a lurking hawk, will swoop over it en masse, hundreds or even thousands strong, evacuating their bowels. In Oakwood Beach, there are people not unlike these thrushes helping us to think in new ways about the Ebro and the Taula d'Acords.

The Library of Alexandria contains a growing number of books raising these types of questions. Questions which are beginning to overwhelm the Nile Delta's inhabitants, who are already considering the possibility of retreating, calculating how and when to do it, imagining where nearby they might be able to build a Delta #2. They can, of course, choose to act or not to act. Moving is an option, a possibility, but having invested so much of their lives there, they find it difficult to envision themselves far from that world of mongooses, crocodiles, and Egyptian clover ideal for forage, fodder, refineries, monumental granaries, cement, cotton, and even the many paint factories. Because that delta is full of paint. And so I think of my father. I think of ways of saying goodbye.

SIÑORS, MOORS, AND EBRENCS

THERE ISN'T A BREATH OF WIND on the night of the boar. Mateo and Karen picked me up in Sant Jaume to drive me to Buda. As soon as we crossed the Migjorn, the eyes of a marten twinkled at us from the riverbanks. The animal stared into the headlights before streaking across the road in front of the vehicle, heading toward the lagoon.

I've left the bike hidden in the foliage next to the river, so I hop on and start pedaling. Mateo drives behind me for a while, lighting the way for both of us, until he passes me with a shout: "See you at La Pantena." He hits the gas and leaves me rolling along in a night whose sky is so starry I don't need a flashlight.

At the start of the straightaway shot to El Mas, I stop to admire the flickering immensity.

So here I am, straddling a bike and staring up at the firmament.

I stand there in the middle of the road, inhaling deep breaths of salty air as if looking to fill my lungs with peace.

The windless night is as impressive as the constellations, perhaps because it's been some time since I could hear the delta in silence.

For the first time, I can make out La Pantena glittering in the distance.

The last human light before the blackness.

A feast is being prepared there.

Let's go.

The living room is hotter than ever. A massive log is ablaze in the fireplace, and the unusually large number of people present only increases the temperature. Artur's father stirs the formidable pot in which the wild boar simmers in a stew of carrots, leeks, onions, and smoked paprika jazzed up with two glasses of cider and two more of beer. There are several side dishes offering fuet, fried potatoes, peanuts, and cockles. Bottles of beer and wine. Mateo is chatting and smiling the most. He's engaging everyone while uncorking a bottle of red wine that slips out of his hands, spilling its spoils across the table and down his pants. He laughs as he pats himself dry.

"When will the boar be here?"

All the men are there, along with Simona, Artur's father, and Karen. After serving the stew and filling the glasses, Mateo announces that he's convened this dinner party to celebrate Dylan's return from Peru, and that Karen will soon become a grandparent for the second time, as will he and Artur's father.

We all toast Dylan and the future baby.

Simona has barely even opened her mouth. She sits at the opposite end of the table, chewing in saturnine silence. I'm next to Karen, who upon finishing her hunk of boar stretches her legs across Mateo's knees. The boss hasn't stopped telling flattering tales of the men who work at La Pantena. "And here's to Dylan, Quim, and Artur . . . the ones who do the real work around here," he goes as far as to say.

The supervisor doesn't bat an eye. The setting invites speculation that the heaping praise is designed to encourage the team, to make sure they realize the boss has their back. And, perhaps, that Simona herself has been apprised of the motivations behind this gathering. Who can say. They ask me how I'm doing in the house and in Buda.

"Really well."

I ask about the significance behind the duck paintings, pointing out that the one in the living room includes three of the creatures. I take a guess and suppose they represent Pep, Ramoneta, and her son Héctor because, in the main bedroom, there are only two ducks in the painting.

"That has nothing to do with it," Simona says. "I chose the décor for the house, and I put the paintings wherever I saw fit."

Well then. I feel almost ridiculous, not to mention disappointed. This poetry is the product of mere chance. I'd have much preferred to stick to my fanciful reasoning. In any case, at this point I distrust Simona to such an extent, and I believe her capable of so much, that I wouldn't be surprised if she'd be willing to undermine an older person's memory simply to deprive me of a lovely notion.

After a brief dessert, everyone leaves except for Dylan and Artur, who go out to check the pantena. They have hauled the basket with the evening's catch, dropping it inside the bedroom nearest the front door, when Gonzalo and his cousin Ignacio appear.

"Seems like a lot's been going on here today," says Gonzalo.

"We were having dinner," I say. "Even Mateo was here."

"Would you like some stewed boar?" Artur offers.

"No thanks, we've already eaten. So how was it tonight? Any fishing?"

Dylan replies that there hasn't been much at all. The last few days haven't turned up what the wind had predicted, and right now it's looking even worse with such a still night.

"There's one person who'll tell you to go out looking for eel," says Gonzalo, who's usually referring to Simona whenever he talks about "one person." "But you should ignore all that. If you want to steer clear of any major problems, then don't go for the eels."

The fishers nod.

Gonzalo opens the door to the bedroom, turns on the light, and inspects the basket at his feet. He looks back to the men and repeats: "Don't go for the eels."

Then he mentions that his cousin Ignacio has come to spend a few days in Buda. Recently he's been dropping by more often. For a long time, Ignacio stayed away from the headaches of rice and lagoons, but after retiring he's rediscovered the space and finds himself increasingly comfortable with every new visit. This cousin of his is also looking into the Budero's daily life, and is starting to think about making some changes to the farm.

When they've gone, Artur shakes his head, insistent on his old song and dance. "I can't. I just can't. Although we didn't happen to catch any today, if Gonzalo were to show up and . . . well, in his case I'd be like Simona. I'd be lying to him. To him, to Ignacio, to the whole family. And I can't go on like this. I just can't."

Within the next forty-eight hours, the hunters will arrive. On the first day of the season, we expect a group that will be going for ducks in the rice field. Day two will bring a reunion of *siñors* invited by Mateo: old friends and one of his brothers-in-law, all of whom are expert shooters. Some own farms of their own, where they also hunt. These are wealthy people, the Saddams and the Fabrizios of Catalonia. Landowners and proprietors who have faced shared problems for decades, perhaps even centuries, and have kept themselves up to date by supporting one another, exchanging stories, opinions, and phone numbers while, for example, hunting. Mateo uses the word "amigo" when referring to Alfons Palau, and emphasizes that Josep Vehí is a very interesting person, someone near and dear to his heart who helped untangle the La Pantena issue, serving as a mediator with La Administración and bringing hunting and fishing licenses back to Buda. These are men who, throughout their intense lives, have shown the ability to both manage and fight. Mateo identifies with that spirit to such a degree that one of his favorite birds is the *Calidris pugnax*, a type of ruff which frequents the island in spring and fall. It's a svelte species, especially during courtship, when the male raises his crest, puffs himself up, and begins to flap his wings, leaping and dancing in his own particular jota of seduction. There are occasions where up to twenty males compete for a female, and the exhibition usually ends in a fight. This is common among plenty of species, but battles among male ruffs are so feisty and sometimes so multitudinous that the bird has earned the nickname with which Mateo has come to identify: el combatiente. The fighter.

There can be no doubt that Mateo is feeling increasingly exhausted. All the years of combat have worn him down, yes, but in this new era there's no room for hesitation or mistakes. And while he's always led the farm with loose reins, he's now ramped up his fighting spirit, knowing he's staring down a decisive period about Buda's future. That means setting aside fatigue and rallying the troops. The *siñors* still make a lot of the decisions within La Administración, so it's good to have a couple on your side. Among those who might support him, though, age has presented itself as a new problem. Many have retired or aren't quite as influential as before, but even when working behind the scenes, they still carry some weight. And, well, if the island ends up falling, at least he'll have honored his friends through gratitude and loyalty. Sharing a way of seeing the world is no easy task, considering that a *siñor* from the delta has little in common with one from La Garrotxa or Empordà. No, they're too dissimilar. Mateo has rolled up his sleeves and planted two thousand trees with his own hands; who else can claim to have done something like that? No, a *siñor* from the delta isn't the same as one from Barcelona because the appellation itself loses all meaning here, where he's gone from being a landowner to a long-suffering local, like all the others. *Siñor* so-and-so, *siñor* this and that. But *siñor* of what?

Nothing in the delta is as the *siñors* once expected. The old Ebrenc elites had envisioned fleets of ships navigating the Ebro and a luxurious Sant Carles de la Ràpita emerging like an Iberian Saint Petersburg, but investors didn't agree. The ground shifts too much, the distance from the big cities is excessive. The money never materialized, and the delta has been relegated to something of a Wild East populated by migrants, fishers, and local farmers. It's one of the only coastal spaces in Spain where real estate speculators aren't allowed to build and where tourism is associated more with adventure than comfort. And that's despite developers' plans to build everywhere. They'd even started referring to Fangar as the Catalonian Venice, because they imagined bunches of little chalets winding their way through the boggy soil, and dreamed of a floating city in the style of what can now be seen farther to the north, in Empuriabrava, a municipality in Upper Empordà. However, before breaking ground in the distant delta, the developers entertained themselves by building thousands of hotels, apartments, campsites, and other such things in the more sought-after areas closer to the big cities, allowing themselves to rake in impressive amounts of money without anticipating that, in the early 1980s, thousands of Ebrencs would protest the large landowners who were drying up the whole Canal Vell lacustrine plain with the intention of converting it into rice fields, thus raising awareness among scientists and, more importantly, politicians—who passed a law converting a good part of the Delta into the Parc Natural. This safeguarded thousands of hectares that, in a short period of time, went from being a hopeless ass of the world to becoming almost as fantastical and attractive as Vietnam, with a kilometric vastness unmarred by even a single tall building and where people of enviable rudeness were often as sincere as they were intimidating.

Such spaces also helped in promoting the delta as an ideal hunting ground. "To a feudal gentleman from Barcelona," Mateo said to me one day, "seeing this immense natural space down here was exciting. It was like they were on safari in Africa."

Yet another space to colonize.

The day Mateo showed La Pantena to his friends from a neighboring farm, a woman from the group told me that her ancestors had acquired La Explanada at the suggestion of General Miguel Primo de Rivera, who had assured them that those impracticable swamps would soon become coveted territory thanks to the administrative operations that were predicted. Thus, a handful of the outsiders became *siñors* by purchasing large tracts of land at bargain-basement prices, reaping the benefits of that information. The result, as Joan Todó wrote, was that most of the delta ceased to belong to the people who lived there. Still, though, many farmers were able to maintain a foothold by creating a cluster of unobtrusive properties, which is why this delta is radically different from, for example, the Camargue, where a small number of landowners lord over immensely vast acreage.

The big, old Ebrenc estates have been mentioned in literature, because the *siñors* would organize hunts to tempt their urban friends to come visit them, and many of these friends happened to be intellectuals who later wrote about their adventures. Josep Maria de Sagarra turned out a few verses depicting a hunting party on the Gallarts' land; some Ebrencs have commented that this poem makes them picture a man from Barcelona visiting the Maghreb. In his *Episodios nacionales*, Benito Pérez Galdós harks back to 1860 to tell of the fictional Juan Santiuste and some of his fellow ditch-diggers encountering poachers in the heart of the delta. These poachers, hidden in a clutch of reeds, insult them and open fire. When the shooters emerge, the diocesan bishop is among them. Juan Santiuste is about to reproach them for their actions, but one of the ditch-diggers cautions against it: "They're out here hunting and fishing all day long . . . There's no way to beat them: they make themselves the masters of wherever they venture." Besides, they add, the bishop is a decent person. He looks after those in need, so it's best not to bother him.

The *cantadors*, artists of oral literature who have dogged, denounced, and mocked individuals from every stratum of society, think differently. And this audacity seems to originate with an Arab, Aben-Jot, a poet who went from town to town performing a song he'd made up which, to many, fell somewhere between excessive and downright sinful, resulting in his expulsion from Valencia. Far from being intimidated, the Moor celebrated his exile by singing in every village he passed through as he left. These townsfolk, however, readily took to his biting and provocative lyrics and the lively rhythms of a musical composition that would come to be known as jota. Thus the jota, one of the delta's two emblematic dances, originated with Jot, the Moor. And to this day the *cantadors* perpetuate his audacious impudence.

The sardana is the most traditional dance in Catalonia, but is promoted by institutions and therefore has not caught on in the delta. It would be more accurate to say, though, that many people prefer the jota because of their native character, their strong and rebellious temperament, their desire to boil over and run rampant, their rule of *rauxa*: that crazy, impetuous side that connects wonderfully with what was first suggested by Aben-Jot.

Jotas glorify leaping, and take it far beyond what the sardana does. The dance might begin with small, tentative jumps, but the music accelerates quickly, often suddenly, offering up a series of fast-paced bounces that situate the dancer somewhere between the eel, with its electric nature, and the nimble-legged frog able to turn on a dime, to stretch out right or left, forward or backward. This is a dance with a bit of a shout to it, something tense like an argument, like any given day for many of these very physical people who make the jump from the fields to the beaches to the wetlands with amazing agility. Sometimes you have to blink to make sure the dance is being performed live, as opposed to a recording playing at too many revolutions per minute. That speed is precisely what distinguishes the jota as one of the most modern forms of classical dance. There is simply no comparison with the sardana.

"Sardana dancers don't have to leap," wrote Josep Pla. "Instead, they sweep through the room like a drab rural conversation. They have to drag themselves along with a heavy, vague, and uncertain uncouthness. When it comes to understanding sardanas, the unawareness and bewilderment of the youth are of no use. One must be at least married and, if possible, the father to a family."

The sardana's sensible rhythm maintains the tempo of bygone eras, while the jota has a more casual flow that makes it chic, suggesting it might endure as a trendy (folk) dance well into the twenty-second century or beyond—if climate change doesn't wipe it out.

In the meantime, we will take note of the droughts, the storms, the hole in the ozone layer, and many other such disasters that announce their presence, because it's also true that, if things take a turn for the worse, the sardana might experience a resurgence. If the people grow increasingly disheartened, if they don't eat, they won't have the strength to perform jotas, making it entirely possible that those who'd still like to dance might prefer the sardana's moderation.

And then there are the *cantadors*, translators of the delta's music. The *cantador*, heir to Aben-Jot, is something of a satirical poet who gracefully improvises songs laced with a biting edge. Descendants of Arabs and troubadours, *cantadors* were forged in taverns where they often challenged one another through singing, as rappers today might battle one another through rhyme. They're clever, playful, sharp, and ultimately their calling is to offer the lyrics people want to hear. Politics, misfortune, current events . . . the *cantador* interprets what's floating through the airwaves and pours it out with verve, holding nothing back, tossing out the occasional obscenity, at once flattering and flustering those to whom the song might be dedicated, and ultimately connecting with an audience that, more than anything else, wants to have fun.

It's symbolic, then, that one of this era's great *cantadors* is Lo Teixidor, a performer who inherited his nickname from his grandparents, both of whom were wool and cotton weavers. Through his songs, Lo Teixidor has stitched together networks of empathy that endure as few others do. He's the final cherry atop the last cake of a splendid tradition of singers that dates from Boca de Bou to Gabriel lo Contadó, Lo Canalero, Terremoto, Caragol, Perot, and Noret, from whom Lo Teixidor learned, as they say around here, *un munt*. A ton.

Lo Teixidor began as a Catalonian peasant farmer spreading guano, *birbant* (harrowing), and harvesting until 1972, when he started selling firewood. He continued on that course, singing all the while. Though he could barely read or write, he'd educated himself as best he could by listening to others, and when he put his wit on full display, the public was amazed. When he performed, he wore a fully formal outfit: a white shirt with a dark-blue *jupetí* or vest and pants. He was accompanied by an orchestra of a clarinet, trumpet, and tenor tuba, as well as a guitar and a *guitarró*, though he was also proficient with *ferrets* (small metal jingles), castanets, a twelve-string, a tambourine, and a violin. He once said he didn't care much about the music, that if he listened to it he only perceived it in the distant background while his mind was composing a story. He knew only too well that he had to come up with six measures at the end, of which three words had to rhyme. And that's exactly what he did.

His talent soon took flight. He started getting calls to perform in towns that took him hours of walking or pedaling to reach. "The world—everything in general—was poor," he says, referring to that period. Before the show, he'd ask for a basket containing a dozen eggs and a wineskin. Whenever he felt faint, he'd crack an egg, drink it, wash it down with a swig of wine, and continue singing. After ten hours, he returned to his village the same way he had arrived.

Lo Teixidor's fame defies explanation. He's become a star of the delta. Everyone wanted him at their parties, at their tables, they were always asking for more, and he tried to give what he could, which was sometimes too much. Like that time in Raval de la Llet. "I sang there, and I don't know how I didn't go insane," he explained to J. J. Rovira Climent in the book *Cantadors del Delta*. "I stood there and sang a hundred and ten songs without moving from that spot. It was crazy! I don't know what fumes my brain was running on. And when we finally finished, the director comes up to me and says, 'Now we're off to the next gig.' So I said, 'Leave me alone! I'm going home! This is nuts!'"

The jota and the *cantador* urge you to let go, to shed your fears and repressions. One afternoon, Dylan, Quim, and Artur tell me, "The only time we'll dance a jota is on the day Simona leaves."

Imagine the old Arab of the Ebro as being like the Romani of the Danube: pilgrims, fugitives, and exiles who gather in the deltas, listening to music in the style of musician, singer, and composer Franco Battiato.

As Battiato's compatriot Claudio Magris writes, "We often come across gypsies, as if this wandering people on the fringes of society were a tribe well-suited to dwelling in the archaic and forgotten world of the delta. A century ago this really was the realm of irregulars and fugitives, a no-man's-land which gave refuge to outlaws from all over the place . . . The guide-books of the last century, the monumental one by Baron Amand von Schweiger-Lerchenfeld, for example, speak of a jungle of men of every type and race, Turks and Caucasians, gypsies and negroes, Bulgars and Wallachians, Russians and Serbs, sailors from half the globe, adventurers, delinquents and escaped criminals."

Now, the Danube Delta is primarily home to Lipovan fishers. They arrived in the late eighteenth century fleeing Russia to avoid religious persecution and remain, above all, people of the river. As Magris describes them, "they live in the water like dolphins or the other sea-mammals."

It's been said that nobody knows whether the fishers were born in the water or on dry land. Their children go to school by boat, and at some point they began rowing to the rhythms of Franco Battiato, the poet who wants to see you dance like a Romani while the ports wave white flags hoisted from a permanent center of gravity.

Most of Buda's boats are nearly a hundred years old. Several may well have passed the century mark. One hundred years: the eternity to which Fabrizio Salina had aspired as a *signore*, happy to have lived in the Sicilian bubble that allowed him to be "the last to have any unusual memories, anything different from those of other families." So happy that, even as he witnessed the end of his lineage and the imminent loss of his property, he didn't wince in the slightest, accepting it all as a natural consequence of the times.

There is a bit of Fabrizio in Mateo, though his uncontrolled vehemence is galaxies away from the Italian's parsimonious ways. Mateo isn't accepting defeat graciously while Fabrizio smiled as he crumbled, and yet both agree on the irony and the love for the land which—and this is particularly important—they've inhabited.

What separates Mateo from the many other *siñors* who own property in the delta is that he lives here. He has for a long time.

For the most part, the *siñors* only show up to supervise their lands, which are invariably being cared for by locals. They can't distinguish a monarch from any other butterfly, nor have they seen bulls loose on the beach. As such, Mateo may not be a *siñor* at all, though his nature does align with the impression formulated by a character from Lampedusa's *The Leopard*: "the 'nobles,' as you call them, aren't so easy to understand. They live in a world of their own, of joys and troubles of their own: they have a very strong collective memory, and so they're put out by things which wouldn't matter at all to you and me."

Regardless, we will soon be hunting with these *siñors*, along with a group of stewards charged with collecting and counting the downed game birds. Each hunter is paired with some of these stewards, who are also responsible for punting their boat to the shooting position, attracting the ducks with calls, and, if necessary, finishing them off. The stewards charge a hundred euros, plus whatever tip the hunter might give them.

As Lampedusa wrote, these hunters are "As avid for power or rather for the idleness which was, for them, the purpose of power." And so-called sport hunting, a leisurely demonstration of power over living beings, is perhaps the best expression of this phrase. In Buda's case, power over coots and ducks. In the Louisiana Delta, otters are the preferred target, with over three hundred fifty thousand having been hunted. There are kings who go for African elephants, and I once met a billionaire who fired over a thousand rounds at camels in Australia. He had to lay the rifle down at times because it scalded his hands. And yet I can't stop thinking about Artur's roe deer, so highly sought-after, and the wild boar we shared the other day. I wonder how many types of game hunters there are.

With the delta being a delta, the Ebrencs will hunt. For decades, it was a way to get ahead. And for a few, this continues to be the case, although most shoot as a hobby while others have taken up poaching to turn a profit. They say smuggling is on the rise, especially now that access to food has become increasingly complicated for many as a result of the pandemic and rising utility bills. But this sounds like a bad excuse in a society that went from malaria to tractors in what seems like no time at all, in addition to reaping the benefits of tourism, which can be rampant even in moderation. In the past, being a southern frontier region had required an economy based primarily on necessity, and water rats were once part of the diet. But all that's done with now, and we're inevitably left with those who poach the past to justify current crimes: the result of pure greed or the pursuit of adrenaline.

Shooting and taking unlawfully killed game are long-established practices in the delta and directly tied to the ancestral pirates, fugitives, and prisoners who once populated it. On the other hand, however, the region is also marked by a lack of self-confidence, meaning people for years tended to comply with—or at least not to protest—the dictates of the prevailing *siñor* or the ordinance from Barcelona. Until the water became a problem for them.

When the Spanish government presented their Hydrological Plan, a scheme to divert millions of liters of water into irrigation canals that would exhaust the river's flow, the Ebrencs organized themselves as never before. They called for demonstrations, blocked highways, printed the now-famous twisted-pipe logo on thousands of hats, banners, and T-shirts. From these demands, something resembling an Ebrenc sense of pride began to emerge: a result which, among others, has made it fashionable again to speak Cavero, the language of La Cava.

The Ebrencs, who previously only presided over what they knew, such as the wind, the tides, the black-winged stilts, or the eels, are now trenchant in their views. Their reaction to the Hydrological Plan has led to an identity overdose which, though, after the initial hurrah, isn't much more than a grandiose adjective, some ostentatious gesticulation which appeals more and more to the *collons*. Spain is such a dutiful country that it constantly appeals to its cojones (or *collons*) to remember that they're there—amazingly enough, *collons* applies to many women as well. This self-confidence or self-worth rarely ends in revolt. "They're not going to rebel against anything," declared one person who lived near the final stretch of the Paraná, referring to his compatriots and therefore establishing a parallel with the inhabitants of the Tigre and the Ebro as precise as it was involuntary. Other reasons why inhabitants of the world's deltas tend not to be excessively rebellious were suggested, also in Argentina, by Rodolfo Walsh: "There are no complaints here . . . If you protest, they call you a communist and kick you right out." It is, however, worth clarifying that Walsh, Haroldo Conti (who depicted El Boga in his novel *Southeaster*), and the Tigre dissidents did put up a bit of a fight, considering that they were under the subjugation of a dictatorship that would, ultimately, murder Walsh and Conti.

Apparently, deltas are full of communists who keep their lips firmly sealed and whose way of venting their anger could well be firing off a few rounds or stealing a couple of eels and a few ducks. Face to face, many of these people, whether communists or not, tend to be curt and brusque. They're prudent in their bluntness, though sometimes we see the emergence of a *pocsaber*: an ignorant charlatan who boasts of his lack of culture. He's the most modern product of the delta, something of an expert nitpicker who knows everything, understands nothing, and never stops talking. His existence invites us to ponder why there are so many people saying too much of the same thing.

In any case, *pocsabers* are rare in nature's meanderings. Foolishness is uncommon when you live life on the outermost bounds, habitats more suited to scoundrels and rogues. Which is why stories of poachers have become local legend. Some have even left records of their incursions. There's Xato de la Serro, who'd sneak into the rice fields to hunt *taus* ("water rats") with his dog. His appearances in Buda were primarily "to gather up the coots that had been wounded and left for dead after a hunt conducted by the *siñors*. This was forbidden, but I went at night by boat with a well-trained bird dog. One night, I was making my way back with a sack filled with forty coots, a heron, and two other *moixons* [birds], but when I got to where I'd beached the boat, it was gone. It had been taken. To avoid being caught by the guard, I tied the coots to a string, looped it around my neck, and swam across the river with the birds floating behind me. On the other bank, a set of dry clothes had been left for me, and so, with the dog and the sack of coots, I headed home. Along the way I ran into a couple of armed officers; I gave them each a coot so they wouldn't say anything. Later, when I was already in bed, asleep in my shack, I heard someone outside talking to my kid:

"'Your father . . . Where did he go last night?'

"'Nowhere, he's right here, sleeping.'

"It was the guard from Buda. But since he hadn't caught me in the act, what was he going to do? Nothing. We just had to be smarter than them."

Natalia Gallart has no tolerance for smugglers, "those sons of bitches." Though she does distinguish between the old-timers like Xato de la Serro, who poached to survive, and the slick new generation who do it as a hobby or to earn a little something extra at the expense of someone else, for example the Gallart family. So, yes, to a certain extent, she understands them. To some it must be a form of revenge, as if they were collecting a portion of the unpayable debt owed to them and their ancestors for the services they've been providing to the *siñors* for more than a century. While across much of Catalonia locals will refer to the landowner as amo, master, it certainly doesn't seem like a coincidence that in the delta they've reduced his rank to *siñor*.

Every time Natalia remembers calling Simona from the discotheque to ask her to take out the trash from the El Pas shack, she can't help but shiver and blush. At the time, it never occurred to her that it might have been inconvenient for the supervisor; Simona didn't have a car or other means of hauling off the bags. But now she's gotten to know the supervisor's other side, seeing how Simona's refused to greet her ever since Artur started working on the island and listening to the stories being told about her, she can almost sense the resentment gnawing at that woman and how much it must have made her stomach churn to have to obey the orders of an indulged child. Even though Natalia didn't turn on the heat and instead kept warm by the fireplace to avoid spending money, and even though she's always been a frugal type, someone who loves and respects people for who they are, not for their money or titles or surnames, evidenced by the man she fell in love with and with whom she's going to have another child, despite all this, she's realized Simona might have had a hard time believing Natalia wasn't asking her to take out the trash out of arrogance or bad faith but because she was simply oblivious. No, she would never have understood that. Simona is going for what motivates her: the euros. And, in her mind, Natalia is an aggravating little rich kid who's now building a new house in Els Reguers with, of course, Mateo's help.

The construction of this house also hasn't gone unnoticed by Ignacio Sagués, Mateo's cousin, who joined Gonzalo at La Pantena on the night of the wild boar feast. Ignacio is one of Buda's twelve shareholders. For years he rarely visited the island, conditioned by the repudiation his mother felt toward a piece of land that was the cause of some harsh family confrontations. The meetings among the three families who have shares in Buda always end in such violent shouting matches that the parties have had to appoint spokespeople. However much these representatives argue, at least the level of rage has been brought down a notch. Ignacio speaks calmly, weighing his words, and his angular face is topped off by a pair of multi-dioptric glasses that lend him a deceptively fragile appearance, since his body is a block of muscle tightened and honed every morning with a dip in the sea or in the canals. What's most relevant, though, is that he detests browbeating, which might well be why he's been chosen to represent the Saguéses at these meetings.

We met for the first time last week at the El Pas shack, next to the snake's enclosure. I was passing on my bike, and since there's never normally anyone else on the El Mas straightaway, I stopped to say hello. He said he's been staying there since Natalia left, that he's been coming to the island more often in the last couple of years, and that he'd like to increase the frequency of his visits.

A few days later he visited me at La Pantena after a swim in the sea, which is how I now know he's displeased with the meager payments Mateo's handed down to them this year. He believes the family isn't being fully and clearly informed about what's happening on the island, and he intends to investigate. He's even participated in a couple of hunts. "I'm not much of a shooter," he said, "but I have to be there if I'm going to find out how everything is going."

Ignacio says he has just enough to live on, neither scarcity nor excess, although now he's retired he'd like to have some semblance of peace and security for himself and his son, and the island could provide them with some additional income. He's not ambitious, he has no intention of getting involved in anyone's personal affairs. He simply wants to follow his own path, as he did as a young boy when he managed to get himself expelled from the religious school where he studied. His life has been staggered between earning a salary as a civil servant and making backpacking trips, especially to Asia, observing from afar the changes coming to Buda, a place he associates with unpleasant disputes. Now, though, he's reached a point where he doesn't want to be made a fool of by allowing someone to cheat him out of a benefit that ultimately belongs to him. After all, he and his cousin Roberto own 33 percent of Buda.

"Thirty-three?" I ask.

"Thirty-three."

"So how much does Mateo own?"

"There are a lot of brothers. I think he owns maybe six."

It was a surprise to learn Mateo ruled the island as he pleased with such a low percentage. Ignacio agreed with what Gonzalo had already told me: that, apart from being the only one who knows the island with any degree of detail, Mateo shouts more loudly than the others. And when they arrive at a critical point in discussions, he gets up, announces that he's leaving, and that someone else can take care of the rice and the tractors and the fishing and hunting licenses and . . . Well, in the end, everyone tries to get him to calm down, assuring him that nobody wants to get rid of him, that they understand his reluctance. And everything remains the same.

"For years, nobody had the time to really dig into the island. Well, now I've got plenty of time, and I want to spend some of it here," Ignacio said. "That's one of the advantages of being a retiree. And I want to get a better idea of how things are going. If there's a change that needs to be made, I don't need to get dragged into those arguments. I've got a 33 percent stake and I'm going to use it."

However late in life it may be, Ignacio's desire to be a *siñor* has awakened, though a cloud of doubt looms over whether a man of such refined disposition will know how to govern in this wild delta. Regardless, he's clear about one of the first decisions he'll make, especially after Simona berated a tractor driver on the Migjorn beach the other day for having towed Ignacio's car to help him cross the river. Fire the supervisor.

In December, I'd set out from the most remote beach at five in the afternoon to arrive home as night fell. Now, in mid-January, the light lasts until half past six. The yawning Migjorn has widened by roughly seventy meters, and crossing the river by car is now impossible. Buda is now definitively an island. One that can only be reached by cranking the helm of the El Sifó barge or via some other boat.

The beach is also wider because the sea has receded two meters owing to the January lows, known in Spanish as *minves*. Atmospheric pressures have flattened the sea, ironing it out, giving it the appearance of a vast lagoon. The anticyclone has turned the sea into a lifeless, languid tin sheet that barely even shimmers. The *minves* seem to contradict those announcing the imminent rising of the waters, but this is a periodic event generally associated with the calm before the storm. As if the sea itself were feigning retreat, playing dead, when in reality it's gaining momentum before a charge.

This year has proven resistant to storms. It has barely even rained. But the cyclones from the previous two years swept through the delta in January. It seems as if Buda is waiting, and the *minves* accentuate a dreamlike, unreal digression that has left the delta unusually still, wide, and silent. With Buda effectively being closed to the public, the animals are able to move freely about the island, roaming through places which until now were forbidden to them. The mammals loose in the fields, covered in mud and rice stubble, increase the sense of strangeness. It is the wildest part of the year.

Every afternoon I walk to Cap de Tortosa at the other end of Buda. I usually do this around the same time, and every day I find, out on the sea, the same motorboat piloted by a Black fisher who seems as methodical as I am. He always cruises parallel to the shore, heading north, dressed either in a light-blue or bright-yellow raincoat that complements the boat's electric-blue paint strikingly. Yes, we're both there at the same time, like those people you meet every day on the subway platform, at the bus stop, or at a traffic light, following a routine so unerring that maybe you've thought about—or even started—saying hello even if your interaction will never go beyond that point. The only difference is that the fisher and I coincide on different surfaces, each as deserted as it is immense.

I could live this monotonous life for quite some time. I'm in no hurry. It's taken fifty years to be able to write something like this. Maybe I'm finally understanding the principles of patience that led my father to die so well. I don't feel death as I've been told I should, no, but I've also been told that when someone dear to me expires, it won't be forever, that I'll continue to sense their company, and that much is true. I always regarded this as an illusion born of both desire and pain, the typical, endearing sort of story you tell yourself as consolation, but today I'm the one feeling my father's unexpected presence, and it's so strong, so real, that I've no doubts whatsoever that he's there. I don't feel as though he's gone. He is. I don't know if the right word is *company* or *companionship*, but I'm certain my father is still here. Because I visit with him. I understand that this is how we will forever be. Forever. Another one of those words I used to avoid using. *Forever. Death. Play*. The great words of the world. The appropriate words for engaging with French philosopher Georges Bataille's theory of "strong play," which is characterized by sovereignty, by an indifference to what others might say. One which is incompatible with the principle of a society based on work and production and with that whole shit show of networks where you can judge and be judged. With regard to "strong play," philosopher Byung-Chul Han writes that "death is not a loss, not a failure, but an expression of the utmost vitality, force and desire." Archaic societies don't establish a clear distinction between life and death, but today's society of production does, and that's why it fears the end. This is why it's terrified by the evidence showing that, ultimately, money is of no use. The afterlife can't be bought. Conversations with my dead father don't cost a cent, and they resolve fundamental doubts. He, who painted walls and giant sets and scenery, who played the roles of women and Egyptians, who played dead on the beach and brought me Tintin comics on Saturdays, says: "There are spirits that lead us. Don Quixote. Moby Dick. Carmen. Dersu Uzala. Félix Rodríguez de la Fuente. El Boga. Madame Bovary. Your mother. Your mother. Their reality has built us with hurricane force. It's time to play strong. You can still do it. In the kingdom of books, you are sovereign."

Understood, Dad. Let's play.

The *minves* don't bode well for the hunters. The calm weather forecast predicts a terrible day for them. The first group has been hunkering in their tubs in the rice fields for half the day, but scarcely a shot has been heard. From the perspective of the hunters' scopes, nothing much is happening today.

I've positioned myself next to Mateo on the wharf's lookout tower, my binoculars trained on the fields where rifle barrels are poking out. Keeping watch over those lying in wait. It's four o'clock on an afternoon gilded by a splendidly warm winter sun, and the rice fields are engrossed in a listless, sleepy air occasionally disrupted by a shot. Over the tubs fly flocks of black-winged grebes, lapwings, the occasional flamingo . . . Plenty of birds, yes, but not many of the ducks which are allowed to be shot even during the closed season. As if they knew this was a dangerous time.

"Look, look, there's three of them right there," Mateo says. "Come on! Come on! Come ooooon! What's going on? Why haven't they shot? I don't get it. It's like they're amateurs."

These hunters are visiting the island for the first time, and it would be ideal for them to take home a significant haul so they might then speak well of the farm. It's the same with everyone who comes here to hunt. And the better their quarry, the better their recommendations. Mateo isn't a hunter himself, but he's running a business, and he's desperate for things to go well.

"They barely got anything this morning, so I thought maybe there aren't many ducks, but no way. I know they're there. Look, man, look . . . Today's not the best day for hunting, but they've had plenty of opportunities. The problem is, they aren't taking their shots when they should. And when they do, they're taking bad shots."

Between our hideout in the lookout tower and the hunters' tubs, nine marsh harriers are gliding. Their lithe, unvarying flight is clearly defined against the immaculate sky. They trace different circles from those of vultures. More anarchic. They don't fly in formation, though their expectations are the same. Mateo keeps the binoculars glued to his face as he reports what's happening right there in front of him, as if he were the play-by-play announcer sitting in the broadcast booth calling some sort of game.

"Look, look, there's five of them . . . They're about to be within range . . . Come on, come on! What are you doing? Shoot! Shoot!"

Three shots ring out.

"Well, they got one, but they waited too long."

Most hunters use twelve-gauge automatics and shells containing size-four pellets. Mateo's phone rings. He puts it on speaker. It's Simona. The supervisor is spending her day out in the fields. I can see her car glinting in the sun next to a distant reedbed. "They're just awful," she says.

"Yes, you're absolutely right. They're the worst hunters. There's no explaining it. Maybe they're trying to break some sort of record. What can we do?"

When Mateo hangs up, I thank him for the broadcast and head out for the beach.

The sea's edge invites us to think more about limits, about other ways of facing them. Of focusing on ourselves. Australian writer Val Plumwood used to explore the wildest parts of the Kakadu National Park, often by canoe. In February of 1985, she was paddling through a strip of swamp when a blindingly intense downpour steered her off course before depositing her in an area densely populated by crocodiles. One attacked the canoe. Plumwood tried to leap into the water, but the reptile's jaws caught her by the leg and she was dragged down into the muddy depths. Her knowledge of crocodiles, her physical strength, and a requisite bit of luck allowed her to escape and fashion a tourniquet. A park ranger, concerned about her absence, was able to locate her in time. The media and the usual pundits pounced on the story, retelling it as they pleased. Plumwood, however, waited years before telling her own version. She said that the attack had changed her perspective. That she had rediscovered both reality and herself in a new and different way. She understood how that animal had seen her: as prey.

Not long ago, I read Joanna Pocock's book *Surrender*, in which she interviews a hunter who loves sleeping outdoors during his expeditions into a wilderness populated by grizzlies and cougars. "He laughed and looked at me like I was crazy. 'I could only ever live in a place where I am not the top predator,' he said." Pocock realizes then that she's never thought of herself as prey. Neither had I, until

I read these women. What I mean is that I'd never really stopped and pictured myself being devoured. That I'd never really considered where I stand in the food chain. Now I know that I'm at 2.2. On par with anchovies and hogs. Very different from the orca's 5.5. I suppose, though, that I've always known and accepted that I'm highly edible, and I can therefore conclude that my internalization of this certainty offers a natural explanation for many of the sympathies, attitudes, and commitments I've acquired in life.

As I sauté the chard I've picked and seasoned with garlic and salt, a shadow skitters past my feet: a mouse has taken up residence in the kitchen. During the nights of fishing, two others snuck in, each on a different day. Both hid behind the refrigerator opposite the entrance door, and as soon as the men saw them, they grabbed the broom and a log from the firewood and killed them.

I tap on the metal of the stove, hoping to drive the mouse outside, with little effect. I'd like to get it out of the house, though I doubt I can do that without catching it first, and who knows how I might be able to accomplish that feat. While I'm eating dinner, I see the mouse scurry toward the fireplace. I get up; it darts back to its hiding place in the kitchen.

Lizards, spiders, mosquitoes, mice. It's impossible to feel alone. I spend a while walking along the straightaway to El Mas, which today shines in the distance. The hunters are having dinner at the table where I'll be seated tomorrow, because Mateo has invited me to spend the night in the house and accompany them on tomorrow's hunt. Since we'll have to get up early to get into position, it only makes sense for me to sleep there. Plus, there are plenty of bedrooms at El Mas. The mansion shines like a great firefly perched on the edge of a black plain.

I feel like doing something I've been thinking about for days. It's cold, yes, but it's a reasonable cold, and so I roll up my pant legs, remove my boots, stuff my socks inside them and sink my feet into the mud of the rice field. I cross it from one end to the other. The silt slips between my toes and I step on clumps of who knows what, feeling the sinuous caresses of adherent surfaces that stir in me a sense of apprehension somewhere between nausea and fear. Each stride comes with its own costs. I'm aware of my body being divided in two. My feet are warmer, sheltered by the sludge and the underground life that spurs curiosity about what might be brewing in this inhabited hell. Meanwhile, my chest and face receive the fresh air which oxygenates my feet. Some bird takes flight nearby, sordidly flapping its wings as I slowly make my way to the other side of the field. Having donned my new mud boots, I make my way to the lagoon, which is all but motionless. Every so often something splashes, sending waves across the surface of the water, and the moon takes the opportunity to provide a different sort of reflection. It's beautiful. The seeker's axiom states that less comfort signifies greater beauty. I don't always agree, but today that's the case. Being barefoot in the dark feels different: you intuit more, so the essence, the nature of beings and things, is revealed without the need for form. Obscurity enables greater understanding. If you want to venerate something, start at night.

I put my feet in the water, and my shoes come undone.

The rest of the hunters start arriving at El Mas in midafternoon. Night was falling when roughly fifteen of us gathered in the great hall with the fireplace, the taxidermy-filled showcases, and old maps of Buda adorning the walls. Josep Vehí has brought a gallon or two of green punch of his own concoction. He's unwilling to reveal the complete recipe, but hints that it includes tangerines and, most importantly, liquor distilled from Buda's own rice, and he suggests we all "baptize" this new drink.

Besides mediating with La Administración to once again allow hunting on Buda's private lands, Vehí is a chemist, an agricultural engineer, and he oversees a massive farm in Prades. "I haven't used pesticides since the seventies," he says, taking a sip from his glass of punch, the rim of which is crusted in salt. "My father worked in textiles, he was the head of the cotton employers' association when a plague of caterpillars came in and started to destroy the fields. The agricultural minister at the time told him, no, Vehí, don't worry. We've got this remedy from America that's already worked in Andalusia. We'll bring in the planes and spray it all over the farm. It's called DDT, it'll solve everything. You'll see. By that time, my father had already started asking around about whether these caterpillars had any natural enemies, and what they told him was that there was a beetle that would be the perfect antagonist. He tried it. Men would show up with matchboxes filled with twenty or more beetles apiece. They released them into the fields and, wow, I've never seen a more bloodthirsty beetle than that one. It was a complete massacre. The beetles would have been enough to control the caterpillars, but the DDT plan had already been set in motion, so the planes came, they started spraying the chemical like crazy, and . . . well . . . that was the end of life as we knew it. The caterpillars died, but so did the blackbirds, the butterflies, the beetles . . . everything. Ever since then I've been clear that it's never going to happen again."

"They flew a DDT plane over us here too," says Mateo. "Everything was dying. We set up a room as if it were a leper colony for dying birds. It was outrageous."

"It's all to do with the dosage," says Vehí. "When properly administered, arsenic can have revitalizing effects."

Rachel Carson would have disagreed with such a statement. She denounced DDT, pointing out that it killed not only pests but all sorts of animals. With regard to humans, it causes multiple types of cancer as well as serious nervous system and blood disorders. Additionally, its use prompted the emergence of super-insects resistant to pesticides, which in turn encouraged the creation of new chemicals that were even more damaging to the ecosystem. For speaking out, Carson was subjected to a sustained and relentless attack from the American version of La Administración, which was supported by powerful businesspeople and scientists with dubious motives. DDT, however, was banned in 1972 when it was found that it accumulated in the air at levels incredibly harmful to wildlife.

Vehí has come with his twenty-one-year-old grandson Pere. Pere has his own rifle, but he's not the youngest member of the group. In the dining room sit a thirteen-year-old and a nine-year-old, accompanied by their elders.

"Do you hunt too?" I ask the nine-year-old. He takes a quick glance at me before turning to his father and then to the table where the servers, Karen's successors, have laid out platters of charcuterie and bowls of olives, chips, and macadamia nuts.

"Yes, he's just starting out," answers his father, who goes hunting every weekend, often to remote locations.

At one point, his phone rings. It's his wife. I take a bit of a risk and ask him how she feels about him spending so many weekends away.

"My wife hunts too. This was a special invitation and it didn't make sense for her to come, but most of the time we hunt as a family."

The thirteen-year-old chats with his father and his grandfather, Alfons Palau, another of Mateo's old friends. Palau is tall and heavy-set, as is Vehí. He's dressed in an elegant sport coat with a silk scarf tied around his neck and impeccably shined shoes. A stroke has paralyzed part of his face and his speech isn't perfect, though he's able to communicate without difficulties. "He's a great guy," Mateo had told me in advance.

As we sit down at the table, and after having criticized the new law protecting wolves, suggesting that a middle ground between cattle ranchers and conservationists should be reached, Palau recalls African safaris. He talks with Vehí about poachers who killed nearly two hundred elephants between Sudan and Cameroon, and how he's glad a Tanzanian leader has been forced to step down after failing to prevent more pachyderms from being slaughtered.

"These kinds of things don't make the news here, but it's important for people to be aware of them. We know little about how poaching is handled in Africa. We might want to start looking to them as an example of what should be done here."

Simona is leaning against the chimney, watching the table with her back to the fire. She's not eating, she doesn't join in the conversation, nor does she help clear the plates. She's simply standing there, a meter or two from Mateo. Vehí has cut up the cork from the wine being served tonight, smells it from different angles, and explains that it's a Portuguese cork of excellent quality. On his farm, which is called El Murrió, they produce firewood, biomass, pine cones, timber, as well as large quantities of cork. The farm is culturally significant, encompassing medieval churches and thirteenth-century ice wells and megaliths, and is also a hunting farm, its star attraction the Eurasian woodcock.

Vehí praises the intelligence of the woodcock, which is extremely difficult to catch. Whenever someone invents a new technique for hunting it, the animal quickly devises an alternative way of escaping. His opinion regarding this amazing intelligence differs from that which Josep Pla offered in *Journey by Bus*. "Naturalists believe that the nature of these animals [woodcocks] is quite obtuse, almost on the verge of stupidity," he wrote. "They say this because these birds do not flee from the vicinity of country houses and because they are easily caught with traps and snares. The confidence these birds display could be due to the sumptuous meals they eat, which might tend them toward a snug sense of epicureanism. If they didn't eat so well, they would be leaner, more elusive and distrustful." And then, perhaps, they'd know how to hide better? Or is their alleged guile simply due to the fact that they're starving?

"The woodcock's confidence comes from its own sense of security, which results from camouflage," Vehí counters. "The dogs will be right in front of one and not even notice. Their weakness is that they can be blinded by lights. When they can't see, they turn dumb. In Goya's time they were hunted with a lantern and a club."

"If there's one thing we know for sure," says Edu, one of Mateo's relatives, "it's that even the smartest of animals sometimes makes a stupid mistake. And that's when an idiot can bag one. Not the hunter who knows the most about them, not the one who respects them the most. No. They get killed by some idiot who happens to be walking by. The typical lucky bastard."

In contrast to Pla, Vehí admires woodcocks. He's studied them for thirty-two years, and has managed to increase their population by 50 percent in El Murrió. He's done this not by banning hunting, but rather by applying the principle of appropriate dosage.

In an extremist country where many fundamental debates with ecology at their core are still seen as impractical battlefields, the argument in favor of controlled hunting sounds cynical if not outright barbaric to many, although it's worth remembering that Vehí, along with a number of other hunters, also manages lands recognized as much for their vibrant biodiversity as they are for their respect for the law. John Muir, Aldo Leopold, David Vann, Pete Fromm, Abi Andrews, William Henry Hudson, Patrik Svensson, Miguel Delibes . . . All were hunters and fishers who shine today as torch-bearing emblems in defense of the natural environment, and there can be no doubt that a good part of their strength lies in their experiences with death. I'm not a hunter myself, but I accept others hunting in accordance with certain laws.

That morning, before leaving for El Mas, I'd found that my shrewish stowaway had nibbled through the paper in which I had wrapped my bread and gnawed off a fair chunk. I tossed half the loaf in the trash. I'm running out of bread, and while I'm eating out tonight, I'd better get smart about protecting my pantry and maybe ask someone to deliver more supplies.

I asked Gonzalo how I should go about getting rid of the rodent and he lent me two spring traps. When I returned from the beach, the hammer had snapped shut, catching the mouse's head and surely bringing immediate death. If it hadn't come into the house and eaten my bread, or if Simona hadn't prevented me from leaving the island, that mouse might have still been alive. But the circumstances are what they are.

Hunters now consider the roe deer the mammalian version of the woodcock: an elusive creature that demands the most from its pursuer. Edu, the husband of one of Mateo's cousins, who was given the La Casa de la Pantena property where I currently live and which he never visits, loves to track partridges, often hiking up to twenty-five kilometers in hope of finding one, wringing out the day in the countryside like a wet rag, pouring every ounce of his physical self into an experience that, he suggests, reunites him with his animalistic nature, with time itself. "Here's the thing," he says. "You have to differentiate between hunters and butchers. Nowadays, there are more butchers than hunters. And they're the ones making the hunters look bad."

"Tracking woodcocks is a great way to have fun without firing a shot," says Vehí, who, on the occasional morning where no ducks are to be seen, has been known to produce a sheet of paper, a set of watercolors, and start painting the landscape. "But you have to forget about the numbers. The catch doesn't matter. You can still have a great time without even hunting."

Then comes a discussion on the abundance of *collverds* in Buda, followed by one on the green-winged teal. There is envy regarding the existence of France's Office National de la Chasse et de la Faune Sauvage and the political party known as Chasse et Tradition. There is talk of the hunt for woodcock, which can leap a full meter off the ground at an invisible speed. Of the increasing difficulties in extracting salt from the delta, which is Edu's business.

Vehí advocates for ecological hunting, in which opportunities must be shared, and it's in keeping with that philosophy that he hunts with a shotgun. He gets up from the table, returning with a very long weapon with a thin barrel. "This is a Remington repeating shotgun. My father brought it here from the United States. These days almost everyone shoots with semiautos, but this one is completely manual and I have to reload before every shot. That means my own natural speed is competing with the animal's. After so many years, I'm shooting at the same rate as anyone else." He holds the shotgun with both hands. "I brought four hundred shells. They're forecasting bad weather for tomorrow, but in Buda you never know."

Bad weather for hunting, he means. Calm weather.

"Time to draw lots," Mateo announces.

The hunters shift in their seats. Some sip the freshly served tea, while others have ordered coffee although it's nearly midnight. Mateo holds up a small bag with the names of the primary hunters.

"Fuck, I'm nervous," Edu says. "I mean, I've been doing this for years and it's always the luck of the draw. I dream about the stalls, about the draw, I imagine myself hunting there . . ."

Mateo announces the stalls. Uncle Raimundo's is the best, and the Palaus have won it.

Edu purses his lips. "Alright. That's fine."

"Come on," Mateo says. "Go get some rest. Tomorrow we set out early."

The nine-year-old has been nodding off in his chair now for some time.

At five the next morning we all reconvene at the table, equipped with our cold-weather gear: camouflage jackets, knee-high rubber boots, and hats. Breakfast is frugal, though a couple of the men dare try scrambled eggs. We open a jar of arbutus berry jam, thanks to Josep Vehí. He spent twelve years trying to figure out how to make it without grinding the seeds until one day, while browsing a bric-a-brac shop in Paris, he came upon a machine that could filter them out from the fruit. The jam retains the fresh, acidic flavor of the plant, an evergreen commonly known as a strawberry tree because of how its fruit appear. Energy for whatever comes next.

Vehí's discovery, and his obstinacy in smoothing out the texture of his jam, are reminiscent of scientist Charles Snowden Piggot's determination to investigate the layers of sediment at the bottom of the sea. Intent on telling the history of water and earth, Piggot invented a sort of cannon-like tube that allowed for the seabed to be drilled perpendicularly to obtain an elongated, cylindrical sample wherein the seriation and respective order of the differing strata would be perfectly preserved. In doing so, he achieved an unprecedented level of precision when it came to studying the seabed. This drill was described as being an instrument not unlike those designed to separate seeds from their fruit, so Piggot's sediment and Vehí's strawberry tree both demonstrate how one person's dedicated perseverance can add knowledge and sweetness to life with something as unexpected as a corer.

Mateo sends me with Josep Vehí and his grandson, who, by the luck of the draw, have been assigned the Canyaret tubs. We pile into Simona's truck and head out across the dark fields toward the wharf.

Under the glow of the headlights, hunters and their secretaries distribute themselves among eight boats.

It's cold, but there isn't much wind.

Our secretary is Raimundo, a relative of the fisher whose name adorns the star spot in Gran Calaix, where most of the hunting takes place.

The boatmen grab the poles and begin punting down the canal in silence, cloistered by the tall vegetation.

There are also two boats equipped with outboard motors, which are now starting up.

"There's no more poetry in it," Vehí says, perched in the bow.

The boatmen sink their poles into the banks of the canal and into the sandy bottom, trying not to run aground.

When we finally materialize before the darkened immensity of the lagoon, gently glistening under the plenilune glow, the punters relax.

Gradually, the boats disperse. We're left alone, gliding across the surface of the not-so-black obsidian sheen.

The water shimmers lugubriously, dotted in the distance by a few tiny amber lights: the hunters from Sant Jaume heading to their spots on the banks of the Parc Natural.

Soon, the Gran Calaix will be rimmed by more than seventy shotguns. The lagoon will become a killing field.

Two fleeting shadows fly over us, but it's not yet time. Raimundo docks along the banks of the Gran Calaix. We disembark, remove the covers from the tubs, and Vehí and his son situate themselves in the cylinders. A bit of moisture has seeped into the floor. The grandfather and the boy are wearing rubber boots, so the only thing that bothers them is the cold. The secretary tosses a few decoys into the water which float out in front of the tubs. The firmament remains hermetic, pierced only by the occasional pair or flock of birds, particularly black-winged grebes. When they fly low enough, we can hear their wings beating.

Raimundo and I take the boat to a *joca* fashioned out of wooden planks and topped with a thatched palm roof. From this outpost, we can't see the shooters. "They won't start shooting here until they start shooting in Sant Jaume," he says.

He's not expecting much from this day, both because of the weather and because the hunters have been wanting to take every advantage offered by the full moon and shots have been ringing out throughout the area for the past three nights. Tomorrow they'll still be gunning for coots, "and we're not doing anything like that." The ducks seem much more prudent than they did ten days ago, when they saw me walking through the cane field.

"There was a time when the ducks were like mosquitoes," Raimundo says. "You'd look up at the sky and they filled it completely. It was all black. They blocked out the moon and the sun."

Raimundo's favorite game bird is the coot, which flocks en masse to Buda, drawn by *llapó*, a green, mat-like aquatic plant it loves.

"I like the ritual of it all. The way the boats herd the coots, driving them across the water to where the hunters are waiting."

Pale wisps open in the sky, and while shadows still dominate, the outlines of birds are beginning to take shape.

A shot rings out in the distance, followed by scattered volleys.

This first burst is over quickly. Silence returns as the sky takes on a vinegary hue. Violet clouds tinged with hints of lilac appear. The horizon becomes more clearly defined, cut by a squadron of geese flying at a significant altitude. They can't be shot.

The birds return from their dinner in the rice fields. Air traffic increases a bit, though not much. The Vehís have yet to fire a single shot.

Raimundo lets loose a round of bird calls, the directions of which depend on the particular duck he sees. He gets a trio of teals to change their route and glide over us. Two shots ring out, yet no ducks fall. He cups his hands around his mouth and blows out the whistler's call, the shoveler's call, and the *collverd*'s call, but the ducks are either flying too high or directly across the center of the lagoon, exposing themselves to the artillery battery of the Palau family which, yes, is unloading on them.

Dawn now gilds the sky, and the first rays of sunlight adorn a few ducks with golden halos. The fresh light reverberates off the surface of the water, creating a fascinating iridescence that distracts intruders like me, because everyone else is looking up. The painfully low inrush of ducks suggests that Vehí might soon be getting his watercolors ready. His tub remains silent. Raimundo suggests we head over to see how they're doing. We make our way along the shore, brushing aside reeds, tallgrass, bushes, and other bejungled thickets toward their location. Both grandfather and grandson are holding their shotguns, scanning the skies above. Raimundo exhales the *collverd*'s call. A flock of birds pass by, too far to hazard a shot. Quira, a wirehaired pointer who's useful when it comes to taking the plunge, sniffs the damp earth with the excitement characteristic of a Drahthaar. Despite her modest height—she barely reaches our knees—she exudes the nerve and power of her breed. Her wet fur clings to her body, outlining her musculature, and her lowered hindquarters give her the torque needed for dragging large game, which is why the Germans have continued to breed and pamper these dogs so much.

Raimundo blows out a teal's call as a northern shoveler passes by. Vehí stands up, his Remington shouldered. He shoots, reloads, and shoots again. The duck falls.

"*Molt bé!*" Raimundo cries out, running with Quira through the reeds toward the downed quarry. I run after them, pushing aside branches, grasses, and reeds. Quira launches herself into the water, takes the duck in her teeth, and returns it to the hands of the secretary, who then delivers it to Vehí's tub, hanging it by the neck from a tree. "If you're not careful," Raimundo says, "the blue crabs will gobble them up."

Back at our *joca*, Raimundo pulls out an egg sandwich. With fingers peeking out from under his convertible mittens, he begins unwrapping the aluminum foil.

"Did you bring breakfast?"

I show him a package of crackers. "I ate something back at El Mas."

He tears off a quarter of the sandwich and hands it to me. "Here, take it."

"No, I'm fine. Really, I'm fine."

"Take it."

I snatch it up and take a bite. The eggs are cold. "So where do you go hunting?" I ask.

"Around La Platjola. With a semiauto. I was hunting there the morning I got married."

The lagoon is now fully illuminated by a sun that promises radiance. Still, though, these warmer colors are enlivened by the colder tones of the dawn.

"My uncle died a few months ago. He had a heart attack in the boat. He was alone, but at least he fell in the boat and not the water."

Raimundo's skin is healthily bronzed after forty-five years of exposure to the elements. His almost mahogany complexion is so rough and yet so cured by the wind and sun that it appears polished, inviting one to touch it.

"You must really enjoy this."

"A lot."

"What do you like most?"

"What do I like most? Everything in this world," he replies, extending an arm across the landscape.

The morning passes, marked by intermittent and generally distant shots. Before noon, I ask Raimundo to take me back to the wharf. We slowly coast across the lagoon, enveloped in an unexpected mist. Maimundo punts with a pole while I sit in the bow, Quira behind me sniffing the air. The canoe quietly cleaves the soft gray sheet.

Everyone returns to El Mas at lunchtime, discussing the day. The Vehís have whiled away the morning, while the Palaus have brought in several bundles of ducks. "Today was a father–son hunt," they say. "Sometimes all three of us were firing at the same time. That almost never happens, but today it did. Three times. All of us shooting at the same time."

Grandfather, father, and son. On the firing line.

IN THE NAME OF BUDA

LIKE EVERYTHING ELSE, BUDA IS GOING TO DIE. This, however, is a singular end: it's being announced beforehand, and the only doubt lies in the quality of the farewell. It's a proclaimed death, a harbinger of many others. It might even serve as a prologue to a great ending. The grand finale.

The pandemic that ravaged the world for two years has begun to subside. And while at first it was said that humans were paying the consequences of environmental abuse, and that we needed to change many of our harmful habits to prevent new diseases, plagues, and cyclones from wiping us out in an avalanche of disasters, little has changed now the situation seems to be under control: the vast majority of factories and engines spew out the same fumes as before, the coasts once again overflow with tourists, and species continue to disappear at a steady rate. I'm told that in the heart of Barcelona, birdsong is once again drowned out by the roar of machines.

I walk along the beach following the footprints I have left. The lack of wind and the *minves* have petrified the coast, at least for a day. Everything remains as it was twenty-four hours ago. Is this even possible? Isn't this supposed to be a tortuous place of flux where nothing lasts? I want to be inspired by movement. By endings, too. To better appreciate the passing minutes, I want to see life from the perspective of death. I want to know how to close the book. To say The End. Ashes. Flooding. Corpse. Goodbye.

It all makes for a day too transparent for my feelings, which aren't sad. I look into the future from a beach that will soon enough no longer exist and to which everyone should come to remember that spaces too can die. To memorize the plovers as they peck, the boggy rice fields, the cohetera, or the mutant minipeninsula of Cap de Tortosa. To tell the story of how there once was a place you saw dying, and to tell it with serenity. Because we need to educate ourselves about closure. For a while now, although not a long time, we've not known how to say goodbye. This globalized planet of ours has opened everything up to such a degree that borders and boundaries have been erased to the point of suggesting that maybe there is no end, depriving us of the ability to find closure that we acquired over millennia. Today we inhabit a seemingly eternal sum of emotions, events, information, information, and more information that leads us to believe we might actually be infinite, jumping from one sensation to the next without ever stopping. We're exhausted.

The other day I asked the men if they'd like to be immortal. Artur shrugged. Quim said yes, provided there was enough money. Dylan figured it would depend on the conditions of eternal life. For now, he wants to be buried in his village cemetery, as does Artur. Rubén Pons wants his ashes spread among the large eucalyptus trees in El Sifó and Tavertet, where, as a boy, he was won over by nature and birds. Mateo will be laid to rest in the Montjuïc cemetery, the same place chosen by Natalia if she were to die before Artur, because if she dies after he does, she'll choose the site where her partner or children are, "and I'll donate whatever organs I can." Quim doesn't care what they do with him after he dies. Xènia, though, is terrified of death and isn't ready yet to speculate on where she'll end up. Karen sees herself being cremated, her ashes scattered across the river or "flowing through the air." Through this air.

As for the rest of us, news reports say that the demand for services to help people die well has been increasing steadily. Who knows what it truly means to die well? It's a bit disturbing to hire strangers to help you bid farewell to the world. I'm proud of my father and my family and all of his friends, none of whom had to pay for the privilege of comforting him as he left, and as he harbored my mother in her days of greatest pain.

The sun glints off the lighthouse, spreading a carpet of sparks out across the water where the flotsam of a small wreck now floats. The wreck had spent months lying on the beach overlooking the Gran Calaix, and who knows how it has been returned to the sea. It's evidence that even what is immobile can move. In Buda, the reed has replaced the *bova*, which suits the bull fine, as it will eat the reeds but not the *bovas*. The eucalyptus is gaining ground on the poplar; the blue crab, having annihilated the cockle, is taking a toll on the eel. And as soon as the *minves* are over, the water will continue eating away at the sand's domain and Mateo will continue cursing angrily, though with the peace granted to him by Christ and the Virgin, because religion is a form of philosophy which—they say—is helpful when saying goodbye.

The feeling spreads that dying is something to be ashamed of, a form of defeat. Mateo has faced defeat so many times he's become a virtuoso of loss. In exchange for this, he's won the ability to live while appreciating the end. He sees death as something undesirable yet not worrisome, because he's convinced there is an afterlife, and that certainty comforts him. In the meantime, his intention is to leave his heirs a comfortable scenario . . . outside of Buda.

So this is the end.

I've brought an old wicker chair. In it, I now sit looking out to sea. Sometimes a bit of theater can better anchor memories, which is precisely what I aim to do. To conduct a farewell ritual as simple as connecting with this great curtain of water and sky. From here, from the last seat in the delta, it seems strange that the world is moving so fast. That it can't find a way to stop, or at least to slow down. There are those who are afraid of stopping only to find they don't recognize themselves, that they don't understand themselves without the inertia of those around them. There are even some who prefer to throw themselves so completely into a state of acceleration that they challenge death by leaping into the void from bridges or cliffs, hurtling down the track in a race car at three hundred miles per hour, cutting down forests, or decimating the eels in a river. This, too, is strong play, and it seems as though the preferred option is for us to flirt with crashing. Then again, one doesn't crash in the countryside in the same way one does in the city. How, then, does one die in a delta?

One of Thesiger's good friends was shot, Tarranda drowned crossing the river, and a few months ago a one-handed corpse was found along the canal connecting Buda to Sant Jaume. A drug deal gone south, it would appear. Raimundo's father suffered a fatal heart attack on board the boat, the shoveler was felled by a Remington, worms succumb to the birds' beaks, mice die in spring-loaded traps, eels in the embers beneath the grill, crabs are split by knives or shattered by gulls and herons, the apple snail is crushed under Pablo's boots, mosquitoes are extinguished in the bellies of dragonflies and swallows as well as my kitchen towel and, occasionally, fumigated. In Alexandria I heard about a man who spent seven long months making his way back to his native delta only to die there. Dying in the delta seems logical. Redundant, even. Especially if you're from here.

A delta is a school that teaches the art of good death. In such a place, one is able to die naturally, or at least with dignity. There's the case of El Boga, who, before dying, suffered pain he'd never imagined possible. "How could he bear it?" asked the fisher lying in the boat, bearing witness to his own agony with the same dignified distance from which he had witnessed his own life.

Pain exists so we may understand that the ship sails on, that humanity is not reliable, and that there are people like El Boga or my father who take a good while to die because they're made of sterner stuff. Or, also, someone like Prince Fabrizio Salina, so splendid and civilized that "if need be he can die well." That's how my father went. With the tranquility that comes with the wisdom of having lived and which, today, allows me to write: "A prince has died."

As hard as it is to believe, Buda is leaving.

How is it possible that so much land can disappear in such a way? And when it does, will the delta endure? The Amazon has no delta. The planet's wetlands are evaporating at an unthinkable speed. Without deltas we're less variegated, flexible, communicative, diverse. They say it was in the deltas of the world that the terrestrial mammals that would become whales once searched for food. Upon discovering an abundance of fish and other marine life capable of satisfying their massive appetites, they stayed in the water, transformed their front limbs into powerful means of propulsion, and began to swim out to sea, never to return again. Today, both whales and deltas share the same feelings of danger.

It would be nice if a human from the future came to tell us how the whales and deltas are doing in 2052, or what's happening in life. If you're still breathing, that is. But who can say how things will be by then? I set my chair to the side and lie down on my dune, as still as can be, to give the seagulls in the sky something to think about.

Our guiding spirits advise us when doubts appear. Through their actions they draw us a line to follow, and my father's actions had to do with pushing fear aside. On a modest scale, my father was unafraid and said what he thought, losing friends and opportunities, enduring reprisals and a litany of problems that, nevertheless, allowed him to come to a peaceful end. From him, I also learned that actions speak volumes and opinions rarely matter.

Are you trustworthy?

For a while I felt like Artur, debating whom to betray, until I understood that everything has already been said.

That the strong play is the story.

This story.

"So how are you going to end the book?" Mateo asked me the other day. He's very interested in the conclusion.

A book is much more than its ending.

A river is much more than its delta.

Our eyes meet.

In his, there are concern, love, and hope.

In mine, my father.

"We all make mistakes," he says.

I close my eyes, as if returning to my dune.

The delta appears.

I can feel the wind.

And the euphoria of seeing how the colors move. The imposing masses of ochers, blues, and greens flutter like a flag tinged with a certain winter light. What a pleasure to again hear the cry of the tern, the buzzing of the dragonfly, the waves withering away. To appreciate someone who swims backward through opaque waters in which beauty is the only certainty, while Mateo stands erect on a slope slicing into the vast sea, surrounded by the flames of paradoxes, schemes, and hopes, because this is a man.

I open my eyes.

A light squall hit the delta the day before, and the news is reporting that the Trabucador sandbar has been affected. They hadn't yet finished repairing the previous breach, and streams have once again permeated the sand. It sounds as though a stretch of it is almost flooded.

"Did it hit anything in Buda?" I ask.

"No, not much at all."

"To me it didn't seem like I got hit by much of anything."

"It'll come. Before long."

On this we agree. And that Buda is as precious as life itself. A treasure.

DELTA AND CLOSURE

I WOULD NEVER have been able to reach the end of this delta without the support and encouragement of those people who pushed me as if they were water, wind, and sun. Without their patience, energy, and understanding, without their time, none of this would have been the same. Ilse listens, steers, and guides; she has learned to swim the big waves. Gael and Katia are always teaching me other forms of the present. My father Gabriel, my mother Eloísa, and my brothers Edu and Cris are the strong and delicate sand that constantly supports me. With Elsa, my family from Seville, Joan Marcet, Pilar Caballero, the Tróspidos, and Jordi Serrallonga, any delta is better.

I can barely understand the process of writing and reading without bouncing ideas off my dear Marina Penalva. And thanks, also, to Elena Ramírez for getting close with flamingos and horses, as well as for appreciating poetry.

To Joan Carles Girbés, for weaving this strange and beautiful thread from giants, *bovas*, and *bous*.

I can't forget to thank the people who inspired this book for the time they spent showing me their most beloved spaces and for recounting great moments with precise, frequently dazzling words. Starting with Santi Valldepérez, who also built the bridge to Buda.

I don't have the adjectives with which to express the importance of the inimitable Guillermo Borés. All my appreciation and gratitude to William Vega, Pau Cuartiella, Abel Subirats, Ricardo and Susana Borés, Letizia, inconspicuous wise man David Bigas, Adela Tomàs, Ágata, and Noe.

I learned much from people I saw less of but who nevertheless gave it their all, from the Vila trio comprised of Joan, David, and Max, to Manolo, Agustí Vallfosch, Sebastià, Iker, Josep Oliver, Sofia Rivaes, Pedro Franch, Oriol Mosso—both father and son—and Joan Botey.

A tribute wrapped in an embrace goes out to Paco Palmer and his work protecting the space. Paco not only takes care of the amazing Margalef cattle but also watches over the territory by promoting initiatives like the *lligallo* project. He is always guided by his dear Àngel Cruzans.

Joan Tort sought out steel. Àlex Farnós, Oriol Gracià, Antonio Sandoval, Pedro Fumadó, David Milà, Marc Masià, Joan Barberà, Josep Juan Segarra, Carles Ibanyez, Ramon Bertomeu, Maria Teresa Folch, Alba Anguera, and Josep Culvi made the delta an even bigger place.

Thanks to Josep Sucarrats, the Arrels team, and the support and energy of the town councils of Sant Jaume d'Enveja, Amposta, and Tortosa, I was able to uncover new ways of telling the delta's tale by spending several days with the Margalef *bous*, as well as those of the Martorell-Gargallo ranch, along with a notable group of artists led by David Carabén, Andrés Cota Hiriart, Marina Monsonís, Natacha Sansoz, Jaume Vidal, Ada Vilaró, and Natalia Zaratiegui.

I would also like to emphasize the importance of the Finestres grant, which enabled me to spend a year absolutely dedicated to a space, freed from thoughts or concerns about anything other than deltas and affections.

When the end comes, if you can spend a bit of time on that threshold, it would be advisable to sense that you understood something—not much, just something—and that this understanding was a boon, assuming that we've come this far and that everything will then continue. To conclude that the painter paints, the fighter fights, the fisherwoman fishes, the writer writes, the delta dies, the book ends, life goes on.

EPILOGUE

A FEW MONTHS after finishing this book, I learned that Artur had resigned from his position in Buda. He'd been hired by a tractor company and is now the father of two children. He still occasionally visits the island to attend family get-togethers, but domestic tensions are behind him. Artur chose peace and the preservation of his marriage over taking on the job of managing the rice paddies and lagoons alongside Natalia.

Mateo is approaching retirement, and his succession is a major topic of discussion. The Gallart patriarch continues to be part of the Taula d'Acords, which has managed to set the Delta Protection Plan in motion. Buda has received several tons of sand with which to reinforce its beaches. Mateo believes it's too little too late, though he expresses satisfaction with the consensus, which he capped off by constructing a log dike: a true palisade that extends across the beach and part of the Gran Calaix. He knows those defenses won't withstand a major storm, and yet what worries him most these days is who'll take on the task of managing Buda when he and Simona are gone. Because he's certain they're both leaving. Mateo can't imagine Buda being run without Simona, even though most of the clan wants her out . . . starting with Gonzalo.

Mateo's brother is recovering from the illness that frequently forced him to leave the island. Now, he observes the daily goings-on, considering possibilities for shaking up old, inert habits. Most of the family seem to support his desire for change. The question is who'll take Mateo's place. Nobody in the clan has the requisite knowledge to ensure a reliable succession, and it's unclear whether the group even wants to keep shouldering the burden of making such a vast expanse of land and water profitable.

Simona is still as rough-edged as ever, though she's reined in her outbursts after a new bout of clashes with Quim and Dylan, who still work on the island.

Karen and Mateo have redefined their relationship. They don't live together, but they see each other regularly.

Pablo Archer is a leading figure on the bullfighting and free-range cattle scene, as well as a father who's managed to connect with his children.

Luzia Galioto moved to Cádiz after almost three decades in the delta, though she recently returned to the region to work with a private foundation on the restoration of freshwater ecosystems.

The Spanish publication of *The Last House Before the Sea* sparked renewed public interest in the Terres de l'Ebre, leading to everything from cultural events to impassioned public debates about agricultural models, hunting and fishing in the area, the receding beaches, and the biodiversity that needs to be protected. Numerous artists came to explore or in some way intervene in the region, and Mateo Gallart now welcomes a range of visitors to the island, from politicians representing the Ministry of Culture—previously, he had only welcomed representatives from the Ministry of Territorial Policy or the Ministry of the Environment—to photographers, writers, painters, musicians, filmmakers, as well as Teresa Vicente, the lawyer who won the Goldman Prize, which is considered the Nobel of environmentalism, in April of 2024. In the months following this book's release, the Delta Protection Plan started to be implemented with real conviction.

David Bigas, the ornithologist who inspired Rubén Pons's character, died unexpectedly on August 30 of that same year. As was his wish, his ashes were scattered among the eucalyptus trees of El Sifó and Tavertet.

In January 2025, a violent easterly storm triggered emergency public works which made it possible to move even more sand to the delta's shores, adding to the sediment that, lately, has been flowing down from the dams whenever the government orders a controlled flooding of the Ebro in its attempt to stem the advancing sea.

La Pantena sits, awaiting the next storm. They say the La Niña phenomenon will soon lash this coast with unprecedented force. The question, then, while gazing upon the beautiful yet fragile house, remains: can it hold on?

Grateful acknowledgment is given to the following works that have enriched this text:

Arbó, Sebastià Juan, *Tierras del Ebro* (Noguer, 1956).

Barbault, Robert, *Un éléphant dans un jeu de quilles* (Points, 2008).

Beston, Henry, *The Outermost House* (Doubleday, Doran, 1928).

Carson, Rachel, *The Sea Around Us* (Oxford University Press, 1951).

Ibid, *Silent Spring* (Houghton Mifflin, 1962).

Conti, Haroldo, trans. Jon Lindsay Miles, *Southeaster* (And Other Stories, 2015).

Dillard, Annie, *Pilgrim at Tinker Creek* (Bantam Books, 1974).

Duperrex, Matthieu, *Voyages en sol incertain: Enquêtes dans les deltas du Rhône et du Mississippi* (Éditions Wildproject, 2019).

Escarpa, Gonzalo, *Quiero decir* (La Imprenta, 2024).

Kingsnorth, Paul, *Alexandria* (Graywolf Press, 2020). Reprinted with the permission of The Permissions Company, LLC, on behalf of Graywolf Press, Minneapolis, Minnesota, graywolfpress.org.

Macfarlane, Robert, *The Wild Places* (Penguin, 2008).

Magris, Claudio, trans. Patrick Creagh, *Danube: A Sentimental Journey from the Source to the Black Sea* (Farrar, Straus and Giroux, 2008).

Pla, Josep, *Viaje en autobús* (Ediciones Destino, 2010).

Pocock, Joanna, *Surrender: The Call of the American West* (House of Anansi Press, 2019).

Rovira Climent, J. J., *Cantadors del Delta: Teixidor, Lo Noro, Caragol* (Tortosa, 2002).

Rush, Elizabeth, *Rising: Dispatches from the New American Shore* (Milkweed Editions, 2018).

Svensson, Patrick, trans. Agnes Broomé, *The Book of Eels* (HarperCollins Publishers, 2020).

Thesiger, Wilfred, *The Marsh Arabs* (Penguin, 2007).

Todó, Joan, *Guia sentimental del delta de l'Ebre* (Editorial Pòrtic, 2018). Used with permission of the author.

Tomasi di Lampedusa, Giuseppe, trans. Archibald Colquhoun, *The Leopard* (Pantheon Books, 2007).

ABOUT THE AUTHOR

GABI MARTÍNEZ is the author of eleven fiction and nonfiction books. He is well known for his outstanding travel writing and literary journalism, and his novels have been selected as books of the year by Spanish literary magazine *Qué Leer*. Martínez was included in Palgrave Macmillan's list of the top five writers of Spanish Vanguardism in the last twenty years.

ABOUT THE TRANSLATOR

EZRA E. FITZ has translated over twenty books, including nonfiction by Grammy-winning musician Juanes and Emmy-winning journalist Jorge Ramos, as well as fiction by Alberto Fuguet and Eloy Urroz. His translation of *Forgiveness* by Chiquis Rivera was a *New York Times* bestseller.